The EU and the European Security Order

This book attempts to conceptualize EU action in the field of regional security.

Drawing on constructivist theory, the framework of the book focuses on the meeting – or 'interface' – of actors, a situation reflecting the mutual construction of self, other and situation. The analytical framework applied here to European security politics is potentially open-ended as the theoretical logic that informs the framework is general and abstract in character, and not limited to state actors in an international setting. The empirical aim of this book is to further our understanding of the EU as a security actor in a regional perspective. The book thus links IR scholarship with that of EU studies. By analysing a number of different interfaces (such as with Russia, the United States, and other states), we can learn more about the circumstances and preconditions and with what resources and power the EU acts in a regional security setting.

This book will be of great interest to students of European security, EU policy, international relations theory and security studies in general.

Rikard Bengtsson is Assistant Professor of Political Science at Lund University, Sweden. He has a PhD in Political Science, from Lund University, Sweden.

Contemporary security studies
Series editors: James Gow and Rachel Kerr
King's College London

This series focuses on new research across the spectrum of international peace and security, in an era where each year throws up multiple examples of conflicts that present new security challenges in the world around them.

NATO's Secret Armies
Operation Gladio and terrorism in Western Europe
Daniele Ganser

The US, NATO and Military Burden-sharing
Peter Kent Forster and Stephen J. Cimbala

Russian Governance in the Twenty-first Century
Geo-strategy, geopolitics and new governance
Irina Isakova

The Foreign Office and Finland 1938–1940
Diplomatic sideshow
Craig Gerrard

Rethinking the Nature of War
Edited by Isabelle Duyvesteyn and Jan Angstrom

Perception and Reality in the Modern Yugoslav Conflict
Myth, falsehood and deceit 1991–1995
Brendan O'Shea

The Political Economy of Peacebuilding in Post-Dayton Bosnia
Tim Donais

The Distracted Eagle
The rift between America and old Europe
Peter H. Merkl

The Iraq War
European perspectives on politics, strategy, and operations
Edited by Jan Hallenberg and Håkan Karlsson

Strategic Contest
Weapons proliferation and war in the greater Middle East
Richard L. Russell

Propaganda, the Press and Conflict
The Gulf War and Kosovo
David R. Willcox

Missile Defence
International, regional and national implications
Edited by Bertel Heurlin and Sten Rynning

Globalising Justice for Mass Atrocities
A revolution in accountability
Chandra Lekha Sriram

Ethnic Conflict and Terrorism
The origins and dynamics of civil wars
Joseph L. Soeters

Globalisation and the Future of Terrorism
Patterns and predictions
Brynjar Lia

Nuclear Weapons and Strategy
The evolution of American nuclear policy
Stephen J. Cimbala

Nasser and the Missile Age in the Middle East
Owen L. Sirrs

War as Risk Management
Strategy and conflict in an age of globalised risks
Yee-Kuang Heng

Military Nanotechnology
Potential applications and preventive arms control
Jurgen Altmann

NATO and Weapons of Mass Destruction
Regional alliance, global threats
Eric R. Terzuolo

Europeanisation of National Security Identity
The EU and the changing security identities of the Nordic states
Pernille Rieker

International Conflict Prevention and Peace-building
Sustaining the peace in post conflict societies
Edited by T. David Mason and James D. Meernik

Controlling the Weapons of War
Politics, persuasion, and the prohibition of inhumanity
Brian Rappert

Changing Transatlantic Security Relations
Do the US, the EU and Russia form a new strategic triangle?
Edited by Jan Hallenberg and Håkan Karlsson

Theoretical Roots of US Foreign Policy
Machiavelli and American unilateralism
Thomas M. Kane

Corporate Soldiers and International Security
The rise of private military companies
Christopher Kinsey

Transforming European Militaries
Coalition operations and the technology gap
Gordon Adams and Guy Ben-Ari

Globalization and Conflict
National security in a 'new' strategic era
Edited by Robert G. Patman

Military Forces in 21st Century Peace Operations
No job for a soldier?
James V. Arbuckle

The Political Road to War with Iraq
Bush, 9/11 and the drive to overthrow Saddam
Nick Ritchie and Paul Rogers

Bosnian Security after Dayton
New perspectives
Edited by Michael A. Innes

Kennedy, Johnson and NATO
Britain, America and the Dynamics of Alliance, 1962–68
Andrew Priest

Small Arms and Security
New emerging international norms
Denise Garcia

The United States and Europe
Beyond the neo-conservative divide?
Edited by John Baylis and Jon Roper

Russia, NATO and Cooperative Security
Bridging the gap
Lionel Ponsard

International Law and International Relations
Bridging theory and practice
Edited by Tom Bierstecker, Peter Spiro, Chandra Lekha Sriram and Veronica Raffo

Deterring International Terrorism and Rogue States
US national security policy after 9/11
James H. Lebovic

Vietnam in Iraq
Tactics, lessons, legacies and ghosts
Edited by John Dumbrell and David Ryan

Understanding Victory and Defeat in Contemporary War
Edited by Jan Angstrom and Isabelle Duyvesteyn

Propaganda and Information Warfare in the Twenty-first Century
Altered images and deception operations
Scot Macdonald

Governance in Post-conflict Societies
Rebuilding fragile states
Edited by Derick W. Brinkerhoff

European Security in the Twenty-first Century
The challenge of multipolarity
Adrian Hyde-Price

Ethics, Technology and the American Way of War
Cruise missiles and US security policy
Reuben E. Brigety II

International Law and the Use of Armed Force
The UN charter and the major powers
Joel H. Westra

Disease and Security
Natural plagues and biological weapons in East Asia
Christian Enermark

Explaining War and Peace
Case studies and necessary condition counterfactuals
Jack Levy and Gary Goertz

War, Image and Legitimacy
Viewing contemporary conflict
James Gow and Milena Michalski

Information Strategy and Warfare
A guide to theory and practice
John Arquilla and Douglas A. Borer

Countering the Proliferation of Weapons of Mass Destruction
NATO and EU options in the Mediterranean and the Middle East
Thanos P. Dokos

Security and the War on Terror
Edited by Alex J. Bellamy, Roland Bleiker, Sara E. Davies and Richard Devetak

The European Union and Strategy
An emerging actor
Edited by Jan Hallenberg and Kjell Engelbrekt

Causes and Consequences of International Conflict
Data, methods and theory
Edited by Glenn Palmer

Russian Energy Policy and Military Power
Putin's quest for greatness
Pavel Baev

The Baltic Question during the Cold War
Edited by John Hiden, Vahur Made, and David J. Smith

America, the EU and Strategic Culture
Renegotiating the transatlantic bargain
Asle Toje

Afghanistan, Arms and Conflict
Post-9/11 security and insurgency
Michael Bhatia and Mark Sedra

Punishment, Justice and International Relations
Ethics and order after the Cold War
Anthony F. Lang, Jr.

Intra-state Conflict, Governments and Security
Dilemmas of deterrence and assurance
Edited by Stephen M. Saideman and Marie-Joëlle J. Zahar

Democracy and Security
Preferences, norms and policy-making
Edited by Matthew Evangelista, Harald Müller and Niklas Schörnig

The Homeland Security Dilemma
Fear, failure and the future of American security
Frank P. Harvey

Military Transformation and Strategy
Revolutions in military affairs and small states
Edited by Bernard Loo

Peace Operations and International Criminal Justice
Building peace after mass atrocities
Majbritt Lyck

NATO, Security and Risk Management
From Kosovo to Kandahar
M.J. Williams

Cyber-conflict and Global Politics
Edited by Athina Karatzogianni

Globalization and Defence in the Asia-Pacific
Arms across Asia
Edited by Geoffrey Till, Emrys Chew and Joshua Ho

Security Strategies and American World Order
Lost power
Birthe Hansen, Peter Toft and Anders Wivel

War, Torture and Terrorism
Rethinking the rules of international security
Edited by Anthony F. Lang, Jr. and Amanda Russell Beattie

America and Iraq
Policy making, intervention and regional politics
Edited by David Ryan and Patrick Kiely

European Security in a Global Context
Internal and external dynamics
Edited by Thierry Tardy

Women and Political Violence
Female combatants in ethno-national conflict
Miranda H. Alison

Justice, Intervention and Force in International Relations
Reassessing just war theory in the 21st century
Kimberley A. Hudson

Clinton's Foreign Policy
Between the Bushes, 1992–2000
John Dumbrell

Aggression, Crime and International Security
Moral, political and legal dimensions of international relations
Page Wilson

European Security Governance
The European Union in a Westphalian world
Charlotte Wagnsson, James Sperling and Jan Hallenberg

Private Security and the Reconstruction of Iraq
Christopher Kinsey

US Foreign Policy and Iran
American–Iranian relations since the Islamic Revolution
Donette Murray

Legitimising the Use of Force in International Relations
Kosovo, Iraq and the ethics of intervention
Corneliu Bjola

The EU and the European Security Order
Interfacing security actors
Rikard Bengtsson

The EU and the European Security Order

Interfacing security actors

Rikard Bengtsson

Taylor & Francis Group

LONDON AND NEW YORK

First published 2010
by Routledge
2 Park Square, Milton Park, Abingdon, Oxon OX14 4RN

Simultaneously published in the USA and Canada
by Routledge
711 Third Ave, New York, NY 10017

Routledge is an imprint of the Taylor & Francis Group, an informa business

First issued in paperback 2013

© 2010 Rikard Bengtsson

Typeset in Times New Roman by Wearset Ltd, Boldon, Tyne and Wear

All rights reserved. No part of this book may be reprinted or reproduced or utilized in any form or by any electronic, mechanical, or other means, now known or hereafter invented, including photocopying and recording, or in any information storage or retrieval system, without permission in writing from the publishers.

British Library Cataloguing in Publication Data
A catalogue record for this book is available from the British Library

Library of Congress Cataloging in Publication Data
A catalog record for this book has been requested

ISBN13: 978-0-415-49723-7 (hbk)
ISBN13: 978-0-415-85110-7 (pbk)
ISBN13: 978-0-203-87203-1 (ebk)

To Marie

Contents

List of illustrations xi
Acknowledgements xii

PART I
Introduction and analytical framework **1**

1 Introduction 3
2 Analytical framework 18

PART II
Neighbourhood interfaces **39**

3 EU recognition of the neighbourhood 41
4 Post-Soviet interfaces 55
5 Mediterranean interfaces 80

PART III
Great power interfaces **105**

6 The Baltic interface 107
7 The transatlantic interface 131

PART IV
Conclusions **145**

8 Concluding remarks 147
   Notes 151
   Bibliography 152
   Index 171

Illustrations

Figure

2.1　The interface logic　27

Tables

1.1　EU interaction in a regional perspective　12
2.1　Types of interfaces　35
3.1　The ENP framework　44
4.1　Post-Soviet interfaces　78
5.1　Mediterranean interfaces　101
8.1　European interfaces　148

Acknowledgements

Looking back at the research project that forms the basis for this book, I cannot help but conclude that it has been an unexpectedly long journey. All the more appropriate then, to take this opportunity to thank those who have made a difference along the way.

The Department of Global Political Studies at Malmö University provided a dynamic and friendly setting for most of the duration of the project. At Malmö, out of many good friends and supporters, my special thanks go to Dr Magnus Ericson, for his long and ongoing friendship and for in various ways contributing to my thinking on the subject matter of the book and on international relations in general.

The Department of Political Science at Lund University, Sweden, is my Alma Mater to which I returned in the autumn of 2008. Feeling a bit like coming home, the research-intense and friendly environment has made the final tiresome months of the project more bearable. In particular, I would like to thank Professor Christer Jönsson and Director of Studies Dr Jakob Gustavsson for accommodating my wish to complete the project while simultaneously taking up the position at the department. My thanks are also extended to Professor Ole Elgtsröm and Professor Magnus Jerneck for their support and suggestions. Last but certainly not least, my gratitude and appreciation goes to Dr Matilda Broman, who at a late stage helped me out with data collection for one of the chapters.

This is also the place to acknowledge the generous financial support provided by the Swedish Institute of International Affairs, without which this research would not have been possible. Moreover, I had the opportunity to conduct a series of exploratory interviews with diplomats and civil servants at EU institutions and the Russian and American missions in Brussels. My sincere thanks to all interviewees for kindly sharing their time!

Let me end on a personal note. Throughout the research process, my wife Marie has been my strongest supporter (and indeed sometimes also the strongest critic!). Not only has the end product benefitted greatly from her engagement, but she has made life a lot more fun in the meantime! I dedicate this book to her.

Part I
Introduction and analytical framework

1 Introduction

The European Union and the European security order

It is no exaggeration to state that the European security order has undergone dramatic changes in the post-Cold War era. Conceptualizations of Europe, security and order have all changed, and the current order is a more complex and diffuse one compared to that of the bipolar era. Europe has taken on a partly new meaning, no matter whether focusing on geography, institutional set-up or identity. The fall of the Berlin Wall and the subsequent break-down of the Soviet Union and the Warsaw Pact imply both that the bipolar division of the continent has ended and that numerous states have gained or regained their independence. As a substantial number of these have entered or have the ambition of joining European organizations such as the European Union (EU), the North Atlantic Treaty Organization (NATO), the Council of Europe and the Organization for Security and Cooperation in Europe (OSCE), geography, institutions and processes of mutual identification have all come into a new light.

Also the concept of security is changing and contested. Some politicians and academics continue to define security in traditional military terms regarding threat perceptions, actors as well as means, while others favour a much broader understanding encompassing also non-state actors, new types of threats and also new levels of analysis. A prominent example of this is the human security discourse. Order, finally, can be interpreted as global polarity in the traditional sense and has in that light changed from a bipolar structure into a unipolar one, most would argue. When focusing on the regional European level, changing ambitions of different states as well as the appearance and/or changing rationale for the institutions named above have effectuated the simultaneous consolidation and differentiation of the European order (enlargement of major institutions, deepening integration not least within the EU, changing patterns of interdependence, and foreign policy redirection of major states, to mention a few important elements). Thus, to state that this book is concerned with the European security order is more of an introductory orientation than a specific research question.

More specifically, this study deals with the European Union as an actor in the European security order. One of the striking features of European security as it is conventionally understood is the arrival of the European Union as a security actor. This process, further analysed below, remains hotly debated, both in terms of whether it is desired (not least the military components hereof) and how fatal and permanent the so-called capabilities–expectations gap remains. In recent years, much attention has thus been devoted to understanding the evolving common foreign and security policy of the EU, both in terms of impact and when it comes to problems in matching expectations and capacities (see for instance Bretherton and Vogler 2006, Strömvik 2005, Tonra and Christiansen 2004, Ginsberg 2001, Hill 1993). Simultaneously, the debate about the profile of the EU in international relations – in the well-known terms of civilian, military and normative power – continues to occupy a central position in the scholarship on the EU (Kirchner 2006, Sjursen 2006, Hyde-Price 2006, Manners 2002, 2006). This book seeks to contribute to both debates.

The European Union as a security actor

The European Union is taking an increasingly active part in international relations. While the EU has been a dominant actor in the fields of trade and aid for a long time, it is a relative newcomer in the foreign and security policy area. A quick glance at the major international events of the last decade, however, seems to indicate that over time the EU has also become heavily involved in these latter aspects of external relations, both in the immediate neighbourhood and on a global scale. The effectiveness of this engagement remains contested and attempts at a common policy are rivalled by numerous examples of diverging national policies and hence conflict – or at least passivity – at the EU level.

The emergence of the EU on the world scene is a principally important issue. New actors in international relations are a rare occurrence; we seldom see the rise of newcomers on the international arena. New actors are potentially threats to the existing order (which may well be the reason for their rarity), but may also come to be seen as contributors to a given order in a complementary fashion. Entertaining this latter perspective, not only are internal processes of institutional development and allocation of funding of relevance for the making of a new foreign policy actor, equally important is the way in which other actors in international relations perceive the newcomer.

In general terms, institutional developments in the EU in the last ten years have increased the potential for effective EU foreign policy making, evident in the creation of the office of the High Representative, and also in how the European Council and the Presidency of the Council of Ministers engage in policy making in this area. The proposed Reform Treaty further develops that potential. Drawing on Ginsberg's (2001) distinction between presence and actorness, where the former denotes a passive or latent form of agency, for a complex organization such as the EU, international actorness is intimately related to the extent to which the supranational institutions are autonomous from their member-states. The whole debate surrounding EU efforts (or the lack thereof) in recent years – be it in the Balkans or the Middle East – is in essence a discussion about the autonomy of the EU-level foreign policy versus the foreign policies of individual member-states. One of the central consequences of this concerns the relationship between what external actors expect and the capacity of the EU to deliver.

Rather than analysing EU-internal developments alone, one of the arguments that informs the logic of this book is that what ultimately determines how effective the EU will be in this sphere is the interplay between how other actors in the foreign policy game perceive the EU as a security policy actor and what the EU does or what capacities it possesses. Hence it is also the *recognition* by external actors, rather than only intra-institutional developments that are of importance. Such recognition in part depends on how these external actors view their own position in relation to the EU. To be sure, there is a link between these processes, which in turn highlights the central importance of *interfaces* – how political actors are mutually constituted in an interactive fashion. One of the aims of this book is to inquire into the constituent factors of processes of interface formation through the recognition of the EU as an international actor in the security policy area. The general (and intriguing!) question concerns what elements help determine the character of interfaces. The more specific question concerns how the EU perceives itself and is perceived by other actors in a regional context.

The argument here is thus, that while it certainly remains important to analyse EU-internal developments (such as various institutional changes) in order to understand the development of EU security actorness, what may in the end be fundamentally important is to also take account of these developments from the perspective of other different actors involved in the current order, and how their actions are influenced by – and influence – EU action. All in all, this implies an analytical framework based on strategic interaction and mutual constitution of actorness.

Present-day developments involving the EU represent major processes of restructuring of the European security-political order that can be hypothesized to influence both how external actors view the EU and how the EU perceives itself. First, the EU 2004–2007 enlargement, often referred to in terms such as 'unique' and 'historical', is unprecedented in scope and character. It leaves the union with 27 member-states and presumably a new logic of inter-state bargaining and decision-making and new sets of institutional linkages.

Second, at the same time and against a complex background of intentional policy development and the unfolding of external events, the EU is trying to consolidate its foreign and security policy collaboration of rather traditional character, primarily through the development of the Common Foreign and Security Policy (CFSP), the European Security and Defence Policy (ESDP) and the attainment of actor capacity in military form (such as the Rapid Reaction Force).

Third, employing a broader notion of security, the EU actively attempts to regulate its relationship to the near abroad – through the European Neighbourhood Policy (ENP), one of the foci of this book – and to major parts of the world, for instance through the Cotonou agreements and increasing institutionalization of relations with Asia, South America and recently also Africa.

All these processes have potentially central implications for the actorness of the European Union in world affairs; that is, the extent to and the terms on which, the EU involves itself in common international undertakings.

Aims and delimitations of the study

This book contains both theoretical and empirical aims. The theoretical rationale of the study is to further an analytical framework concerning the cognitive dynamics of political interaction. Drawing on constructivist logic, the framework of the book focuses on the meeting – *interface* – between actors, a situation reflecting the mutual constitution of self, other and situation; thus, implying an agency-structure approach to politics. While, in this book, applied to European security politics, the analytical framework is potentially open-ended as the theoretical logic that informs the framework is general and abstract in character and not limited to state actors in an international setting.

The empirical aim of the book is to further our understanding of the EU as a security actor in a regional perspective. By analysing a number of different interfaces, we can learn more about under what circumstances and preconditions, and with what resources and power, the EU acts in a regional security setting. Against the background of these aims, the general empirical research question that guides the book can be formulated in the following manner: What characterizes the EU as a regional security actor? More specifically, we may ask: How does the EU perceive other actors involved in the regional security order? How is the EU perceived by other actors involved in the European security context? What resources and strategies does the EU use in regional security affairs?

The general subject matter of the book is thus how to conceptualize the EU in a regional security perspective, where EU interaction with outside states is very intense, both in frequency and scope. This issue is obviously a complex and broad one, impossible to do justice in this limited volume. Hence, a word on limitations is necessary. The book does not attempt to give a full overview of the relationships between the EU and the various other actors/sets of actors. Rather it is strictly focused on processes concerning the formation of EU-related security interfaces.

Likewise, the book does not seek to give a complete characterization of EU external policy; here, the focus is on the EU in a regional security setting. Given the ambiguous nature of security, the finer points of such delimitation may still be disputed. And, quite obviously, the book does not attempt to analyse the whole of the foreign policy of the countries covered by this analysis, but rather focuses on narrow aspects of it, as pointed out by the analytical framework.

Theoretical ports of entry

In contrast to many writings on security, this book rests on the idea that the regional level of analysis is a central one when attempting to understand interstate security. At the regional level, global and sub-global (regional) power dynamics are played out in a setting characterized not only by material capabilities, strategic interaction and manifest relations and institutions, but one in which also historical and ideational dimensions presumably influence political decision-making and behaviour. From such a perspective, the contribution by Ole Wæver and Barry Buzan around the notion of *regional security complexes* is a particularly fruitful perspective, since it combines a rationalist conceptualization of the structure of world politics with constructivist ideas of actorness and interaction (focusing among other things on learning, change and securitization processes). The basis of the analytical framework, as well as the initial categorization of cases, in this book in part draws its inspiration from the Buzan and Wæver framework. In essence they argue that security interdependence is regional in character; the regional level of interaction is the primary one in security politics. The patterns of such security interdependencies result in a number of mutually exclusive regional security complexes, made up of a relative interdependence within the complex and relative indifference vis-à-vis the outside. In the words of Buzan and Wæver: 'RSCs [regional security complexes] are defined by durable patterns of amity and enmity taking the form of subglobal, geographically coherent patterns of security interdependence' (Buzan and Wæver 2003: 45). The nature of securitization and desecuritization processes of the states within the complex determines the character of the security interdependence (for instance in terms of amity and enmity).

Security complexes/regions may be thought to come in different types. Buzan and Wæver differentiate among conflict formation (conflictual relations within the complex), security regime (a mixed picture of cooperation and conflict) and security community (defined in accordance with Karl Deutsch (1957) as a cooperative situation in which military means are no longer considered for conflict resolution, see also Adler and Barnett 1998a and Adler *et al.* 2006). This corresponds roughly to distinctions made in the literature on qualities of peace between precarious, conditional and stable peace (see Kacowicz *et al.* 2000).

There are two primary analytical dimensions of interest in the Buzan and Wæver framework. One concerns power, where actors are categorized as superpowers, great powers and regional powers, with the remaining set of states left unattended; in this book, however, this category of what may be labelled tertiary powers are also included. Buzan and Wæver characterize the current system as consisting of one superpower (the United States) and four great powers – Russia, China, Japan and the EU (Buzan and Wæver 2003: 34–37). The other dimension concerns boundaries, in that security complexes are defined by the boundaries between zones of interdependence and surrounding indifferences. Against such a logic, it becomes possible to identify a number of regional complexes (all in all nine distinct complexes: North America, South America, Europe, the Post-Soviet space, Middle East, Central Africa, Southern Africa, South Asia and East Asia). There is an interesting variation among these regarding the presence or absence of great powers (the only superpower can be assumed to be of political relevance in all cases, albeit in different ways). The European complex is further of interest in the sense that the great power identified is not a sovereign state in the traditional sense, but an international institution with state-like qualities acting in a 'hyper-institutionalized' setting. Moreover – and perhaps related – is the European complex, together with the North American complex, the one most easily labelled a security community in which military force or threats thereof have ceased to be used in intra-complex conflict resolution and where securitization processes encompass other issues, such as energy, environment, migration and international terrorism (see Buzan and Wæver 2003: 356–372; Wæver 1998; and Bengtsson 2009a for analyses of the European security community).

In two important ways, this book seeks to develop the Buzan and Wæver framework, first, by further problematizing the meaning of boundaries and second, by going beyond the focus on the internal logic and character of complexes and instead analysing relationships across the boundaries of security complexes. In doing so, this analysis employs a looser conceptualization of region – rather than viewing the pattern of security interdependencies as delineating distinct groupings of countries, it is here perceived in terms of degrees of intensity from core areas (corresponding to complexes in the terminology of Buzan and Wæver) to surrounding areas. More specifically, the analysis aims at understanding more about the relationship of the EU to neighbouring countries that geographically fall within other complexes. Involving actors from different complexes, it becomes impossible to a priori label these relationships in terms such as security regimes or communities; rather, such labelling will be the outcome of empirical analysis. In that process, existing research on regional community-building, such as that of Emanuel Adler *et al.* (2006), as well as on the relationship between security communities and their neighbours (Bellamy 2004; Bengtsson 2009a) becomes of interest. Furthermore, the assumption of *regional* security logic comes under scrutiny, if it is the case that there is great variation in the character of different bilateral relations between the EU and countries geographically and conventionally grouped together.

How are these relationships to be conceptualized? This study attempts to contribute to the conceptual toolkit by using the concepts of interface, recognition, actorness, power and identity. Developed in further detail in the next chapter, here it suffices to say that an *interface* denotes a meeting between *actors* which involves the perceptual *recognition* of actors (self and others) in terms of *power* (configuration and resources) and *identity*. If only focusing on resources/strategies/power in a traditional rationalist manner, we risk overlooking central elements in understanding the interactive nature of perceptions (who 'we' are is of importance when determining who 'they' are, and vice versa) and may also miss important processes of change, continuity and feed-back. If only focusing on the images/identities of self and other, we risk overlooking the power/resources dimension of interaction. Hence, the *interface* concept – a relational identity-based concept which builds on the mutual recognition of two or more actors in interaction – allows for a more sophisticated analysis which includes both strategic interaction and mutual perceptions.

This framework, elaborated in the next chapter, is potentially open to all sorts of political analysis. In this book we limit ourselves to EU interaction in a regional (European) security setting; that is, relationships between the EU and a number of other actors. This task involves an extra challenge due to the non-state nature of the EU. While easily overlooked or underestimated in traditional state-centric analyses, this book departs from the notion that the EU potentially has actor qualities that states have, but that it simultaneously faces a different or specific set of challenges because of its non-state composition. Its unique nature at the same time provides it with special opportunities for impacting on international relations (compare Ian Manners' argument that what ultimately makes the EU important is not what the EU does or says, but what it is (Manners 2002: 252)). In consequence, it is one of the aims of the book to contribute to a deeper understanding of the EU as a security actor.

Methodological remarks

The methodological approach embarked upon in this book falls within social constructivism. The constructivist spectrum is a broad and complex one, and the approach chosen here draws on rationalist (however, realist rather than positivist) assumptions, rather than reflectivist such (see Christiansen *et al.* 2001: 2–11; Hollis and Smith 1991: 10–12). It combines a rationalist epistemology with a hermeneutic ontology, thus ending up in the same kind of constructivism as in some of the writings of Alexander Wendt, Emanuel Adler and Jeffrey Checkel, to name a few leading contributors.

From such a point of departure, a number of interesting issues follow. First, reality is assumed to be complex and multi-causal, which means that it is not feasible to argue that there exists clear, singular, and unitary actor perceptions (on the impact of ideas and societal aspects on actors, see Moses and Knutsen 2007: 178–187). We know from previous research that there are often competing impressions, world-views and policy conclusions within for instance the security elite of a given country. In the United States, for example, variation can be found within the Administration, in Congress, and between the institutions of government. Likewise in Russia, with the added complexity of a regional dimension which may bring, or contribute to, the outcome of inconsistent and internally contradictory policies. To conclude, to argue that there exist official perceptions other than on a rhetorical level is certainly problematic.

Second, it is necessary to address the question whether, and how, perceptions may change over time. This inherently difficult question involves both fundamental theoretical assumptions regarding actors and rationality in international relations, and psychological processes such as the search for cognitive consistency. This book departs from the assumption that perceptions may change – not least as an effect of what Hollis and Smith (1991: 190) refer to as interlocking rational expectations – and that this is of relevance for policy change; this is, after all, a central tenet of constructivism as applied in this book. While seemingly reflecting real world developments, such an assumption includes an obvious methodological challenge, in that it cannot be argued that perceptions just are the way they have been in the past irrespective of context, but are formed in interpretations of reality. All in all, what follows must by necessity, then, be one among many possible interpretations and represents to some extent an inherently subjective exercise on behalf of the analyst.

Third, to add to the problem, there is also the difficult issue of operationalization – how to study perceptions. The way forward in this particular book will be to focus on what the collective actors themselves (the EU, the neighbourhood policy countries, Russia and the United States) express in official contexts about the EU as a security actor and their own place and role in the European security order. By focusing on official rhetoric that is deliberately intended for public consumption, we reduce the problem of establishing perceptions by not being dependent on what certain individuals think in private or what ideas they have internalized.

Fourth, the data utilized in this book needs to be commented. The analytical framework draws on readily available data concerning material resources and overt political actions (speeches, documents and the like) in establishing a descriptive understanding of EU security interaction with actors in a regional context. The framework however also includes – more challenging from a methodological point of view – the analysis of perceptions of political actors, in this case both EU perceptions of self and other, and others' perceptions of the EU. The primary material for the study consists of statements, speeches, and policy documents of governments and EU institutions, used against the background logic that values influence actor interests and manifest behaviour. These sources are complemented by the use of secondary sources, both academic and journalistic in character, and a number of interviews with EU representatives and diplomats in Brussels. Interviews can at best be complementary sources due to problems of representativity, but may still be helpful in interpreting the official rhetoric.

In concluding, establishing perceptions of different actors represents a major methodological challenge. While not impossible, caution is necessary regarding inference-drawing and reliability of data.

European interfaces: research design

This book aims at contributing to the logic of cross-border relationships between actors of different security complexes. More specifically, the book seeks to analyse the relationship between the European Union, as the great power of the European regional security complex, and various kinds of actors adjacent to, but outside of, the European security complex proper.

As noted above, in the European regional security complex, the EU stands out as a pole, the great power of the complex. Within the complex, this means that the EU is in a superior power position vis-à-vis the members of the complex. This is most obvious in the case of the enlargement process, where candidate countries are forced/induced by the EU to comply with certain standards if they want to change their relationship to the core (become members). This goes equally well for regional powers such as Turkey and lesser powers such as

Croatia, albeit within rather different political logics. (From this follows that this author readily includes Turkey in the European complex, based on the recognition by the EU concerning Turkey's candidate status regarding EU membership.)

Outside of the complex, the issue gets more complicated. How does the great power EU function in different kinds of power relationships with neighbouring countries outside of the security complex? What similarities and differences are there in terms of how the EU performs as well as how it is perceived by these countries in the 'near abroad'?

In answering these and related questions, the following analysis seeks to study interfaces between the EU and a number of other actors in a regional security perspective outside the European complex proper. As observed above, the current polarity of international relations can be described as a 1+4 system, with the United States as the only superpower, and the EU, Russia, Japan and China as the four great powers. From this follows analytically that there is only one power superior to the EU – the United States, of relevance in all complexes – and in a regional perspective only one power equal to the EU in great power status, namely Russia. These two distinct and principally important cases are included in the subsequent analysis of this book.

Drawing on the Buzan and Wæver framework, the remaining countries neighbouring on the European complex can be geographically categorized into two primary and four subordinate groups. First, cases belong to either the post-Soviet complex or the Middle East complex. These two complexes display an interesting difference in that the post-Soviet case is centred around Russia as a great power (with a special relationship to great power EU), whereas the Middle East complex contains no great power, but is an environment in which the superpower – the United States – is heavily involved in parts of the complex (see Buzan and Wæver 2003: 201–218, 403–436 for general characterizations of the complexes).

Second, in each of these complexes, formations on lower levels (within complexes) can be found. In the post-Soviet case, four sub-regions appear, according to conventional categorization: Central Asia, Caucasus, the Western group of states and the Baltic states. After EU and NATO membership, the Baltic states must now readily be seen as part of the European complex rather than the post-Soviet one, a transformation process that is empirically as well as theoretically interesting but left unattended here. Of the remaining three sub-regions, two – Caucasus and the Western group of states – border on the European complex and are thus of interest to the analysis of this book. The Caucasus sub-region has an internal logic strong enough to categorize it as a mini-complex (Buzan and Wæver's terminology), whereas the Western group of states, while interdependent, is not a complex formation on its own. What brings them together as a group is in part their European linkages, hence the label 'Wider Europe' employed in this book. Shifting focus, in the Middle East complex, there are three distinct sub-complexes, according to Buzan and Wæver – the Maghreb, the Levant and the Gulf. Whereas the latter falls outside of this analysis since it is not adjacent to the European complex, the other two can be utilized as relevant categorizations of countries on the borders of and in interaction with the European complex.

In policy terms, these four groups are concurrent with the set of countries that are covered by the EU's European Neighbourhood Policy (ENP). The Wider Europe group consists of Belarus, Moldova and the Ukraine, whereas the Caucasus group is made up of Armenia, Azerbaijan and Georgia. The Maghreb countries are Algeria, Libya, Morocco and Tunisia and the remaining countries, in the Levant, are Egypt, Israel, Jordan, Lebanon, the Palestinian Authority[1] and Syria. While all 16 countries are part of the same policy framework, they simultaneously enjoy rather different individual relationships to the EU, and also different institutional contexts, for instance regarding the existence and relevance of regional arrangements, such as the Black Sea Synergy or more importantly the Euro-Mediterranean Partnership (the 'Barcelona Process'). All in all, while often categorized geographically, it is argued here that it would be unwise to assume that ENP countries in the same group all stand in the same relationship to the EU; rather, the rationale for the chosen methodology calls for investigating whether there exists different interfaces between the EU and neighbouring countries, not based on geography but on the *character* of recognition in terms of power and identity.

Regarding research design, all countries in Table 1.1 are analysed by employing the analytical framework elaborated in Chapter 2. Having said that, the cases of Russia and the United States, respectively, stand out as principally important cases and will receive extensive attention. The analyses of the neighbourhood countries will be somewhat shorter. These analyses will be grouped into two chapters, one concerning the post-Soviet space, the other concerning the Mediterranean space. This structure enables comparisons among interfaces sharing a great-power presence (Russia in the post-Soviet space) and among interfaces without great-power presence (the Mediterranean) as well as comparisons among the same kind of interfaces irrespective of geographic location. Moreover, this design allows for potential conclusions about the viability of discussing security in geographic terms.

In what follows, the different initial sets of interaction are presented. First, however, a brief look at the EU-centred European complex.

Table 1.1 EU interaction in a regional perspective

EU interaction	Countries
Wider Europe	Belarus, Moldova, Ukraine
South Caucasus	Armenia, Azerbaijan, Georgia
Levant	Egypt, Israel, Jordan, Lebanon, Palestinian Authority, Syria
Maghreb	Algeria, Libya, Morocco, Tunisia
Baltic	Russia
Transatlantic	United States

The EU-centred European regional security complex

According to the logic of Buzan and Wæver, there is a distinct European security complex with the EU as the great power. The complex is not limited to the membership of the EU strictly, but also encompasses other states with which the EU countries entertain intense security interdependence (such as Norway, Iceland and Switzerland and recognized candidates for membership). The EU-centred complex is unique – perhaps paralleled by North America – to the extent that the nature of that security interdependence is of such kind that internally, the issue of military conflict resolution has given way to the securitization of a number of other aspects, ranging from environmental matters to minority rights, identity and conclusions about Europe's own past (Buzan and Wæver 2003: 356–361).

There are a number of interrelated points to be made against such a background. First, concerning the character of the European security complex, conventional wisdom holds that the European complex is a security community, defined in parallel to Karl Deutsch's (1957) notion of expectations of peaceful change and involving the notion of stable peace, understood as a situation in which the parties do not consider the use of military force for conflict resolution (see further the next chapter). Second, the EU is at centre stage of this security community, which in turn means that the EU is attributed actor capacity both internally in the complex and externally in relation to outside states/actors – a 'security provider', to use Kirchner's terminology (Kirchner 2006: 951). Third, drawing on the two previous observations, EU enlargement can be seen as the great success story in the field of European peace and security – through the attractiveness and conditionality of the EU, most obviously played out in the Copenhagen criteria, the security community has gradually been expanded. Fourth, this means that it is the acknowledgement of candidate status, rather than formal membership as such, that determines the scope and character of the EU-led European complex. In consequence, the countries of the Western Balkans, now negotiating for membership or being acknowledged by EU representatives as prospective members, are part of the security complex, along with – most importantly from a geopolitical point of view – Turkey. Fifth, against the background of that conclusion and the observation that 'voluntary' non-EU members, such as Norway and Iceland, obviously belong to the community, it needs to be recognized that institutional membership cannot serve as the sole determinant of the scope of the community. Sixth, directly related to the perspective of this book, although the relationship between the EU and the candidate states can certainly be analysed in terms of an interface, it is not a case of inter-complex relations but, rather, a case of internal relations (within the EU-led complex), and hence falls outside the realm of this book. Seventh and final, the nature of the EU's borders may compromise these conclusions to some extent. As James Anderson notes: 'The EU's internal borders have generally been weakened, its external ones strengthened; and there are further 'internal' distinctions due to some states opting out of the euro currency and/or the Schengen Agreement to suspend passport controls' (Anderson 2002: 230). This process is furthered by the probable differentiated application of the reform treaty from 2009 onwards.

Neighbourhood interfaces: the EU and the ENP countries

Enlargement can be viewed as the true foreign policy success story of the EU. Enlargement holds a fundamental dilemma, however. It will not go on indefinitely, and there will always be states outside of, but deeply interdependent with, the EU. As the EU-centred European complex expands (most obviously through the EU enlargement process) and consolidates, the border between the inside(rs) and the outside(rs) becomes increasingly sharper, both in substantive and cognitive terms (Bengtsson 2009b); the very rationale for borders in general and membership in particular, is to distinguish and divide, rather than unite (see Hassner 2002). Indications of this can be found, for instance, in the challenges that the Schengen arrangement poses to new member-states as well as non-members, in the Kaliningrad issue, and in new obstacles to cross-border trade and investment.

A number of attempts have thus been launched by the EU to handle this situation. The most ambitious of these, and the one getting most political attention currently, is the European Neighbourhood Policy (ENP). This policy, initially outlined in March 2003, 'was developed ... with the objective of avoiding the emergence of new dividing lines between the enlarged EU and our neighbours and instead strengthening the prosperity, stability and security of all concerned' (Commission 2009a; see also Council 2004: 11 for identical reasoning). The underlying logic rests on ideas of liberal internationalism, in that communication, organization and exchange are seen as mechanisms to achieve political outcomes.

Hitherto in this text used only as a geographic marker, over the longer run it is substantially more interesting and relevant to inquire into how and to what extent the ENP transforms the interfaces between the EU and various countries in the neighbourhood. This is an especially interesting issue against the background of quite common arguments that the ENP in its construction of conditionally and rewards draws on the enlargement logic, but is set to experience problems since membership is either politically or geographically out of the question. Through the ENP, the EU can be said to sharpen its normative (ideational) profile vis-à-vis countries on the outside of the security community that the EU leads. At the same time, these countries are quite different in nature and belong to different regional formations. This in turn brings the question of the feasibility of the ENP as a singular policy, albeit with bilaterally designed cooperation schemes between the EU and each partner country (Bengtsson 2008).

Following the logic above, the countries covered by the ENP are grouped into two complexes. These are rather different from each other in terms of the theoretical logic elaborated. First, as observed above, the complexes as such are different from each other in the sense that Russia is deemed a global great power around which the post-Soviet complex converges, whereas no great power is at centre stage in the Middle East complex (although – or perhaps due to the fact that – American superpower presence thus far has been greater in the Middle East than in the post-Soviet area). Second, the character of the borders between the EU and the groups of countries considered here is also different – land borders to the east and southeast (Wider Europe and South Caucasus), sea borders to the southeast and south (Levant and Maghreb). Also the disposition to the EU varies, with the membership issue a politically significant card in the post-Soviet case, especially in the Ukraine, given that other parts of the same complex have been allowed to join once they have fulfilled formal requirements, as compared to membership being a non-issue in relation to the Middle East, which is well-known to both sides. Finally, in terms of institutionalization of cooperation beyond the ENP, interesting differences appear. The post-Soviet cases have individual forms of association to the EU, whereas the Middle East countries are part of the Barcelona process, launched in 1995 as a way to promote closer and more stable relationships among the actors in the region.

The Baltic interface: the EU and Russia

In the parlance of the European Union, the EU and Russia are engaged in a 'strategic partnership' which can be seen as highlighting the reciprocal great power status of the two sides. Both parties figure prominently in the strategic thinking of the other, to the extent that Buzan and Wæver see them as two great powers within a 'loose supercomplex'. Their security interdependencies are not intense enough, however, to warrant the identification of a single European complex (2003: 343), a statement that is of particular interest given the Cold War background, during which the 'most thorough securitisation on either side was the other side as threat' (Buzan and Wæver 2003: 353). Conversely, if judging by the increasingly global agenda of both sides, it seems obvious that while each party deems the other as central and of strategic importance, it is not the only actor/relationship of security importance.

A number of agreements for the institutionalization of the relationship have been set up (Commission 2009b; Bengtsson 2004). Among these, the four Common Spaces agreed to in 2003 form the current platform of the relationship, although the Partnership and Cooperation Agreement (PCA, from 1997) remains the formal basis for interaction. It should be noted that Russia is not part of the ENP (due to its strategic standing), but is covered by the same financial framework – the European Neighbourhood and Partnership Instrument (ENPI) – as the ENP countries.

It is in the Baltic Sea area that the EU and Russia interact most intensively (hence the interface label), in part through the EU's Northern Dimension programme, in part through the Council of Baltic Sea States (CBSS), which holds Russia as well as a number of EU countries along with the Commission as members. While further institutional arrangements regarding the four common spaces are still awaited, a process of establishing an EU Baltic Sea strategy has begun in the Commission.

The transatlantic interface: the EU and the United States

As a superpower the United States is present in various ways in all regions of the world. It is however deeply embedded in the European institutions such as NATO and the OSCE and keeps particularly strong political relationships to a number of European countries to an extent that it seems as if its European engagement goes beyond that in other regions, to the degree that the United States may even be considered a European power, while not being a designated member of the European regional complex.

The relationship between the EU and the United States is characterized by a low degree of institutionalization, but simultaneously appears within a rather dense context, especially obvious through the existence and relevance of NATO, and the great overlap in membership between the EU and NATO. The formal grounds for engagement – common institutions – are not at all as developed as in the case of Russia or the neighbourhood countries, although there are annual summits and a number of working groups within the so-called New Transatlantic Agenda that provides the framework for interaction (Commission 2009c).

It is especially evident in external policy settings that there is an obvious degree of like-mindedness and similar approaches to many international relations issues based on normative conclusions regarding liberal democracy and market economy. Against the background of such value commonality, there are at the same time obvious elements of competition not least in economic matters and different approaches to multilateralism as well as to the utility of military means. All in all, Robert Kagan's famous characterization of the relationship between Europe and the United States in terms of 'paradise and power' (Kagan 2003) is well-taken, interestingly enough against a logic of mutual constitution as explicated in this book – the United States superpower is constituted in part by the European paradise it helped create, a paradise that in turn depends on American power.

Concluding remarks

Whereas the global picture is a complex one, in a regional European perspective – through enlargement, the ENP policy development and interaction with Russia and the United States – the EU clearly poses as an important actor. These processes cannot be viewed in isolation from each other as they obviously are connected in various ways – the ENP was after all developed in relation to the upcoming 2004 enlargement, and relations with Russia are for instance influenced by the fact that the EU as an actor changes in relation to its expanding membership as well as the success of its policies to the east, southeast and in the Mediterranean. The events in Georgia are a good case in point. The strategic relationship with Russia is of importance to the ENP logic; American involvement on the European continent potentially influences political interaction on lower levels. Against this complex background it remains a challenging yet fruitful endeavour to try to understand the variations across interfaces regarding the EU as a security policy actor.

Disposition of the study

The disposition of the book is as follows. Following these introductory remarks, Chapter 2 outlines an analytical framework for the study of interfaces, focusing on concepts such as interface recognition, power and identity in the ambition to construct a general framework based on constructivist logic that can be applied also to studies beyond those of this book. It also discusses the logic of regional security and potential expressions thereof. Part II concerns neighbourhood interfaces: Chapter 3 holds an in-depth study of EU self-image in relation to the neighbourhood as well as a characterization of the general EU perception of the neighbourhood; Chapter 4 analyses the various interfaces stemming from the post-Soviet space; whereas Chapter 5 in a parallel manner takes on the Mediterranean interfaces. Part III deals with the strategic 'Baltic' interface with Russia (Chapter 6); and the 'transatlantic' interface with the United States (Chapter 7). Each of the chapters analysing EU interfaces is set up in a parallel manner: after providing the general setting of the type of relationship in question, each case is analysed in detail regarding strategic interaction and processes of recognition involving perceptions of self and other; ending with a characterization of the interface(s) in terms of central parameters drawn from the analytical framework. In conclusion, Chapter 8 presents a comparative analysis of the findings of the case studies. It also contains reflections in relation to theoretical and empirical observations of the study and regarding the future of the EU as a security actor.

2 Analytical framework

Introduction

The analytical framework of this book, hinted at in the first chapter, is founded on two sets of theoretical propositions. The first such point of departure concerns the subject area of the book and can be summarized in an argument that security in international relations is fruitfully studied on a *regional* level of analysis. In consequence, this is in essence an idea that security cannot be reduced to systemic logic or only understood through consecutive studies of bilateral security relationships at the inter-state level. On the contrary – while not ignoring these two levels of analysis, it is here hypothesized that there is also a regional dynamic of security interaction, which in the end may turn out to be the primary one.

The second theoretical proposition is general in scope and inspired by both rationalist and constructivist reasoning. In essence, it is an argument that any political order (defined as a set of actors, institutions and relationships) consists of a set of *interfaces* which reflect the mutual recognition of the actors involved. Recognition, in turn, denotes a process through which actors establish their disposition towards each other. Recognition presumes actorness, which in this book is understood to follow from mutual perceptions of identity and power. Such perceptions result from considerations regarding material and ideational aspects of self, other and context as they play out in the concrete behaviour of actors.

This chapter in consequence has two main ambitions. One is to elaborate the concept of regional security. For that purpose, regional security complex theory, as developed by Barry Buzan and Ole Wæver, is critically conceptualized and complemented by other works regarding the regional dimension of security as well as the variation in the character and quality of inter-state relations. The second ambition is to develop a general framework for the study of political interaction based on a combination of rationalist and constructivist reasoning. For that purpose, the central concepts of interface, recognition, actorness, identity and power will be elaborated on to some extent. The concluding analytical framework is conceptualized in general terms and may be applied to all cases of political interaction. In this book, the framework is utilized in a regional security setting, more specifically regarding the European Union as an actor in European security matters. The EU does present a challenge by way of its hybrid nature (intergovernmental and supranational dimensions interacting), which is discussed in the final part of this chapter.

Regional security

Regions and regional security

This book rests on the assertion that there is a regional dimension to international relations in general and international security in particular. Striking a critical note, not everyone is convinced that this is a fruitful or necessary supposition. Traditional realist analyses and globalization studies do not generally include the regional dimension as a distinctive level of analysis. Drawing on Andrew Hurrell, there are three kinds of arguments that can be employed to underline the regional dimension. The first one concerns the character of interaction among units of the international system – if levels and character of interdependence vary significantly among different parts of the international system, it may be worthwhile to speak of regionally distinct logics. Second, the character of the units of the system – for instance, the political organization of the 'state' – may also display fundamental differences according to a regional pattern. This aspect is also related to the extent to which non-state forms and actors of governance are of importance. Third, there may be differences in societal approaches – culture, some would say – according to regional patterns. If – and this is the fundamental condition – these dimensions influence policy outcomes, it is worthwhile, even necessary, to allow for a regional, sub-systemic level of analysis (Hurrell 2005: 39–40). At the same time, it is fundamental to underline, as Stadtmüller (2005: 114) does, that the regional dimension of security cannot be separated from the global order. Actors of any subsystem of the international are also actors in multilateral fora, and competition among regional actors sometimes has global impact. In conclusion, regional security consists of the interplay of the global powers at the systemic level and clusters of close security interdependence at the regional level.

Conceptualizations of 'region' have traditionally centred on geographical proximity as the key component. This book, along with numerous writings in the field of 'new regionalism', takes a different point of departure, instead focusing on social (cultural), economic and political interaction. This starting point includes key assumptions regarding the logic that informs both theoretical propositions of the book. The constructivist thinking rests on the assumption that interests of political actors as well as their sense of security are relative and dependent on their identities (Adler and Crawford 2003: 15). In a regional context, that means that regional security is intimately related both to material configurations (manifest power), patterns of intense interdependence and issues of identity formation and change.

Theoretical approaches to regional security

How is, then, regional security to be conceptualized? Although we frequently think of regional security in terms of manifest regional institutions addressing common problems, it is fundamental to underscore that regional distinctiveness is not related only to positive forms of interaction – cooperation – but may equally well stem from intense competition and conflict within a subsystem of the international (Ayoob 1999: 249). From such a point of departure, Barry Buzan and Ole Wæver have developed what they label *regional security complex theory*. Their basic argument is that as 'most threats travel more easily over short distances than over long ones, security interdependence is normally patterned into regionally based clusters: security complexes' (Buzan and Wæver 2003: 4). This is to say that neither a global or systemic power-political perspective such as neo-realism nor a strict focus on domestic politics give a complete picture of security relations between states or other units. Rather, there is a need to focus on the interaction – perceptions and actual practice – of political units and in doing so, the regional level appears as prominent. The regional security complex can thus be defined as 'durable patterns of amity and enmity taking the form of sub-global, geographically coherent patterns of security interdependence' (Buzan and Wæver 2003: 45). In this perspective security interaction at the regional level is predominantly internally directed – high intensity among the units of the region, low intensity or indifference between that group and surrounding states or groups. 'Insulators' are units that face both ways, but are not strong enough to unify its two worlds into one.

Although the logic rests on realist assumptions about international anarchy, the importance of territoriality and the distribution of material power, it nevertheless ends up in constructivist reasoning, which is evident in at least two important points. First, their framework employs a wide conceptualization of security and threats, drawing on the importance of securitization processes, which in turn yields the important implication that the meaning of security is never fixed and cannot be objectively defined, but is a result of political processes involving material considerations, ideational components and cognitive processes, such as perceptions. Second, their framework employs a conceptualization of region not as an objective entity, but as a social construction resulting from (among other things) the security practice of actors. Systemic factors influence but do not determine regional outcomes, which are the result of security interdependence as perceived and acted upon by the states themselves. The resulting patterns vary in quality (see section below); the outcome in each individual case (complex) can be expected to influence the future of the security relationship.

Buzan and Wæver are primarily concerned with the internal logic of security complexes. With the assumption that such complexes exist comes, however, also the issue of the relationship between the complex and actors outside of that complex. Naturally, their framework is rather brief in this regard. It is, however, a principally important issue not only because it is methodologically challenging to establish the boundaries of complexes but also because it challenges the central assumption about the defining logic of regional security complexes – relative intensity of security interdependence among a group of units and security indifference between that set and surrounding units. If regions are socially constructed in the sense that they are contingent on the security practices of different actors, it becomes problematic to stress the distinctiveness of regional complexes in terms of mutually exclusive membership too much. On the contrary, numerous countries can be seen as natural parts of one complex, but at the same time are of security relevance to other complexes. This certainly applies to powerful states (traditionally understood), but also smaller states in the neighbourhood of a given complex.

The empirical field of investigation in this book is Europe, a complex and evasive concept. The important point to make here is that if we accept that there is a distinct EU-centred European complex, as Buzan and Wæver quite reasonably do, there is attached a principally important issue of the relations between that complex and other actors that are of relevance to the European complex, either geographically in a traditional understanding, or more importantly, instrumentally through interaction of various kinds (not necessarily of a positive nature), or cognitively, based on self-perceptions and processes of identification. This means, in consequence, that 'Europe' is not synonymous with the EU.

In important ways, the work by Buzan and Wæver coincides with that of Emanuel Adler and others on cognitive regions and security communities (Adler 1997, Adler and Barnett 1998a, Adler and Crawford 2003: 11–18). Security complexes, cognitive regions and security communities all acknowledge the social construction of political relations and all are concerned with the idea of a common security space among actors on a sub-systemic level. While the metatheoretical logic of the concepts is parallel, there is, however, a major difference between the two in terms of normative foundation – whereas the cognitive region as well as the security community revolves around a sense of collective identity, mutual trust and community, the notion of security complex is a broader one as it is merely an aggregation of socially constructed relations of intense security interdependence. As such, it is more appropriate in terms of the research design and rationale of this book, as it does not limit itself to relationships of positive security interdependence only. The dynamics of cognitive regions and security communities still makes a fruitful contribution to understanding the variation in character of security complexes (see further next section).

Distribution of power

Bringing attention to the importance of powerful actors within regionally distinct contexts, Ayoob discusses the complex yet central role of pivotal powers, which on the one hand may make the region more distinct by giving more coherence to the region and provide collective goods and in the process exercise power in relation to other actors of the region, but which at the same time find themselves in a vulnerable position depending on the degree of legitimacy they maintain and may increase the level of conflict if their claims for primacy are disputed (Ayoob 1999: 252, 256). Moreover, it could be argued that a regional hegemon may play a role in upholding the regional distinctiveness by resisting extraregional influence and in the process contribute to a sense of security among weaker members of the region (Ayoob 1999: 256).

Naturally, Buzan and Wæver readily acknowledge the importance of distribution of power; as pointed out in Chapter 1 of this volume, they distinguish among superpowers, global great powers, regional great powers and lesser powers and describe the current system as a 1+4 system, with the United States as the superpower, and China, Japan, Russia and the EU as global great powers. To their mind, regional security complexes come in two different versions, one being what they call a standard complex among roughly equal states in terms of power, and where the security interdependence results in rather traditional security interaction and logic. The alternative, they argue, is a so-called centred security complex in which one actor is clearly more powerful than the others, which in turn also means that differences in power among lesser states are eradicated – countries that would otherwise be regional great powers are diminished in power terms if there is a global great power, not to speak of a superpower, included in the complex (Buzan and Wæver 2003: 55–57). In this way, power is relative (and relational, as we shall see later in the chapter).

The role of formal institutions

In line with general logic of international cooperation in the form of formal institutions, Charles Kupchan argues that security organizations in a regional setting can play an important role for at least three different reasons. First, formal institutions affect the distribution of power among actors and define centres of power, to the effect that some states are benefitting from a certain institutional design whereas others do not. Second, organizations encourage further cooperation among the members of the institution, for material and ideational reason alike (by establishing rules and norms, by decreasing transaction costs and suspicion and by increasing transparency and trust). It should be stressed, however, that it is empirically quite evident that the mere existence of institutions, although perhaps necessary, is not sufficient for closer relations to develop. Third, international institutions are not only an effect of strategic choices among states, but do also affect domestic politics and the construction of foreign policy in individual states. As Kupchan argues, 'security institutions are political communities.... Participation in these communities, as well as exclusion from them, helps shape national self-images and encourages polities to identify with a certain grouping or region' (Kupchan 1997: 219–220).

It is fundamental, however, to make the point that formal institutions do not make up a region. Applied to the European case, it means that the European Union, although a (the) key regional institution is not synonymous with the European region. Institutional membership thus cannot be used as an indicator of the scope of socially constructed regions – by way of obvious examples; EU non-members such as Norway and Switzerland are naturally part of any European region. Principally more interesting from the point of view of the interface logic spelled out below, the same logic applies to countries such as Russia and the United States, due to the centrality of the security interdependence with the EU and its member-states, and countries that border on the EU-led security complex, again referring to security interdependence, which means that the fate of the EU-led complex to some extent is dependent on perceptions and political choices made in countries in, say, North Africa, the Middle East or among CIS states. This way of reasoning renders the conclusion that cognitive regions are (normally) larger notions than security complexes, as the former also include interaction across the borders of the complex.

It should be noted at this point that to the mind of this author, countries that are recognized as prospective members by a formal institution (membership then being conditioned on the rules and procedures laid out by the institution), can be considered part of the security complex although they are not (yet) members of the formal institution. In concrete terms, that means that the countries of the Western Balkans, and more importantly Turkey, are to be seen as part of the EU-led security complex although their EU membership is yet to be determined. This has at least two important implications – first, that the nature of the boundary between these countries and the formal institution has taken on a new meaning through the possibility of membership (a strict inside–outside dichotomy does not apply, it has become an issue of transformation), second – and principally more important – it means that countries that are formally recognized as candidates for membership are assumed to share the same set of values and interests as other members of the institution. In the EU case, this has great weight as it can be argued that the EU-led complex is a so called security community in which conflicts are settled without referring to the use of military means (see further the section on variations in outcome below).

The nature of boundaries

The claim that distinct regional orders can and do exist also pinpoints the intricate question of the nature of the boundaries vis-à-vis actors outside of the regional complex. In their discussion of cross-border cooperation in Europe, Henrik van Houtum and Anke Strüver employ a constructivist perspective on boundaries as mutually constituted but simultaneously with real consequences and effects (van Houtum and Strüver 2002: 142). What is the role of boundaries? In everyday language a boundary (or border, in the legal sense) denotes the geographical demarcation of separate territories and power hierarchies (and involves the function of social control, see Anderson 2002: 231). When utilizing a perspective of social construction, however, the psychological aspects of boundaries are also illuminated, problematizing the 'imagination of togetherness' (van Houtum and Strüver 2002: 144). Van Houtum and Strüver draw on George Simmel in using the metaphors of bridge, door and stranger. The role of the bridge, they argue, is to bring together parts that are at the outset separated from each other. The door is symbolizing something more – that the blocking and permitting effects of boundaries are actually two sides of the same phenomena, following logically from each other. The label of stranger, finally, is acknowledging the alienating effect of boundaries: 'being spatially close, but socially remote is being neither insider, nor outsider, but "near and far at the same time" and a strange, yet constitutive non-member of a group' (2002: 143). From this perspective, discussions about inclusionary versus exclusionary boundaries and soft versus hard borders underline that these are not only, perhaps not even primarily, administrative phenomena but political constructions involving not only legal but also ideational aspects (Bellamy 2004: 43–45). In that sense, the construction of border regimes becomes an issue of power. Employing an institutional perspective, it may be hypothesized that the character of boundaries between a security complex and surrounding actors may in part be a reflection of previous interaction, and in part determine the character of future interaction. Focusing on the European context, this is one of the reasons why the Schengen border regime of the EU becomes interesting – what is the impact on surrounding states of the increasing territorialization of the EU that can be claimed to follow from the Schengen process and the finalization of the internal market (Bengtsson 2009b)?

Outcome: variation in character of security

The very argument that there are distinct regional orders implies that there may be variation in the quality of political relations of different such orders. In other words, the character of international anarchy is different in different parts of the world – a conclusion that has relevance both in the academic community (what general assumptions about the logic of international relations can we make?) and in political circles (what are the foreign policy implications of such variation and what are the mechanism that allow for some regions to develop higher-quality peace than other regions?).

Security complexes, argue Buzan and Wæver, reflect 'patterns of amity and enmity' (2003: 40) on a regional basis; amity then being understood as relationships of 'genuine friendship' or 'expectations of protection or support' and enmity denoting relationships characterized by 'suspicion and fear' (Buzan 1991: 189–190). Analytically, complexes come in different types, ranging from conflict formation (predominantly conflictual relations) to security regime (mutual recognition of conflictual as well as common interests give rise to dispute management) to security community (mutual expectations of peaceful conflict resolution), thus roughly corresponding to Hobbesian, Lockean and Kantian versions of anarchy (Buzan 1991: 218–219; Buzan and Wæver 2003: 53–54). This typology corresponds roughly to general IR scholarship on variation in the quality of peace, distinguishing, for instance, between precarious, conditional and stable peace (Kacowicz *et al.* 2000). Precarious peace denotes the negative form of peace that is most easily thought of as the absence of war, a relationship in which fundamental conflict and the use of deterrence is present and which includes only limited forms of intergovernmental contacts and strict regulations on societal interaction. In contrast, under conditional peace (although it may still involve certain elements of deterrence), relations among political actors have normalized and include also societal contacts. Although conflicting elements may still be present, common interests also form part of the rationale for interaction and policy formulation. Stable peace, finally, refers to the kind of high-quality peace that does not involve military means for deterrence or actual use in situations of conflict among the parties. Such a situation is naturally conducive to advanced forms of societal interaction, and also to the development of not only common interests but also common values, norms and identities. The main distinction among these forms of peace is the degree of trust or distrust among the actors involved – relationships of precarious peace rest on distrust as the main psychological mechanism, whereas conditional peace denotes a situation of trust, and stable peace – the central dynamics of security community – is based on a kind of blind trust, some would say confidence, to the effect that the parties involved never contemplate using military violence for conflict resolution, no matter the severity of conflict (Bengtsson 2000a, 2000b, 2009a).

The logic of stable peace is at the heart of the notion of security community, as developed originally by Karl Deutsch and a number of colleagues and more recently advanced by Emanuel Adler and Michael Barnett (1998a). Security communities – zones of peace in which actors entertain dependable expectations of peaceful change – are based on shared norms, collective identity and high levels of trust and are based on benign security practices, such as dialogue and persuasion, that is, social communication (Adler and Barnett 1998b: 37–48, Adler and Crawford 2003: 11–18, Bellamy 2004: 6–11, 27–29). This characterization is connected to the concept of cognitive regions, which are transnational, constituted by people's shared values, norms and practices, and, it could be argued, non-territorial, as they exist independent of geography (Adler 1997).

This also relates to Ayoob's continuum of regional order, where he distinguishes among regional system (merely a set of interacting units), regional security, regional society and regional community. Focusing his analysis on regional society, he argues that what distinguishes regional security and regional society is that a regional society requires the 'conscious recognition on the part of regional states that they have certain common interests which they need to preserve despite the existence of differences, even disputes, among them' (Ayoob 1999: 248). Moreover, regional society requires that the states of a region perceive state- and nation-building processes as complementary rather than competing processes, a condition, argues Ayoob, that is difficult to fulfil in many cases due to the disputed borders in many parts of the world (Ayoob 1999: 256). Regional security, on the other hand, can be maintained through balance of power logic and need not include any common interests, let alone the build-up of some degree of trust through common interests and undertakings. Regional community, on the other hand, rests on great levels of economic and political interdependence but includes, moreover, not only rational/material incentives but also, importantly, 'cognitive regionalism' (Ayoob 1999: 248, see also Wendt 1999: 247 on the importance of the degree of internalization of different roles in interaction), understood to include the same notions of we-feeling, trust, shared identity etc. as in the logic of Deutsch *et al.*, Adler and Barnett, Bellamy, and others.

What determines the patterns of amity and enmity that are the defining dimension of security complexes? This empirical question needs to be studied in individual cases, but generally a whole array of factors is potentially relevant, such as history, religion, culture, geography, and economics, but what ultimately matters is how these factors are perceived by different actors in processes of mutual constitution. Additionally, proposing an institutional perspective on patterns, Buzan and Wæver argue that 'to a large extent they are path dependent and thus become their own best explanations' (2003: 50). Such a perspective implies that orders are durable rather than permanent and thus that change is possible. It is in this context that the literature on cognitive regions, security communities and stable peace becomes politically relevant, as it addresses the question of how to devise political programmes to achieve such desirable outcomes.

Concluding remarks: regions and regional security

Acknowledging such variation in the internal character of security complexes begs the question of the relationship between complexes and actors outside of them. Is there, for instance, any significant difference between relations of security communities and their neighbours compared to those of conflict formations and their neighbours? Returning to the initial argument based in constructivist reasoning that security interfaces among actors are socially constructed renders a conclusion in the positive, that there may be relevant differences and these, in consequence, need to be empirically studied in order to learn more not only about improvements in intra-complex relations, but also in regional politics generally. That said, it remains an open question what the nature of those interfaces may be. Generally speaking, some may be rather friendly in nature, others of more hostile character, some may involve limited material interaction, others rather advanced transnational collaboration – as Alex Bellamy points out regarding security communities, their external relations may be of varying character, depending in part on the outside actor involved and in part on the nature and political profile of the security community as such (Bellamy 2004: 11–12, 60–62).

The discussion above points out a number of potentially relevant aspects for studying the nature of security interfaces – the nature of borders between actors, the character of power relationships, the degree of mutual identification, the nature of material interaction and the scope of common formal institutions. We turn now to a fuller conceptualization of interface and related concepts in order to establish an analytical framework around these notions.

The general logic of interfaces

The general logic of interfaces can be summarized according to Figure 2.1.

Before embarking on various conceptualizations, a couple of general comments may be in order. First, the framework rests on the importance of perceptions. The content of these remains an empirical issue to be settled; here, the point to be made is about the inherently subjective nature of perceptions and the need to take into account actor subjectivity: Actor A's self-image may or may not correspond to actor B's image of A. In turn, it becomes a relevant issue to try to locate the main parameters for such similarities and differences. Second, the interface logic builds on an idea of mutual constitution of relationships, in that experiences of contextual change or continuity and image transformation and permanence may lead to changes in perceptions – through feed-back mechanisms, the meetings of actors are translated into perceptual experiences and potential reframing of self, other and context.

A brief conceptualization of interface

In its simplest form, an *interface* is constituted by two actors (or sets of actors) through their respective recognitions. It builds on the idea that actors are mutually constituted through their actions. This in essence means that it is the interplay of internal dynamics within collective actors' perceptions of each other and actual behaviour that ultimately determine the character of any relationship (for instance domestic politics within states). The concept can thus be said to be relational and identity-based in character, although perceptions quite naturally in part may be (are) determined by material conditions. This means that for each actor, both the self-identity and the image of the other contribute to the interface – who 'we' are is of importance when determining who 'they' are, so to speak. Such a way of reasoning rests on constructivist logic (for an overview, see Adler 2002) and focuses on cognitive processes on the part of political actors. In conceptual terms, the notion of interface is in consequence open to analysis of various kinds of actors as well as types of interaction.

Regarding actors, the notion does not in itself presume any particular actor category, although it should be underlined that there is an obvious delimitation to collective actors rather than individuals, given the focus on internal dynamics of actors in terms of learning, competition and change. In terms of types of

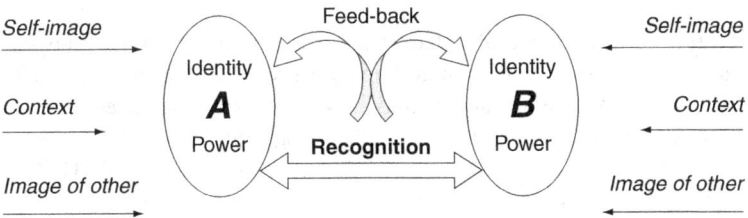

Figure 2.1 The interface logic.

interaction, again, there is no theoretical foreclosure: the notion potentially includes various types of interaction, such as economic, political (diplomatic) or violent; the concept does however assume a perceptual process when translating experiences of interaction into image input.

In principle, there are two kinds of interfaces. On the one hand, an interface may consist of actors with a common understanding of the nature of relationship and the actors involved, that is, mutual recognitions are identical/overlap greatly (for instance, both parties to a relationship agree that one is the employer and the other is the employee, and from that joint conclusion (not to be mixed with harmony) follows expectation, obligations and rights). Such mutual recognition thus rests on an agreement in terms of understanding and can be expected to be a rather stable form of interface. Such agreement in terms of recognition is, however, not to be confused with identity in content, for instance that the actors are of the same kind – as the example of the employer and the employee illustrates, this is not necessarily the case.

On the other hand, parties to a relationship may be in complete disagreement regarding how to recognize each other. This is, for instance, the case in severe political conflicts, such as the relationship between governments and freedom fighters/terrorists (depending on the labeller) – in such relationship there is disagreement about expectations and identity, legitimate claims and long-term outcomes, right to resources and agenda-setting etc. Such interfaces rest on disequilibrium – cognitive imbalance – and will presumably change as a result of the concrete behaviour of actors. In summary, it seems fruitful to distinguish between *agreement interfaces* (in which A recognizes B in the same way as B recognizes A) and *disagreement interfaces* (in which A recognizes B in a different way than B recognizes A).

On recognition

What is, then, the substantive logic of recognition? The concept of recognition has traditionally been employed in international law concerning acts of acknowledging state actors in the international system based on a general principle of sovereignty. That such acts take place at the intersection of law and politics is illustrated by the recent and contested cases of Kosovo, South Ossetia and Abkhazia. Hans Kelsen makes the distinction between political and legal aspects of such recognition. He argues that the

> [P]olitical act of recognition of a state or government means that the recognizing state is willing to enter into political and other relations with the recognized state or government ... political recognition of a state or a government is an act which lies within the arbitrary decision of the recognizing state.
>
> (Kelsen 1941: 605)

This means that political recognition is declaratory and deliberate and that it signals a readiness to interaction vis-à-vis the recognized entity. Kelsen goes on to argue that 'declaration in itself has no legal consequences, although it may be of great importance politically, especially for the prestige of the state or government to be recognized' (Kelsen 1941: 605). This relates to the importance of legitimacy and other resources that the recognized actor comes to possess in the process (Yu and Longenecker 1994: 476–477, 480). Recognition in this sense refers to actorness being conveyed or acknowledged by other actors rather than simply being stated by the entity in question. Recognition, argues M.J. Peterson, 'is the way in which the major actors in the system identify each other, since there is no central agency to pass on a new regime's qualifications' (1982: 324). In a legal sense, recognition refers to the dichotomous concept of statehood, but in a political sense, recognition can be thought to denote a number of other characteristics/forms. This is also the way to interpret the position of the EU in the international system – while the union is not legally recognized (although the European Community is), there is the political recognition of the EU in the world. The character of this political recognition depends on other actors' expectation of EU actorness in various processes and events (see further next section).

From these initial observations, it can be concluded that mutual recognition is a processual concept, denoting the process through which actors in a relationship establish their disposition towards each other. Since recognition refers to the identification of an actor by others, in our case as a potent international actor, such a process necessarily involves subjective elements – perceptions – that are influenced by a number of factors, such as general world-view, experience, self-image and understanding of context along with more concrete aspects such as instrumental power and capacity for institution-building. The concept of recognition thus seems rewarding in pinpointing a process through which an actor is judged by others to have certain qualities and capacities, thus tying together internal and external developments and underlining the inherently subjective character of international relations as understood in this book. This way of reasoning is in line with that of Peterson, who explains:

> Political uses of recognition may be classed into two main categories: expression of friendship or hostility toward a new government (expressing opinions), and exchange of recognition for a particular act or promise regarding future policy (influencing a new government's conduct).
> (Peterson 1982: 328)

There is, a priori, no reason to exclude either material or non-material factors in such processes; rather, it seems fruitful to note that recognition is based on the perceived actorness of others, and such actorness may involve both material and non-material expressions (see further discussion in the next section).

As Erik Ringmar argues, processes of recognition are fundamental to social relations:

> To desire recognition is not to desire an object that provides utility, pleasure or profit, but instead to be a *subject* of a certain kind. The desire for

> recognition is the core human desire, central to our sense of who and what we are. Hobbes was wrong: the self is a relational, not an atomistic concept.
>
> (Ringmar 2002: 119)

We find processes of recognition all the time in international relations. Recognition as a great power, for instance, may both yield external expectations and bring increased room for manoeuvre. In recent years, preparation for EU enlargement by a dozen countries is an interesting case in point. These countries have ultimately aimed at becoming recognized by already existing actors as democratic and based on market economy principles. In his own research, Ringmar brings forward the example of the Russian civil war, which 'did not primarily concern who should get what, but instead *who should be who*' (Ringmar 2002: 124). One of the central lines of thought in the democratic peace literature also focuses on the idea of mutual recognition (although this particular term may not be used). The rationale is that recognition by outside players is what in the end determines the impact of an actor, rather than how the actor himself perceives his capacity.

An interesting issue in this context concerns how recognition takes place; that is, the dynamics through which dispositions are established and reproduced. Figure 2.1 above hypothesizes that through feed-back mechanisms, mutual recognition may actually influence images of self and other (both material and ideational components) which in turn may alter the character of the interface at a later time. Ringmar understands the recognition process as deliberate interaction:

> Since recognition never will be automatically forthcoming, however, each person has to fight for who he or she takes him- or herself to be.... The struggle concerns not the distribution of utilities, but instead who should have the right to impose what description on whom. This is how the master is separated from the slave, the superior being from the inferior.
>
> (Ringmar 2002: 120)

This way of thinking runs parallel to a conceptualization of 'framing' as a process through which actors compete for determining the meaning of events, processes and concepts and subsequently change their stance in relation to actors and/or issues (see Payne 2001 and Benford and Snow 2000).

Actorness: identity and power

Recognition – the mutual constitution of a relationship through parallel actor-internal developments and external expectations – helps us conceptualizing the elusive notion of actorness. The basic argument is rather straightforward. Focusing solely on developments in internal capacity of a given actor misses the fundamental point that what is ultimately decisive is how other actors perceive such developments. These developments may be overvalued or undervalued by the external actors, attributed more or less value than the actor himself (or other actors) would assert. Hence, although an actor may hypothetically have great ambitions in a given issue area, this matters little as long as others do not recognize the impact of the actor. Conversely, external expectations may be rather substantial in some cases, while at the same time preconditions in terms of actual capacity to deliver may be limited. The argument rests on constructivist logic in focusing on how perceptions shape and are shaped by actual behaviour in a constantly ongoing process.

It is this behavioural approach that for instance forms the basis of the analysis of Charlotte Bretherton and John Vogler (2006) regarding the EU as a global actor. A central argument on their part is that internal and external factors are mutually constitutive in the evolution of actorness – both internal capacity ('capability') and external events ('opportunity') are of importance, and how the former relates to the latter influences the 'presence' of an actor on the international stage. Presence is not regarded in terms of concrete (purposive) action, but rather as a 'consequence of being' (Bretherton and Vogler 2006: 12–36, quote on p. 27).

Their analysis highlights that there are essentially two elements to actorness. One concerns the power resources of an actor in terms of ability or capacity to influence a desired outcome. The other concerns the image of the actors in the eyes of others. In what follows these two constituent factors are discussed. The substantive interest in this book concerns EU actorness in the field of foreign and security policy, an area in which the EU traditionally has not been recognized as a potent actor, but one in which both external events (EU activities in the Balkans, the Middle East and Africa) and EU-internal developments (ENP, CFSP, ESDP) may have contributed to changing the perceptions of different actors of the current order, thus influencing the recognition of EU actorness.

Identity

The relevance of identity in international relations is one of the core debates of current IR scholarship. This short section cannot do the rich debate full justice, but merely seeks to highlight the principal assumptions that inform the analysis of this book. While realist and other traditional perspectives on IR assume that identities have no independent explanatory power and that interests stem from material considerations (and systemic factors), the constructivist logic rests on the assumption that processes of identification do matter (and change) (Adler 2002: 103–104). Moreover, identities are assumed to precede interests; as Peter Gourevitch argues, 'prior to interests and institutions lies the formation of an identity and a framework of discourse' (Gourevitch 2002: 313). Ringmar follows the same line of reasoning: 'states not only pursue their "national interests", but also – and before anything else – they seek to establish identities for themselves. In fact, questions regarding a state's identity must always be more fundamental than questions regarding its interests' (Ringmar 2002: 116).

For the purposes of this analysis, identity can be understood in terms of values of a (collective) actor and the role these play in relation to oneself and other actors (see further Herrmann 2002) – in this way, values, interests and action are linked together. As a conclusion, through policy interaction, self-image and image of others are constantly related to each other (see Jepperson *et al.* 1996: 53 for a fuller elaboration). What matters in the end, then, is the degree of value compatibility.

Processes of identification thus involve the drawing of boundaries between self and other. The attributes, roles and actual practice of an actor simultaneously yet subjectively establish the actorness of an actor as seen by the actor himself and by surrounding actors. As Eric Clark and Bo Petersson note:

> The corporeal and semiotic construction of identities and boundaries are intrinsically intertwined. Identification involves de*fini*ng oneself, commonly as one among a group or set with common characteristics, tastes, styles, preferences, beliefs or the like, in contradiction to others who do not share these characteristics. *Finis* is Latin for boundary.
>
> (Clark and Petersson 2003: 12)

In this way, identity is inevitably linked to the issue of boundary formation, and the consequences thereof, as discussed above.

While there naturally exists no comprehensive typology of identities, it seems fruitful for an analysis of value compatibility to draw on Bjørn Møller's distinctions among perceptions of the potentially dangerous 'hostile Other', the neutral and distant 'different Other' and the 'transient Other', one that is in transition in the direction of the actor in question (Møller 2005: 40–41). In a regional security context, the 'different Other' is empirically unlikely against a logic of security interdependence – actors can be assumed not to be indifferent to the actions of geographically adjacent others. To Møller's categories could be added that of the 'friendly Other', one that is based on amity and an identification of value compatibility.

Interfaces based on these different kinds of identification can be assumed to include different levels and forms of interaction. In interfaces involving hostility, interaction can be expected to be competitive in nature and limited due to perceived self-sufficiency, the presence of threats as well as the distance in terms of value commonality. Also in interfaces involving perceptions of difference interaction can be expected to be limited (or be part of general/multilateral processes), but based on a different rationale – that of disinterest vis-à-vis the Other. In interfaces of transience, on the other hand, interaction may be expected to be quite intense, against the background of the potential realization and upgrading of common interests. This goes equally well for parties in symmetrical relationships (in power terms), in which actors converge to a value base and relationships of asymmetry (influence and leadership on the part of the superior and the management of dependence on the part of the inferior). The same logic applies in friendship interfaces, where interaction stimulates the further promotion of common values.

Power

As is the case with the concept of identity, power is an elusive concept that has rendered a whole array of attempts at definition and clarification. General social science distinctions regarding 'power over' versus 'power to' and internal dimensions of power (capacity for action) versus external dimensions of power (capacity to control the behaviour of others) have their specific reflections in IR scholarship, for instance in Joseph Nye's well-known distinction between soft power (the ability to get 'others to want what you want' (Nye 2005) and traditional hard power mechanisms to enforce compliance through military and/or economic means. Even so, power remains an essentially contested concept and it is necessary here to somewhat further problematize the concept for the subsequent analysis to be worthwhile.

A useful framework for understanding power is presented by Michael Barnett and Raymond Duvall. They define power as 'the production, in and through social relations, of effects that shape the capacities of actors to determine their own circumstances and fate' (Barnett and Duvall 2005: 3). Their typology of power fruitfully integrates many of the aspects that other scholars have discussed as central to the concept. The typology identifies four different forms of power: compulsory, institutional, structural and productive. Very briefly, compulsory power corresponds to traditional understandings of power as one actor's direct control over another. Institutional power, on the other hand, is indirect in nature so that actors exercise or are affected by the impact of institutional design choices that were made at a prior point in time; it may also be the case that institutions themselves possess power mechanisms (reflecting the degree of autonomy of institutions). Structural power relates to ability to influence or alter the positions and interests of actors that stand in a direct relationship to each other. In a dialectic manner, one actor is constituted by the existence of another actor, as, for instance, in a master–slave relation; structural power refers to the capacity to change this relationship. Productive power, finally, refers to the ability to define and/or interpret terms, symbols, events and actors according to one's own belief systems or frames of reference. The typology rests on two core distinctions, first, regarding whether power is relational (concerning direct interaction between specific actors) or constitutive (concerning the constitution of social relationships), second, whether the social relations that encompass power effects are direct or diffuse in character. Compulsory power is thus relational and direct, whereas institutional power is relational but diffuse. Structural power is constitutive and direct, while productive power is constitutive and diffuse (for an elaboration of the logic of this framework, see Barnett and Duvall 2005: 9–22).

The framework highlights that resources for political action – the operative aspect of power – can be of either material or ideational character. Material resources may for instance consist of military force, natural resources, or economic capability, whereas ideational resources come in the form of norms and values which are translated into aid conditionality, diplomatic skill, and not least, framing, a process in which the resourceful actor is able to stipulate what is expected and/or acceptable behaviour. Whereas compulsory power utilizes material resources, institutional and structural power potentially draw on material as well as ideational resources. Productive power is principally based on ideational resources. In this vein, Adler notes:

The imposition of meanings on the material world is one of the ultimate forms of power, and this is where constructivism's added value with regard to power lies. The added value that results from interpreting power from a constructivist perspective also includes what Hacking (1999) has called 'making people'; in other words, labelling people in such a way that they change their identity, status and functions in reaction to the labelling.

(Adler 2002: 103)

This discussion can be specified regarding the EU in terms of the well-established distinction regarding the EU as a military/civilian/normative power (Manners 2002; Manners and Whitman 2003). Military power builds on material resources, whereas civilian power utilizes material as well as ideational resources. Normative power – the ability to shape conceptions of 'normal' (Manners 2002: 240) – draws on ideational resources and results from cognitive processes on the part of both possessor and object, with both substantive and symbolic components. In conclusion, the normative power often discussed regarding the EU is a case of the more general category of productive power.

A central implication of the Barnett and Duvall framework is that the resources that political actors may potentially use can come in many forms and actors that can draw on, or combine, various forms of power find themselves in an advantageous situation. At the same time, it may be the case that different forms of power may contradict each other. Regarding the EU, for instance, it can be argued that the increasing salience of military power in EU international action jeopardizes its normative power impact.

Logically, although difficult to specify empirically, political relationships can come in one of two different guises – symmetry and asymmetry. Symmetrical power relationships imply equality and denote perceptions of actors as being of the same status in terms of relative power position. Asymmetry, on the other hand, denotes an inferiority/superiority situation defined by the understanding that one actor is superior to the other in power terms.

Analytical framework

The logic of the discussion above can thus be summarized as follows: A regional security complex is made up of a set of interfaces, internally as well as across the boundaries of the complex. An interface consists of the mutual recognition of two or more actors. Recognition denotes the process through which actors establish their dispositions vis-à-vis other actors. The process comprises three analytically different elements: self-image, perception of the other, and of context. In that process, material and ideational resources of actors become decisive.

The character of the interface – the outcome – is determined by two variables – degree of value compatibility and the power configuration internal to the interface. Both variables are investigated in terms of manifest behaviour of the interface actors: what they say about themselves, the other and context, and how and on what terms they interact with each other. Drawing on the typologies discussed above, six types of interfaces are possible (see Table 2.1).

Table 2.1 Types of interfaces

Values/power	Symmetry	Asymmetry
Incompatibility	Hostility	Resistance
Interaction: competition		
Transition	Convergence	Adaptation
Interaction: socialization		
Compatibility	Community	Inclusion
Interaction: integration		

On mutuality of values, a crude distinction between value incompatibility (disparity), value transition and value compatibility (commonality) can be maintained. Regarding power configuration, a crude distinction between power symmetry and asymmetry internal to the interface can be applied. Combining these two dimensions, six types of interfaces appear: the *hostility interface* denotes symmetrical power configuration and value incompatibility and implies a situation of competition and rivalry, such as great power enemy interaction. Asymmetrical power configuration and value incompatibility implies a competitive situation of (attempts at) control and domination by the superior power, and resistance on the part of the weaker power. Significantly enough, however, the power of the dominant part is not so strong as to push the resistant actor in the value direction of the dominant actor, resulting in a so-called *resistance interface*. Symmetrical power configuration and mutual value transition is a form of *convergence interface*, whereas value transition against the background of power asymmetry implies an *adaptation interface*, in which the weaker part adopts and adapts to core values of the dominant actor. For both sides, but with different rationales, this means utilizing interdependence in a pro-active fashion to achieve desired (welfare and security) goals. When value compatibility is at hand, finally, we may either consider *community interfaces* against the background of power symmetry, or *inclusion interfaces* against the background of weaker parties being included in the group of similar value base. It should be underlined at this point that this does not imply harmony or identity of interests, but rather that shared fundamental values determine the nature of negotiations and dispute settlements.

The analytical framework to be used when establishing the nature of different interfaces in subsequent chapters consists of the following dimensions:

Variable: identity

Key questions

- What are the key features of the self-perception of the actor in question?
- How is the other party perceived in terms of the typology above (hostile, different, transient, friendly)?
- To what extent are there signs of value compatibility between the actors?

36   *Introduction and analytical framework*

Indicators

- Statements about self, other and relationship
- Interaction in key spheres, such as general foreign policy, strategic issues and/or security concerns as defined by the actors themselves
- Existence and growth of common organizations
- Joint activities
- Collaboration to combat common threats/alleviate problems

Primary data

- Official documents including joint statements
- Key political speeches
- Media communication
- Opinion polls
- Printed interviews

Variable: power

Key questions

- What kinds of power mechanisms are found in the relationship (compulsory/institutional/structural/productive)?
- What power resources/strategies do the different actors utilize?
- How does each side perceive its relative power status vis-à-vis the other?

Indicators

- Origin and logic of formal interaction
- Formal agenda-setting (e.g. renegotiation of agreements)
- Rhetorical agenda-setting (e.g. terminology)

Primary data

- Official documents including joint statements
- Key political speeches
- Printed interviews

Concluding remarks: analytical framework

While traditional security studies have been concerned with state actors, and not least with the great powers, recent developments in this scholarly area has brought a broadening of the concept both in substance (scope and hierarchy of issues) and in terms of subjects (not only states but also other collectives – ranging from terrorist groups and private military enterprises to non-governmental organizations and trans-national corporations – and, importantly, individuals). It is in this increasingly complex realm that the EU as a security actor appears centre stage. The EU presents a challenge due to its hybrid nature, combining intergovernmental and supranational dimensions. As is evident in the analysis by Bretherton and Vogler, the balance between these dimensions – in essence, the competence granted to EU-level institutions – varies from issue-area to issue-area (Bretherton and Vogler 2006). In the foreign policy field, there are historic differences, for instance, among the areas of foreign economic policy, aid and development policy and military security policy, related to differences in the original treaties and not least the set-up of the treaty on the European Union (the Maastricht Treaty) that entered into force in 1993. Apart from the general conclusion that we should be very cautious when generalizing about this complex institution, this means for the purposes of this book that for outside actors trying to grasp the EU, how they perceive the EU is in part an issue about what policy fields and what institutional aspects they focus on. For instance, both Russia and the United States has increasingly recognized the EU as a major player in world affairs (Bengtsson 2004), but as will be evident in subsequent chapters, the rationale and conditions of this recognition differ between the two.

What assumptions can be made about the EU as a security actor in a regional European setting? While it is disputed what the global impact of the EU amounts to, and while cases such as Iraq and the war on terrorism brutally show that in terms of crisis, temptations at national foreign policy-making are hard to resist, in a regional context, the EU is generally – for material as well as ideational reasons – perceived to be a great power in relation to most other actors in the region. That can be expected to give a different logic regarding how others view the EU and what they expect from it – here, to use Hill's well-known distinction (Hill 1993), may the gap between expectations and capabilities not be as great as in other places, or no issue at all. Here, on the other hand, may the ideational impact be greater.

Interestingly enough, it may be the *sui generis* character of the EU entity that is providing the organization with part of its resources for influence. Ian Manners argues that what gives the EU its normative difference is its historical context, hybrid polity and political–legal constitution (Manners 2002: 240). It can thus be understood, in Manners and Whitman's (2003) language, as a 'difference engine'.

From a regional security complex perspective, there are two related ways of approaching the EU. The first concerns the EU as a distinct complex in the form of security community, in which the members (formal members, recognized candidate states, and voluntary non-members) enjoy such a high degree of mutual trust that they rest assured that conflict will be settled peacefully. The other understands the EU as a great power in a larger regional context (not synonymous with the EU itself), interacting with various units that are not part of, but border on, the security community. Although fully agreeing with the characterization of the EU as a security community, it is the latter approach that is in focus in this book, as it investigates relationships between the EU and various neighbouring states. It could be added that the two approaches are connected to the effect that the security community is a dynamic construction due to the potential for enlargement, if community members and states currently on the outside entertain consolidated expectations of peaceful change. That in turn means that the boundary between the community and bordering states changes character, not only geographically, but potentially also politically, if the community and/or outsiders change their policies as a result of enlargement.

In conclusion, there are two fundamental points that inform the analyses of subsequent chapters. First, drawing on various characterizations made in the literature about EU institutional capacity and external relations, it could be hypothesized that the EU stands in a superior power relationship to neighbouring states, apart from Russia, with which it entertains a symmetrical great power position. In relation to the United States, most analyses posit the EU in an inferior position, in that the United States is the only superpower in the international system, and the EU does not entertain such a comprehensive or aggregate hegemonic power. Alternative analyses do, however, point to specific issue-areas – democracy promotion being one – where such power disparity seems not to be at hand. The empirical analyses will initially take this hypotheses as points of departure, but through the empirical analyses qualify them in important ways, and moreover – in consequence of the discussion above – show that a given power distribution does not imply one particular interface.

Second, regarding the concept of *Europe* as applied to discussions of regions, complexes and communities alike, the constructivist logic that informs the analytical framework of this book renders the conclusion that it is indeed impossible to objectively determine the boundaries of the European entity. This forms an assumption – partly in contrast to that of Buzan and Wæver – that underlies the design of this enquiry, along the lines that a number of states that border on the EU-led community can be argued to belong to other complexes but are still of significance to the European security community, against the background of different levels of security interdependence and resulting interfaces of various kind. If anything, it could be concluded that for the notion of a European regional security complex to make sense, also states in the post-Soviet complex, as well as in the North African and Middle East complexes, are, potentially to be considered part of the European complex. That, in turn, gives rise to important policy conclusions, discussed further in the final chapter of this book.

Part II
Neighbourhood interfaces

This second part of the book deals with interfaces between the EU and the countries bordering on the European security complex, collectively referred to as the neighbourhood. Empirically, this is equivalent to the countries covered by the EU's European Neighbourhood Policy (ENP). Russia is excluded from this analysis and is dealt with in a separate chapter in Part III of the book. Based on theoretical as well as empirical justifications, the analysis of this book rests on a distinction between Russia and the other neighbouring countries. In theoretical terms, the power relationship between Russia and the EU can be hypothesized to be of a different nature (great power interaction) than the power relations between the EU and other neighbouring states, in which the EU can be expected to play the role of the superior power and the neighbouring states in different ways are situated in an inferior position. Having said that, it is one of the ambitions of the subsequent analyses to investigate the power dimension between the EU and other actors, and it is quite evident that in the neighbourhood group, there are great variations in this (and other) respects. Empirically, there is also reason for separating Russia from the rest of the neighbouring group. While relations between Russia and the EU take the form of a traditional bilateral arrangement, all other neighbours (beyond those recognized as candidates for membership) – 16 in total – are part of the ENP, and the majority, moreover, part of the Euro-Mediterranean Partnership (EMP). Although there is an important bilateral dimension between the EU and all ENP (and EMP) members, there is thus nevertheless a regional perspective that provides the framework for various bilateral relations and implies that the context of EU interaction is different from the Russian case.

For reasons of reader feasibility, the rather extensive analysis of EU-neighbourhood interfaces is divided into three chapters. Chapter 3 applies a regional perspective on EU recognition of the neighbourhood and contains an analysis of EU-self-images as expressed in official statements and interviews with EU representatives. Chapter 4 takes on interfaces between the EU and neighbourhood countries in the so-called post-Soviet space. The chapter thus analyses EU recognition of Belarus, Moldova and Ukraine (labelled as Wider Europe) and Armenia, Azerbaijan and Georgia (under the heading of the South Caucasus) and, conversely, these countries' recognition of the EU. Chapter 5 is constructed in a parallel manner but deals with the Mediterranean neighbourhood, in terms of EU recognition of Algeria, Libya, Morocco and Tunisia (the Maghreb countries) and Egypt, Israel, Jordan, Lebanon, the Palestinian Authority and Syria (the Levant) and these countries' recognition of the EU. It should be underlined at this point that the geographical group labels are used for convenience only – the constructivist logic that informs the theoretical framework of this book implies that geography need not be the most decisive parameter, which in consequence means that interfaces within the same geographic sub-group need not be of the same kind. This is also the reason for not a priori using the sub-group level as the level of analysis. Interfaces are dynamic and reciprocal processes that can be – and are – rather different also between geographically adjacent states.

3 EU recognition of the neighbourhood

Introduction

A quick glance at the current events that mark international relations grants the picture that it is in the areas surrounding the European Union that many of today's pressing security issues are played out. Examples such as the recent conflict between Russia and Georgia and the deteriorating and violent situation in the Middle East are obvious cases in point, but we could also refer to energy politics in south-eastern Europe and elsewhere as well as migration and terrorism issues related to North Africa. All these events and topics impact importantly on the European Union and its member-states; at the same time, these issues are affected – albeit to different degrees and in different ways – by EU behaviour. Against such a background, there is an obvious need for systematic study of relations between the EU and states in its immediate vicinity.

Utilizing the theoretical language spelled out in the previous chapter, the analyses conducted in this and following chapters rest on the assumption that it is fruitful to talk about a European regional security complex, in which the EU is the assumed great power. Importantly, this in effect means that the European complex is not synonymous with the formal membership of the European Union, but a larger entity encompassing also states that have voluntarily opted for non-membership and, perhaps more importantly in the context of this analysis, states that are seeking membership and are recognized by the EU as potential members; i.e. countries that have been granted formal candidate status. This means for instance that Turkey and the countries of the Western Balkans are to be considered as part of the EU-led security complex, although their formal membership may be a possibility for the distant future. While it certainly would be fruitful to study the enlargement process from an interface perspective, the process itself and the countries included in it fall outside of this analysis – these countries are no longer part of the neighbourhood; instead, they are part of the complex per se. Rather, the neighbourhood consists of countries that are intensely interdependent with the EU, but are simultaneously part of a different complex.

This chapter is divided into four main parts. The first section describes the institutional framework for neighbourhood interaction, focusing primarily on the

European Neighbourhood Policy (ENP). The second section deals with EU self-image as the motor and guarantor of European security and prosperity. The following section focuses on general EU perceptions of the neighbourhood. The final substantial part of the chapter brings up the issue of potential EU power resources in the context of interaction.

The EU and the European neighbourhood

The relationship between the EU and its neighbourhood rests on a combination of bilateral and multilateral/regional arrangements. As shown by Table 3.1 below, the large majority of neighbourhood countries to the south have entered into bilateral association agreements with the EU, whereas most countries to the east are involved in bilateral partnership and cooperation agreements with the EU. In addition, there are a number of sub-regional institutional arrangements. The most prominent of these is the Euro-Mediterranean Partnership established in 1995 and encompassing all Mediterranean neighbouring countries except Libya, and also Turkey. In the post-Soviet space, a number of recent initiatives have been introduced, both by post-Soviet states themselves, such as the GUAM (consisting of Georgia, Ukraine, Azerbaijan and Moldova) and the Eastern Dimension, put forth by EU members Sweden and Poland and aiming at all six post-Soviet states of the ENP. In this context it is also worth mentioning the Black Sea Synergy, which brings together littoral states of the Black Sea and thus includes Russia, ENP countries, Turkey (recognized candidate for membership) and current EU members. The bilateral arrangements between the EU and the different partner countries as well as sub-regional processes of institutionalization will be referred to in subsequent chapters containing analyses of the individual relationships. Here, focus is on the regional level, and specifically, on the European Neighbourhood Policy (ENP).

The European Neighbourhood Policy

The origins of the neighbourhood policy are intimately related to the historic Eastern enlargement of 2004–2007. In the summer of 2002 External Relations Commissioner Chris Patten and High Representative Javier Solana suggested in correspondence with the Council that as enlargement negotiations were coming to a close, the EU ought to 'fully exploit the new opportunities created by enlargement to develop relations with our neighbours' (Patten and Solana 2002: 1). At the time labelled 'Wider Europe' and focused on Belarus, Moldova and Ukraine, as thoughts progressed, the countries south and east of the Mediterranean – Algeria, Egypt, Israel, Jordan, Lebanon, Libya, Morocco, the Palestinian Authority, Syria and Tunisia – were also included and the European Neighbourhood Policy (ENP) took form, formally endorsed by the Council in June of 2004. The Council then also decided to include Armenia, Azerbaijan and Georgia in the process, thereby sending a significant signal about increased EU engagement in the Southern Caucasus. All in all, this makes 16 neighbours covered by one single framework – the ENP. Russia is not party to the ENP but instead maintains a 'strategic partnership' with the EU on the basis of an agreement on four so-called Common Spaces (see further Chapter 6), but it is part of the same financial framework as the ENP countries – the European Neighbourhood and Partnership Instrument (ENPI) – for the period 2007–2013.

The logic of the ENP draws its inspiration from the set-up of enlargement negotiations in terms of positive conditionality, socialization and monitoring. In essence, the ENP offers deeper economic and political integration – ultimately a share in the internal market of the EU – if neighbouring states adapt to core EU liberal norms. This logic has been described as a 'virtuous circle, a policy based on shared value and enlightened self-interest' (Landaburu 2006). More specifically, two broad areas are in focus: adherence to core values (commitments to democracy, rule of law, human rights, honouring international obligations) and functional cooperation (closer relations to the EU in areas of economic and social development). In fundamental contrast to the enlargement process, there is no formal connection to the issue of future membership, however.

Although there is a common platform for cooperation with all ENP countries, it is fundamental to stress that there are individual profiles of EU engagement – in the form of individual action plans with different content and time of entry into force – for the different countries. Actions plans are mutually agreed by the EU and individual neighbouring countries. This bilateral logic means that regarding concrete cooperative measures, differentiation among the ENP countries is a possibility as well as a necessity. This has been acknowledged many times, as illustrated already in the first overall assessment of the ENP (December 2006), where the Commission noted: 'The circumstances of each country are very different, and the jointly-agreed reform agendas set out in the Action Plans are likewise different' (Commission 2006b).

By the end of 2008, concrete action plans had been agreed and are now being implemented with 12 countries (Israel, Jordan, Moldova, Morocco, the Palestinian Authority, Tunisia and Ukraine in 2005, Armenia, Azerbaijan and Georgia in 2006 and Egypt and Lebanon in 2007) (Commission 2009a, 2008a: 2–3, see Table 3.1), but how far collaboration has progressed is radically different from case to case (see further chapters). As regards Algeria, an Association Agreement was signed in 2005 and numerous political contacts have been taken to activate and implement it properly. There is not yet any development in the direction of an Action Plan, however. Belarus, Libya and Syria have no such contractual basis for interaction (an Association Agreement for Syria is pending ratification) and are not in the process of establishing action plans. The main reason given by the EU for this situation is the lack of commitment to and progress towards domestic reforms and democratic consolidation (2008a: 3).

As noted above, the initial policy steps were reviewed by the EU in the autumn of 2006, and generally deemed to display good results. A number of measures were introduced to strengthen and develop the ENP framework further, through attributing more money (in the form of €700 million to a Neighbourhood Investment Fund – to which also member-states are invited to contribute – to complement development banks and €300 million to a Governance Facility to economically assist reforms underway in the partner countries), improved visa procedures, strengthened political cooperation, further EU engagement in conflict resolution processes in the region (Commission 2006a, endorsed by the Council in March 2007 and formally concluded in June the same year, see Council 2007d and European Parliament 2007a). The Council has subsequently reaffirmed the main rationale and mechanisms of the ENP and more concretely initiated negotiations on 'deep and comprehensive free trade agreements' (DFTAs) with the most pro-active ENP members, notably Ukraine (Council 2008a, Commission 2008a: 2). The Commission has implemented the above-mentioned measures, further developed means for cooperation, for instance regarding visas, and identified areas where more effort is needed, such as in relation to the frozen conflicts in the neighbourhood (Commission 2007a).

In conclusion, the ENP is of particular interest as it represents a very decisive attempt on the part of the EU to structure its external relations. It simultaneously highlights a central policy dilemma – how to rely on the means of enlargement to induce reforms and value change without offering the prospect of membership.

The EU self-image: the motor of European security and prosperity[2]

In order to fully understand EU recognition of the neighbourhood, it is necessary initially to make a few analytical remarks about the EU's self-image. Analysing EU rhetoric in the context of European security and specifically the ENP, three interrelated elements of the EU self-image stand out. The most prominent one

Table 3.1 The ENP framework

ENP partner country	Contractual relation	ENP Country Report	ENP Action Plan adoption
Algeria	AA (September 2005)	–	–
Armenia	PCA (1999)	March 2005	November 2006
Azerbaijan	PCA (1999)	March 2005	November 2006
Belarus	–	–	–
Egypt	AA (June 2004)	March 2005	March 2007
Georgia	PCA (1999)	March 2005	November 2006
Israel	AA (June 2000)	May 2004	April 2005
Jordan	AA (May 2002)	May 2004	June 2005
Lebanon	AA (April 2006)	March 2005	Jan 2007
Libya	–	–	–
Moldova	PCA (July 1998)	May 2004	February 2005
Morocco	AA (March 2000)	May 2004	July 2005
Palestinian Authority	Interim AA (July 1997)	May 2004	May 2005
Syria	–	–	–
Tunisia	AA (March 1998)	May 2004	July 2005
Ukraine	PCA (March 1998)	May 2004	February 2005

concerns *the EU as a primary contributor to the European peace*. In the first major speech (December 2002) on what was to become the ENP, Commission President Romano Prodi argued that the

> [C]urrent enlargement is the greatest contribution to sustainable stability and security on the European continent that the EU ever made. It is one of the most successful and impressive political transformations of the twentieth century. And all this has been achieved in less than a decade. The EU looks certain to remain a pole of attraction for its neighbours.
>
> (Prodi 2002)

Enlargement Commissioner Günter Verheugen returned to much the same idea in late 2003:

> During the past fifty years the European Union contributed decisively to transform a large part of our continent, previously ravaged by devastating wars and nationalist divisions, into an area of peace, freedom, integration and prosperity. This major achievement was accomplished in full respect of the identity of our peoples and nations. This is why the EU is arguably the greatest success story in the second part of the 20th century.
>
> (Verheugen 2003)

Continuing along the same lines, External Relations Director General Eneko Landaburu later stated: 'We are a "pole of attraction" for our region – countries along our borders actively seek closer relations with us' (Landaburu 2006: 5), and in the same vein, ENP Commissioner Benita Ferrero-Waldner has noted the EU's 'growing role as an anchor of stability and modernization, which is the logical consequence of ... enlargement' (Ferrero-Waldner 2006g). Commenting upon the Commission's adoption of a renewed enlargement strategy in November 2006, the current enlargement commissioner Olli Rehn observed: 'Enlargement is the essence of the EU's soft power to gradually extend peace, democracy and prosperity in Europe' (Commission 2006j).

This relates to the second aspect of EU self-perception, concerning *the EU as a value community based on a set of core norms*. The Commission in 2003 highlighted democracy, respect for human rights and the rule of law as central EU values (Commission 2003: 4), reiterated shortly thereafter by the Council (Council 2003a); in an ENP strategy paper from the following year it added human dignity, liberty and equality (Commission 2004: 12). Ferrero-Waldner has also included good governance on this list (Ferrero-Waldner 2005a; 2006g) and more recently, in the aftermath of the controversy surrounding the cartoons of the Prophet Mohammed, freedom of religion and freedom of speech (Ferrero-Waldner 2006f). Most of these elements can be recognized from the enlargement criteria established by the Copenhagen European Council in 1993, and they are in the same fashion at the centre of the conditionality of the ENP. The main elements are furthermore broadly in line with public opinion. In a special

Eurobarometer survey in 2006, when asked which three values best represent the European Union, respondents (from member-states and candidate states) underscored human rights (39 per cent), peace (38 per cent) and democracy (37 per cent) (Eurobarometer 2006). The standard Eurobarometer of 2008 conveys a similar picture: human rights (37 per cent), peace (35 per cent), and democracy (34 per cent) (Eurobarometer 2008).

In connection to the point above, there is also evidence that the Commission sees the need for actively promoting these values; Ferrero-Waldner noted in early 2006 that the EU has a moral obligation to values in contacts with all international partners (Ferrero-Waldner 2006a, see also Ferrero-Waldner 2006k on the ENP as 'our newest democratization tool'). From this perspective, the ambition of the ENP can be seen as extending 'the idea of Europe', which points in the direction that in contrast to a static geographical definition of Europe, it could be argued that 'Europe may be more appropriately understood as one defined by a European identity' (Møller 2005: 41), an identity which revolves around the points above (see also Manners 2002: 242 on core norms). This is most vividly elaborated in the Berlin Declaration of 25 March 2007, on the occasion of the fiftieth anniversary of the signature of the Treaties of Rome (Berlin Declaration 2007).

The third element of EU self-image is the idea of *the EU as global political actor*. Prodi noted that if 'we want to satisfy the rising expectations and hopes of countries abroad and the peoples of Europe, we have to become a real global player' (Prodi 2002). Verheugen (2003) reiterated much the same point: 'The bigger the Union is, the greater its global interests will be.... Our weight on the international scene will increase'. The European Security Strategy, adopted by the European Council in December 2003, notes that 'the European Union is inevitably a global player ... it should be ready to share in the responsibility for global security and in building a better world' (European Council 2003: 1). The ENP, the Council later stated, is in accordance with the goals of the ESS (Council 2004). Ferrero-Waldner has argued that 'both EU citizens and our partner countries want the EU to play a greater role on the international stage' (Ferrero-Waldner 2005b), and later added that there is

> [S]trong public support for EU action to meet global challenges like terrorism, poverty, AIDS and other pandemics, energy security and the environment ... The European Commission alone provides aid to more than 150 countries, territories and organizations around the world. We are a reliable partner over the long term, and as the world's biggest donor we help bring stability and prosperity to many parts of the world. And we are a champion of multilateralism, standing at the forefront of a rule-based international order.
> (Ferrero-Waldner 2006d)

It could be added here that the Eurobarometer survey published in November 2008 reflects public support regarding the international actorness of the EU to the effect that 68 per cent of the respondents favour a common foreign policy

(20 per cent against), whereas 76 per cent support a common defense and security policy (15 per cent against). On both issues, the figures are very consistent over time, with only marginal variations (Eurobarometer 2008). Moreover, regarding relations with neighours, there is substantial support for developing policies to promote democracy and handling common security threats such as terrorism and organized crime, but no strong support for spending financial resources to help solve internal conflicts in the neighbouring countries (33 per cent for, 38 per cent against) (Eurobarometer 2007).

All in all, this points to the EU holding a self-image of a successful peace community with global aspirations and responsibilities. Out of this arises the need for policy development in relation to the near abroad. In its communication to the Council and the Parliament, the Commission in March 2003 argued that these aspects should form the basis for future policy, in that 'the EU should aim to develop a zone of prosperity and friendly neighbourhood – a "ring of friends" – with whom the EU enjoys close, peaceful and co-operative relations' (Commission 2003, see also the report of the European Parliament (2003) on the Commission's proposal). In a speech in March 2004, Verheugen returned to the same point:

> The Union has always exerted a strong pull on its neighbours even beyond the circle of countries to which we have held out prospects of membership ... the European Union has major interests in the stability, prosperity and democracy of its neighbours not to speak of its moral and political obligations towards them.
>
> (Verheugen 2004)

Ferrero-Waldner recently argued in a similar fashion that

> Europe cannot be an 'introspective bystander'. On the contrary, we are and must remain a key actor in the region; a political and economic partner who supports and manages change and who helps reap the opportunities that flow from it.
>
> (Ferrero-Waldner 2006g).

The EU image of the neighbourhood: interdependence, incentives and inferiority

Turning to the EU perception of the neighbouring countries as a group, three main elements again stand out. One concerns the mutual dependence of the EU and these countries, another concerns the perceived need for the neighbours to develop economically and politically in the direction of the EU. The third – perhaps the most sensitive – concerns the link to enlargement.

Although being a 'pole of attraction', the idea that *the EU is dependent in various ways on the neighbourhood* figures prominently in official documentation throughout the period studied here. It is, for instance, the original assumption by Patten and Solana (2002: 3): 'When the frontiers of the Union shift eastwards, the opportunities and challenges raised by our eastern neighbours will affect us more directly than today'. Repeatedly, the security and stability of Europe is made dependent on the outcome in the EU neighbourhood. In late 2005, Ferrero-Waldner, when talking about the ENP as a 'virtuous circle', argued that by 'investing in our neighbours and by helping to create prosperous, stable and secure conditions around us, we extend the prosperity, stability and security of *our citizens*' (Ferrero-Waldner 2005c). This point was reiterated the following year: 'ENP ... promotes ... reform, both for reasons of solidarity, but also because we want stability in our neighbourhood and thus added security for ourselves' (Ferrero-Waldner 2006e). In a different context she added that it 'is not just a political imperative, but a matter of self-interest. If Europe did not 'export' stability, it would import 'instability'. The European Union is neither an island nor a fortress' (Ferrero-Waldner 2006g). The same point – expressed in terms of a 'vital interest in seeing greater economic development and stability and better governance' – is stressed in the subsequent official Commission communication on strengthening the ENP (Commission 2006a: 2).

There are a number of areas where the interdependence of EU and the neighbourhood is obvious. Energy may be the most prominent one: 'Enhancing our strategic energy partnership with neighbouring countries is a major element of the European Neighbourhood Policy' (Commission 2004: 17). Commissioner Ferrero-Waldner later underlined 'the vital role that the EU's neighbours play in the EU's energy security either as suppliers or transit countries' (Ferrero-Waldner 2006j), whereas Commission President Barroso has argued that 'reinforcing energy security in the EU–ENP area is a key priority for cooperation with our neighbourhood partners' (Barroso 2007a, also see Ferrero-Waldner 2007b). Transport and environment are two other such fields (Commission 2004: 18–19; Ferrero-Waldner 2006h). Migration is yet another area of common concern. It is not viewed as an EU-internal issue, but needs to be managed in collaboration with the neighbours, and features as one of the main issues of the action plans (Ferrero-Waldner 2006c). This relates to the issue of border control, where the EU is heavily dependent on how the ENP countries manage their borders (Commission 2004: 16, 2006: 9).

The second element – the imperative for reform – follows from the EU perception that *the neighbourhood is in need of political and economic development*, both against the background of EU dependence discussed above, and as an end in itself. Ferrero-Waldner was very explicit on this point in a speech about the Middle East and the Mediterranean in the summer of 2006, focusing on 'insufficient investment in people ... low education rate for women and a very low labour force participation for them, [and] poor quality of governance ... weak rule of law, undemocratic decision-making in major parts and serious human rights issues' (Ferrero-Waldner 2006g, see also Ferrero-Waldner 2007a). The change needed in the South Caucasus has also been stressed, as the conflicts in the region show small signs of being solved; on the contrary, defence expenditures of the countries in the region have been increasing rapidly in combination with harsh rhetoric on the part of political leaders (Ferrero-Waldner 2006i). The general and principal conclusion for EU policy-makers is that in the end it is the performance of the neighbours – their political will – that determines the quality of the relationship. In the logic of Ferrero-Waldner: 'An important part of the ENP is the commitment partner governments make to political reform' (2006e); 'the more you do, the more we will offer. But the decision is entirely yours' (2006h; also see Prodi 2002). Barroso explains further:

> The closer you [neighbours] want to be to the EU, and the greater your commitment to reform, the more we will offer you in terms of both assistance to reach those goals, and opportunities to expand and deepen our relations.
> (Barroso 2007a)

That places heavy responsibilities on the neighbours, but interestingly enough also underlines the dependence of the EU on these countries.

When it comes to the issue of *the relationship between the ENP and enlargement*, finally, such connections are consistently downplayed in most EU rhetoric. It is quite clear, however, that the EU holds the perception that the neighbours want more, in some case even membership, than the EU is prepared to offer. Commission President Prodi argued already in 2002 that enlargement 'creates legitimate expectations in the EU's future neighbours which, in turn, wish to reap benefits from the current enlargement' (Prodi 2002). But Commissioner Verheugen made perfectly clear, as early as 2003, that this was not to come in the form of membership – the ENP 'concerns countries for which accession is not on the agenda' (Verheugen 2003: 7, also Verheugen 2004). Commissioner Ferrero-Waldner has recognized the wish for closer relationship on the part of some neighbours, but argues that the ENP is 'a way of responding to our neighbours' desire for closer relations with the EU, without entering into discussions of membership' (Ferrero-Waldner 2005b). Landaburu has more strongly underlined that 'continuing to view our neighbourhood from an enlargement angle is an unhelpful distraction' and adds that through the ENP, 'we respond to the desire of our neighbours ... for closer relations, without entering into premature or unrealistic discussions about possible eventual membership' (Landaburu 2006: 2, 5). It is of interest, however, to take note of the Parliament's partly opposing view in this respect. While not arguing that the membership should be included in the ENP process per se, it nonetheless opens for the possibility of future membership regarding the eastern European neighbourhood – 'democratic neighbours which are clearly identifiable as European countries and which respect the rule of law may in principle apply ... for membership of the EU' – and have particularly Ukraine but also Moldova in mind (European Parliament 2007a).

In conclusion, the EU image of the neighbourhood holds partly contradictory aspects. The neighbourhood is a source of potential insecurity for the EU, the logical conclusion of which is to engage in a self-interested fashion to promote change in the direction desired by the EU. At the same time, the EU's position is weakened by the fact that for a number of reasons, ranging from the relational character of security to material aspects such as energy supply, the EU is involved in an interdependent relationship with the neighbourhood. The EU is clearly the superior power, but there are obviously various incentives for engaging the neighbouring states more intensely. Regarding EU power, it is easy to agree with Michael Emerson that the EU 'retains an extremely elastic continuum of degrees of functional inclusion in its policies – even as the full membership issue becomes increasingly difficult' (Emerson 2005: x).

EU power in relation to the neighbourhood: conditionality, differentiation and assistance

Turning finally to the specific issue of EU power, it seems a suitable start to return to the idea described above that the contractual ENP arrangements, for instance the action plans, are mutually agreed to, and thus rest on the notion of joint ownership. Notes Verheugen (2004): 'Of course, we cannot impose the policy on any neighbour.... The action plans will contain nothing that does not have the full approval of both sides'. In a communication from the Commission it says:

> Joint ownership of the process, based on the awareness of shared values and common interests, is essential. The EU does not seek to impose priorities or conditions on its partners.... There can be no question of asking partners to accept a pre-determined set of priorities. These will be defined by common consent and will thus vary from country to country.
>
> (Commission 2004: 8)

Ferrero-Waldner has reiterated much the same point: the ENP 'is not about imposing specific models from the *outside*. "State building" is about sowing the seeds of change at the *inside*, not least through the "soft power" of persuasion of the international community' (Ferrero-Waldner 2006g, also see Council 2004 and Commission 2006a: 3).

The notion of joint ownership does, however, downplay power dimensions inherent in the relationship. The EU has a number of resources to utilize in the process. These resources correspond to the different forms of power discussed in the previous chapter. An example of the EU's compulsory power is the possibility to impose sanctions of different kinds on states. The EU exercises institutional power to the effect that it constructs political frameworks, such as the ENP and the Barcelona process (and not least when determining the character of membership negotiations in relation to candidate countries). Once established, institutional frameworks yield opportunities for influence at a later point in time. As for structural power, this most obviously relates to financial and technical assistance (and at a later stage participation in segments of the internal market). Through the use of incentives, the EU hopes to attract both the initial interest of neighbouring countries and their future reform in the direction of the values discussed above (Commission 2004: 8–9, 23; 2006: 3; Ferrero-Waldner 2005a; 2006a, e.g. Landaburu 2006: 5). Productive power, finally, refers to the EU's ability to determine the core principles and value base of interaction as well as establishing the normative conceptual framework – the discourse – on various topics. This can be summarized as the power of leading by example – Ferrero-Waldner (2006d) speaks of the most prominent source of influence for the EU as 'our power of attraction'.

It could thus be argued that the construction of the ENP potentially includes a number of the power dimensions discussed above. While there is no compulsory component to the arrangement as such – EU leaders continually assert that the process is voluntary and rests on an idea of joint ownership – institutional, structural and productive power dimensions can all be found in the ENP. In essence, there are three practices that potentially bring about EU influence – conditionality/normative framing, differentiation and assistance.

As we have seen, the basic logic of the ENP revolves around the notion of *conditionality* – as the neighbouring countries develop their societies in the direction of the core norms of the EU, the EU in turn agrees to deepen political and economic relations. It is thus an attempt from the Commission to combine conditionality and socialization in influencing the neighbourhood countries, the very same idea that has previously been successfully applied in the enlargement process (see for instance Kelley 2006, esp. 34–36). 'Our aim' argues Verheugen (2003: 5) 'is to build special relationships with our neighbours, based on shared values and common interests'. In that process, conditionality appears as the central mechanism for inducing change preferred by the EU: 'In return for concrete steps being taken towards economic reform, and our shared values – good governance, human rights, democracy, and the rule of law – it offers our partners deeper political and economic integration with the EU' (Ferrero-Waldner 2005a; this logic is also shared by the European Parliament in its December 2005 report on the ENP). Landaburu adds: 'We offer advice and support on relevant reforms and offer deeper relations to those partners who make progress towards good governance' (2006: 2). Ferrero-Waldner (2006b) underscores 'the essential role of Community conditionality in the triumph of democracy and the market economy in most of our continent' and stresses that 'ENP is based on the same kind of positive conditionality underpinning the enlargement process ... progress is rewarded with greater incentives and benefits' (Ferrero-Waldner 2006e).

This relates to the notion of *differentiation*. Within the overall framework of the ENP, individual countries have different approaches to EU cooperation and the EU maintains different positions for different countries. The principle of differentiation has been a core idea throughout the process – as Verheugen explains, 'differentiation is a key notion in our neighbourhood policy. Our relations also reflect different sets of common interests, and different extent of values shared' (Verheugen 2003: 6). This approach was agreed upon by the member-states at the outset (Council 2003b, 2003c). Ferrero-Waldner (2006e) notes that each country's action plan contains an individual, specific balance of needs and capabilities. Differentiation is a reality – the spectrum ranges from implementation well underway, for instance in the case of Ukraine, to neighbouring Belarus, with hardly any institutionalized contacts at all and no ENP Action Plan in sight (see further next chapter). Argues Barroso: 'As the policy develops, this differentiation will become more pronounced' (Barroso 2007a).

Differentiation has an obvious power component to it. In parallel to enlargement negotiations, the EU has the power to determine the rules of engagement – the process through which individual third parties interact with the EU institutional machinery, creating a very asymmetric power situation where EU-internal negotiations generally leave very little room for change and compromise in negotiations with third parties. This situation holds both institutional power in terms of the constitution of interaction and productive power as far as the norms and principles that third parties are to agree to are concerned.

Finally, EU assistance to neighbouring countries represents practices of power. Regarding financial assistance, this may be thought of as structural power of the donor in a rather traditional manner. As an example, the financial instrument of the neighbourhood policy – the ENPI – contains an increase in financial assistance of 32 per cent in real terms for the period 2007–2013 compared to the period ending in 2006 (Commission 2006b). While naturally attractive to most ENP partners, and arranged by the EU deliberately to increase concrete help and also achieve better efficiency in its foreign assistance, it nonetheless contains an explicit power dimension. Expert assistance – ranging from twinning and TAIEX actions to legal and administrative expertise – combines structural and productive power, as the EU has the means as well as the ideational frameworks for development of various sectors.

These power dimensions play out differently in different individual relationships, as will be evident in the following chapters. Here it suffices to say that through a combination of ideational primacy and institutional mechanisms, the EU is generally in a superior power position vis-à-vis the countries in the neighbourhood.

Concluding remarks: EU recognition of the neighbourhood

Returning to the analytical framework discussed above, the ENP can be viewed as a collective representation of the interface between the EU and its neighbours. It is an institution through which different actors recognize each other against the background of self-images, perceptions of others and of the context/situation in which they interact. The EU image of the ENP as displayed in the analysis above is well captured in the following way:

> The ENP is a virtuous circle, a policy based on shared value and enlightened self-interest: by increasing our neighbours' prosperity, stability and security, by projecting our prosperity, stability and security beyond our borders, we increase our own. In a very real sense, 'by helping our neighbours, we help ourselves'.
>
> (Landaburu 2006: 2)

Here it is obvious that the EU is seen as the superior power in the relationship, a potent actor possessing forceful resources (money, knowledge and normative framing) that can bring about change for the EU as well as others. In the words of Ferrero-Waldner: 'The momentum of ENP has already enabled us to mobilise the best expertise from the Commission and Member States, sharing our know-how and best practices' (Ferrero-Waldner 2007b). The neighbouring countries, on the other hand, are inferior to the EU, in need of help and dependent on the EU for their future security and prosperity. They are not without influence, however. To some extent they determine the agenda, in the same way that some of those countries entering the EU in 2004 pushed for closer relations in the mid-1990s against the will of the EU. More importantly in the short run, perhaps, is that in the security sphere, not least in the fields of energy, environment, and migration, the EU is dependent on the actual behaviour of the neighbours.

ENP policy dilemmas

The ENP represents the EU's most advanced foreign policy framework and a lot of energy and attention has been devoted to it thus far. It involves, however, a number of policy dilemmas. First, the neighbourhood demand for closer cooperation provides the union with a dilemma about how to strike the best balance between engagement (trans-border cooperation) and exclusivity (membership). As noted already by Patten and Solana at the outset of the ENP process, the fundamental issue concerns 'the dual challenge of avoiding new dividing lines in Europe while responding to needs arising from the newly created borders of the Union' (Patten and Solana 2002: 1, see also Commission 2004: 12, 16). Ferrero-Waldner has repeated that same point: 'the ENP is not about "exclusion" of new dividing lines between "ins" and "outs". On the contrary, we want to expand the EU's zone of prosperity – to our mutual benefit' (Ferrero-Waldner 2006g). In a critical light, one could ask how successful a policy based on enlargement conditionality but without the incentives of membership will be in the long run. If the distinction between neighbourhood policy and enlargement is upheld, is it logically and empirically possible to avoid new dividing lines in Europe as a result of the ENP?

Second, the institutional structure of the ENP holds potentially contradictory elements. To begin with, the conditionality at the centre of the ENP is perceived as the key mechanism for inducing reform in the neighbourhood. There is an inherent tension between this governance approach and the idea of joint ownership played up in some of the speeches and documents, which is evident when analysing the asymmetric power situation. To what extent is it possible to avoid or overcome the tensions between these two concepts? Moreover, the ENP is constructed as an overall framework for neighbourhood cooperation, and, the Council concluded already in 2004, 'it will be essential to maintain the coherence and unity of this policy, in its content, instruments and final goals' (Council 2004: 11). Simultaneously, there are individual action plans and related forms of practices for all participating countries, reflecting the very different nature of their EU interaction as well as political and economic profile in general. In a Commission evaluation, it is noted: 'Thus far, the ENP has been largely bilateral, between the EU and each partner country. This is essentially due to large differences between partners' (Commission 2006a: 8). How can the EU avoid the ENP concept as such losing meaning against the background of the differentiated approaches?

4 Post-Soviet interfaces

Introduction

This chapter deals with EU interfaces vis-à-vis the neighbouring countries to the east and southeast of the EU area, countries that were part of the Soviet Union before gaining independence in the 1990s. These countries – Belarus, Moldova and Ukraine to the east, and Armenia, Azerbaijan and Georgia to the southeast – thus share some important elements in terms of common history, political institutions and economic practices. They can all be referred to as transition countries. At the same time, there are vast differences among them, in terms of how the transition process in general has developed, in terms of the character of the relationship to Russia, and also in terms of integration with European and Euro-Atlantic institutions. Regarding the latter point, with the exception of Belarus, all countries have embarked on a path of Europeanization on a combined basis of manifest cooperation with the EU and attempting to adopt European democratic standards. As noted by the EU Commission, in the east and southeast, 'all ENP partners that have agreed Action Plans are members of the OSCE and the Council of Europe, which contributes to a particular reform agenda aiming at close approximation to the fundamental standards prevailing in the EU' (Commission 2008a: 3). Yet, as this chapter will show, there are dramatic differences not only between Belarus and the other five countries, but also within the group of European orientation.

For practical reasons, the analysis below is structured around the concepts of Wider Europe and South Caucasus, respectively. These are geographical distinctions that can be traced back to the early ENP policy development (as the initial thoughts of what later became the ENP were focused on Belarus, Moldova, Ukraine – and Russia – and labelled 'Wider Europe', whereas the South Caucasus countries were included later). It is also a distinction employed in the analysis of Barry Buzan and Ole Wæver regarding what they label the post-Soviet regional security complex. As will be evident in the coming pages, however, these geographical distinctions carry little value in terms of interface characteristics, neither in terms of group-internal similarities, nor in terms of distinct differences between the groups. Before embarking on analyses of individual interfaces, we need to briefly review the scope and nature of regional cooperation involving the countries of interest to this chapter.

Regional frameworks of interaction

In terms of regional cooperation within the post-Soviet context as delimited here, much attention focuses on the Black Sea. The Black Sea Forum for Dialogue and Partnership was set up in June 2006 by Armenia, Azerbaijan, Bulgaria, Georgia, Greece, Moldova, Romania, Turkey and Ukraine, aiming to promote democratic consolidation, good governance, civil society capacity-building and explicitly seeking cooperation with EU institutions (Black Sea Forum 2006). Against that background, the EU developed its so-called Black Sea Synergy initiative in 2007, aiming at developing cooperation among all littoral states of the Black Sea (see Commission 2007a for the original proposal). It is an interesting endeavour not least from a cognitive perspective as it includes EU member-states, Turkey, Russia and ENP countries. The synergy is set up as a complementary measure to the ENP, the enlargement policy for Turkey and the strategic partnership with Russia. While still too early to claim results, some concrete cooperation has been intensified (for instance regarding energy) and an intensified dialogue on trade and frozen conflicts has taken place (Commission 2008m).

Second, as a reaction to the ideas of a Union of the Mediterranean, the Swedish and Polish governments in May 2008 jointly introduced the idea of an 'Eastern Partnership' aiming at deepened cooperation, for instance regarding visa matters, economic affairs (the creation of a DFTA) and people-to-people contacts with Ukraine, Moldova, Belarus, Armenia, Georgia and Azerbaijan (CEPS 2008b: 6–7). This idea was subsequently formally endorsed by the European Council in June 2008, calling on the Commission to present an official proposal in the spring of 2009 (European Council 2008b). The Extraordinary European Council of 1 September 2008 asked the Commission to speed up the process further, and in December the Commission presented its proposal, along the following lines:

> The EaP [Eastern Partnership] should bring a lasting political message of EU solidarity, alongside additional, tangible support for their democratic and market-oriented reforms and the consolidation of their statehood and territorial integrity. This serves the stability, security and prosperity of the EU, partners and indeed the entire continent.
>
> (Commission 2008n: 2)

The EaP proposal opens up for closer contractual relations in the form of association agreements, involving deep and comprehensive free trade agreements and including a specific programme – the so-called Comprehensive Institution-building programme – to assist partner countries in meeting the requirements of the association agreement (Commission 2008n: 4).

In this context could also be mentioned the Northern Dimension initiative between Russia and the Baltic Sea EU member-states (further discussed in Chapter 6), a framework in which Belarus and Ukraine are observers.

Third, the GUAM initiative –formally known as the Organization for Democracy and Economic Development-GUAM – represents, as the label indicates, an attempt by Georgia, Ukraine, Azerbaijan and Moldova and to intensify cooperation in the areas of democracy, human rights/fundamental freedoms and establishing free trade among the partners, securing energy supply and energy transit to the European market. GUAM was set up in May 2006 in Kyiv, where its permanent secretariat is located (GUAM 2006). There are, furthermore, attempts by some states (EU members and ENP countries) to create a framework for linking the Baltic, Black and Caspian seas in the energy sector (see further below). In conclusion, this means that the structure of EU interaction with neighbours is multi-level and dynamic in nature, and that changes in the set-up of inter-institutional relations may be expected.

Wider Europe interfaces

Two short remarks are appropriate at this point. First, it needs to be repeated here that what follows in this and subsequent sections are not complete reviews of bilateral interaction between the EU and the respective ENP country. Rather, it is a focus on perceptions of identity in terms of core values and displays of power in terms of logic of interaction. Second, while the chosen methodology and theoretical framework merits a bilateral research design, such an approach risks overlooking important political processes among the countries under study. Such processes will be alluded to in the respective analyses, which imply some repetition in the respective interface analyses. In the context of Wider Europe, one important such item concerns the Transnistria conflict and the EU border assistance mission (EUBAM) involving both Ukraine and Moldova, and hence of interest to the respective interfaces. A second example concerns the GUAM cooperation referred to above.

The EU–Belarus interface

The political relationship between the EU and Belarus is characterized by competitive practices, harsh rhetoric and limited contractual relations. There is no Partnership and Agreement Cooperation between the EU and Belarus (the standard legal basis for interaction with eastern neighbours), and there is no ENP Action Plan in place or developing in the foreseeable future. At the heart of the situation is the perception by the EU regarding the government of President Alexander Lukashenko as authoritarian and the resistance on the part of the Belarus government to change in a democratic direction as desired by the EU. EU reactions to the presidential election and its aftermath in March 2006 are telling in this context. First, the European Council 'condemns the action of the Belarus authorities' regarding the arrest of peaceful demonstrators who reacted against the conduct of the presidential election. Second, the European Council 'deplores the failure ... to meet OSCE commitments to democratic elections and considers ... the Presidential elections ... fundamentally flawed' (European Council 2006). In a resolution from

November 2007, the European Parliament states that 'Belarus has the same European vocation and perspectives as Ukraine and Moldova, once it embraces democracy, respects fundamental human rights and freedoms and enhances the rule of law' (European Parliament 2007a).

A focus on the strategies used by the EU to induce change is quite illuminating. There are essentially three such strategies. One concerns rhetoric, as an attempt to draw on productive power to influence a more democratic path. In that context, the EU has repeatedly used normative statements to condemn activities by Belarusian authorities, such as the sentencing of opposition leader Alexander Milinkevich in April 2006 to 15 days in prison for active participation in an unauthorized event, when, according to the EU, he was exercising fundamental freedoms such as freedom of speech (Council 2006f) and the sentencing of presidential candidate Aleksandr Kozulin in July 2006 to five and a half years in prison for hooliganism and disturbing political order, a sentence deemed politically motivated by the EU (Council 2006g). The EU has also tried to use positive rhetoric when deemed possible, as in a presidency declaration in March 2008 welcoming the release of a number of political prisoners in Belarus, but, significantly enough, at the same time condemning – in the language of 'strong disappointment' – the arrest of a large number of demonstrators on the occasion of Freedom Day (25 March) in Minsk (Council 2008b). In the same vein, upon the signature of a Memorandum of Understanding concerning the establishment of an EC delegation in Minsk, Commissioner Ferrero-Waldner stated: 'The opening of the EC delegation and the release of several political prisoners over the past days can help us build a positive momentum' (Ferrero-Waldner 2008a). Recently, the EU has acknowledged some positive sign in relation to the parliamentary elections in September 2008 (although fundamentally deemed undemocratic) and offering to assist Belarus on its path to democracy and human rights (Council 2008i).

A second strategy contains manifest activities to punish the Belarus authorities: a good example being the restrictive measures in the form of a visa ban taken by the EU against high officials (31 individuals singled out, President Lukashenko included) following the elections of 2006 (Council 2006a). Also economic sanctions were imposed (Council 2009). Of interest in this context is also the decision by the Council in October 2008 to extend the travel restrictions for yet another year, but – importantly – not apply this for six months, which is subject to renewal in order to 'encourage dialogue with the Belarusian authorities and the adoption of positive measures to strengthen democracy and respects for human rights' (Council 2008i; those involved in the disappearances in 1999 and 2000 and the president of the Central Election Commission are exempted from the moratorium).

The third strategy is to support civil society and try to communicate with the public at large. Again in the context of the 2006 election, the EU in various ways – financially, rhetorically and by increasing access to information – offered support to Belarus civil society (European Council 2006, see also Council 2006a detailing the statement by the External Relations Council in April 2006). In subsequent communications, EU representatives have tried to communicate with the general public. In November 2006, for instance, the Commission launched a non-paper on 'What the European Union could bring to Belarus' should Belarus turn to democratic reforms. Stated ENP Commissioner Ferrero-Waldner in this context: 'Our message is that as soon as the country indicates a willingness to move towards true democracy, human rights and rule of law, we will be ready to enter into full partnership with Belarus'. Among the benefits of engagement, the EU notes trade opportunities, improved healthcare and education, improved transport and energy networks and greater cross-border cooperation (Commission 2006n). Of symbolic importance, Commission President Barroso gave a statement to the Belarus people in connection to the Berlin Declaration celebrating the fiftieth anniversary of the EU, in which he stated that the EU is built on

> [D]eep-rooted values of democracy, human rights and the rule of law, and [that he wanted] to reiterate to the people of Belarus that the European Union is ready to enter into a full partnership with Belarus on the basis of these values and towards these goals. I hope that we will soon see a willingness to move in this direction.... I very much hope that the government of Belarus will reciprocate.
>
> (Barroso 2007b)

It is evident, however, that the attempts by the EU have thus far not induced the desired change. The European Parliament, for instance, in a resolution in November 2007 was 'seriously concerned, however, by the lack of positive response on the part of the government of Belarus to the conditional cooperation offer formulated by the Commission' (invitation for Belarus to attend as an observer the ENP conference on 3 September 2007; European Parliament 2007a).

Regarding the Belarus recognition of the EU, a number of statements by President Lukashenko convey a picture of the EU as a dominant actor furthering its own interests and pointing to moral high-grounds when suitable against a general background of politics as essentially economic in nature. Lukashenko thus acknowledges the inferior economic dependence relationship to the EU, stating for instance:

> We wish that the EU will open its internal market for our products so that we can compete.... Precisely the energy conflict with Russia revealed that we need more investors from Europe and the United States ... we need the EU as a partner in diversifying our energy policy.
>
> (*Die Welt* 2007)

On value compatibility between the EU and Belarus, Lukashenko has argued that

> Belarus is located in the center of Europe, our values are identical; only that we have specific national interests.... Equal access to mass media exists

nowhere in the world.... Regarding the development of the freedom of the media that you were speaking about we may still have deficits. But the EU has to acknowledge that people can feel safe here. Our crime rate is one of the lowest in Europe and everybody has a job.

(*Die Welt* 2007)

In such a perspective, European reactions appear inappropriate to the Belarus leader: 'I want Belarus to look like Germany or Sweden one day. But so far we have mainly received kicks in the back from the West' (*Die Welt* 2007). He goes on to argue:

Belarus helps to protect its [the EU's] borders in the East. We catch most of the illegal migrants and criminals, streaming into the EU from the East and send them back to where they come from. We use a considerable amount of financial resources for this end and form a protective barrier for Europe. Today illegal migrants manage to come into the EU via the Balkans and Ukraine. In contrast, our border is closed for them. And how does the EU thank us for that? It imposes economic sanctions and withdraws preferential tariffs.

(*Die Welt* 2007)

Quite evidently, Belarus does hold an antipathy towards the West in general, particularly the EU and the United States. This is evident in manifest behaviour in relation to Russia (despite the energy conflict with Russia in 2006, the idea of a Union State between Russia and Belarus persists), but also in the constant references of Lukashenko to 'Russian brotherhood' (see for instance *Die Welt* 2007). Interestingly enough, Belarus is engaged in an increasingly closer relationship with Iran. President Lukashenko has visited Teheran twice (in 2001 and 2006), and Iranian President Ahmadinejad visited Minsk in 2007, the event at which Lukashenko described the relationship as a 'strategic partnership' (*International Herald Tribune* 2007). The material background is one of mutual interest – Iran has gained access to Belarus technology and expertise regarding civil nuclear power, whereas Belarus gains an energy source (Iranian oil, which still, however, needs to pass through Russian territory on its way to Belarus).

In conclusion, the EU–Belarus interface has the character of a *resistance* interface. In essence, the superior power – the EU – is unable to use its channels of influence (successful in many other cases) to impact on the value incompatibility at hand on the basis of Belarusian non-democratic credentials and human rights violations and the EU embracing exactly those particular values. Belarus signals that it is firmly outside of any aspirations for membership or close association and seems willing to sacrifice economic benefits for maintaining political stability. In that context, the EU instruments of conditionality and socialization are rendered inefficient. Limited financial assistance returns marginal structural power impact. Moreover, due to the nonexistent contractual relation, the EU has limited institutional leverage. EU attempts at exercising productive power have thus far been ineffective. In conclusion, EU efforts at changing the Belarus regime are resisted and the value incompatibility remains. In that situation the EU has, however, relied on its compulsory power (the Council decision in October 2008 to pause the travel restrictions for leading Belarus officials is interesting in this context).

The picture is made more complex by recent signs that the Belarus society may be deeply split regarding Belarus political orientation. An opinion poll carried out during the period 3–13 March 2008 by the Independent Institute of Socio-Economic and Political Studies (IISEPS) shows even fractions in favour of and in opposition to Russian–Belarus integration (35.8 per cent for, 41.6 per cent against) as well as in favour of and in opposition to Belarus joining the EU (35.4 per cent for, 35.4 per cent against). As regards perceptions of President Lukashenko, 47.3 per cent of respondents said they trust him, 38.0 per cent claimed they distrust him (CEPS 2008a: 11).

The EU–Moldova interface

In institutional terms, the relationship between the EU and Moldova rests on a Partnership and Cooperation Agreement from 1998 and an ENP Action Plan adopted in February of 2005. Negotiations for a new PCA agreement are expected to start in the middle of 2009 (Moldpres 2008). The basic EU recognition of Moldova as a pro-EU country embracing core EU values and interested in further integration, albeit currently lacking full administrative implementation capacity. The Commission progress report of December 2006 is illuminating in this respect:

> Faced with an extremely difficult internal and external situation, Moldova has begun implementation of the Action Plan. Overall, while progress was made since 2005, implementation of reform strategies remains a problem, even in areas where there has been good legislative progress. Moldova needs to concentrate resources in implementation and clearly prioritise action. Good progress has been made with regard to Moldova–Ukraine border management and some progress has been made towards resolution of the Transnistria conflict.
>
> (Commission 2006d: 2)

In the perspective of the EU, there are a number of problems/weaknesses with regard to democracy and human rights that need to be settled, and which imply uncertainty in terms of long-term outcome. In 2006, the Commission noted: 'Freedom of media is still far from ensured. Corruption is widespread ... Moldova needs to ensure better respect for human rights. Further reform of the judiciary, in particular to ensure its independence, is needed' (Commission 2006d: 2–3). Reporting on subsequent progress, the Commission in 2008 points to major achievements in terms of advances on completing a trade agreement, entry into force of visa facilitation and readmission agreement, 'positive cooperation' with the EU Border Assistance Mission (EUBAM) and full cooperation on the Transnistria issue. It furthermore stresses 'good progress in most areas during the reporting period. The 2007 local elections were generally well administered and voters were offered a genuine choice' (Commission 2008i: 2). However, returning to issues of administrative capacity, the Commission notes that 'in spite of the progress made, effective implementation of reforms remains a challenge' (Commission 2008i: 2). The link between European cooperation and the Transnistria issue can be seen in that the EU clearly seeks to strengthen Moldova's capacity to interact with the EU, a prerequisite for effective implementation of ENP Action Plan measures as well as regional stability. Hence, the EU publicly declared not to recognize the outcome of the so-called referendum on Transnistrian independence and subsequent accession to Russia, instead stating that the EU 'fully supports Moldova's territorial integrity' (Council 2006d). The prolongation of the EUBAM mandate, for another two years as of December 2007, can be seen in this light (Council 2008g).

The positive perception of Moldova also became clear in November 2007, when the European Parliament passed a resolution saying that in principle, EU membership could be open to countries in the Eastern neighbourhood that are democratic and respect the rule of law, and pointed to Moldova as a possible candidate in the future (European Parliament 2007a).

Moldova's European orientation – embracing core values and embarking on a path of increasingly closer ties – is evident in a number of ways. At the outset of the ENP process, President Voronin (elected in 2005) explicitly declared the ENP 'a very positive change' (quoted in Kelley 2006: 48). In addition to the PCA and ENP organizational frameworks and concrete cooperation in relation to action plan goals, Moldova's extensive participation in regional arrangements embracing EU values is significant. Moldova is, for instance, a founding member of GUAM – the Organization for Democracy and Economic Development whose charter explicitly points out the 'strive of the GUAM States to deepen European integration and enhance relations with the European Union' (GUAM 2006). Participation in the Community of Democratic Choice and the Black Sea Forum – both forums set up in relation to EU core values – point in the same direction. The pro-EU stance is also obvious in its extensive alignment with the EU on CFSP matters. Notes the Commission in its progress report for 2008: 'The Republic of Moldova actively co-operated with the EU on regional and international issues and aligned itself with nearly all EU CFSP declarations open for alignment' (Commission 2008i: 6, see also Council 2008c, 2008g). The Transnistria issue is also of interest in this perspective, as Moldova (and Ukraine) has turned to the EU for assistance, and the EU has reciprocated by the Council appointing a special representative in 2005 (Lavenex and Schimmelfennig 2006: 146) and the border mission mentioned above. Moreover, Russian involvement in the Transnistria issue (and gas price increases and Russian import bans of Moldovan – and Georgian – wines and water) have brought the Moldovan government and EU institutions together in non-recognition of Transnistria as a politically and economically independent entity as well as of Russian calls for honouring the results of the Transnistrian referendum, something that neither the EU nor the OSCE has agreed to (Ferrero-Waldner 2006l).

In conclusion, the EU–Moldovan interface is best described as a case of an *adaptation interface*. Moldova is gradually adapting to core EU values, which is recognized and further supported by the EU. 'The EU welcomes the recent increase in the pace of its relations with ... Moldova' the Council concluded in October 2008 (Council 2008h), and was said to be

> Ready to have a deeper relationship ... and to negotiate a new and ambitious agreement with Moldova soon. This agreement will go beyond the current Partnership and Cooperation Agreement and will include the aim of a comprehensive and deep free-trade area.
>
> (Council 2008g)

Thus, Moldova is the object of processes of conditionality and socialization. Both parties to the relationship recognize the EU as the more powerful actor – as argued by Nicu Popescu, 'EU ... normative superiority and attractiveness cannot and is not challenged in Moldova' (Popescu 2005). This power asymmetry is quite significant. The EU utilizes productive power resources, generally through the normative framing of European values and specifically in channelling the Transnistria issue through the lens of border management. Moreover, institutional power resources are employed, generally in the ENP framework (determining the character of the process) and specifically in CFSP alignment. In structural power terms, financial assistance is of relevance for the poverty-struck Moldova. Through the ENPI, the Commission allocates (in the so-called National Indicative Programme) €209.7 million for the period 2007–2010 (Commission 2008i: 18).

The EU–Ukraine interface

The formal foundations for EU–Ukraine interaction mirror those of EU relations with Moldova, and hence are made up of the Partnership and Cooperation Agreement (from 1998) and the ENP Action Plan adopted in 2005. In substantive terms, however, EU–Ukrainian cooperation has advanced significantly further. Ukrainian leaders have consistently adopted a pro-active stance and pushed for advanced cooperation, and have stated numerous times that the long-term goal of Ukraine's European policy is EU membership. The EU has mainly responded by deepening or increasing measures within the frameworks mentioned above, i.e. measures that are open also to other ENP countries. In the Ukrainian case, this has included visa facilitation, enhanced preparation for a deep free trade agreement with the EU and increased cooperation on foreign and security policy. In addition, the EU has assisted Ukraine in its successful quest for WTO membership. A principal recent step, moreover, is the decision to initiate negotiation for an association agreement, as decided in September 2008.

EU recognition of Ukraine

EU recognition of Ukraine rests on the idea of a successful transformation to democracy and market economy, and encouraging signals of democratic consolidation. For instance, in the concluding statements of the EU–Ukraine summit in December 2005, EU leaders welcomed 'Ukraine's firm commitment to shared values of democracy, rule of law and respect for human rights' and also noted the developments in reforming the economy (EU–Ukraine Summit 2005). In the Commission progress report of 2006, it was noted: 'Considerable steps have been taken towards consolidating respect for human rights and the rule of law' (Commission 2006c: 2–3). In sharp contrast to the Belarus presidential election at the same time, the Ukrainian parliamentary election of March 2006 was deemed free and fair according to the International Election Observation Mission of the OSCE (OSCE 2006). The European Parliament has subsequently welcomed the democratic development and growth of liberal values in Ukraine and urged the Commission and the Council to support the consolidation of democracy in Ukraine, to strengthen the ENP and to take steps in the direction of a non-visa regime (European Parliament 2006a). The Commission later stressed that 'Ukraine's positive record in the conduct of democratic elections of 2006 was broadly confirmed during the 2007 early parliamentary elections, and the freedom of the media further consolidated' (Commission 2008k: 2).

Also in other areas the EU takes note of Ukrainian efforts to adopt pro-EU policies, which is then acknowledged in concrete measures of intensified interaction. The Commission brings out a number of major achievements in 2007, such as the finalization of Ukraine's WTO accession, start of negotiations regarding a DFTA, entry into force of visa facilitation and readmission agreements, increasing cooperation on transport, energy and foreign and security policy (see further below) and 'positive cooperation' with the EU Border Assistance Mission (EUBAM) (Commission 2008k: 2). As the current PCA nears expiry, a new agreement is necessary, which seems unproblematic from the EU side: 'Building on the strong progress achieved previously, in March 2007 the EU and Ukraine opened negotiations on a new Enhanced Agreement (NEA) aiming to draw Ukraine significantly closer' (Commission 2008a: 2, see also Commission 2008k: 2).

It is also of interest to note that earlier signs of problems regarding implementation of reforms – 'progress is being hindered by endemic corruption ... and by the lack of a truly independent judiciary' (Commission 2006c: 2) – do not appear to the same degree in more recent evaluations. In the Commission progress report of 2008, it is noted that 'Ukraine continued to make progress in most areas, although the pace of progress stalled somewhat compared to the previous years, in particular as regards economic and structural reforms, also due to the political instability which characterised most of 2007' (Commission 2008k: 2).

In essence, then, EU representatives recognize Ukraine as a country that embraces core EU values and increasingly orienting itself in the direction of EU. Against the background of interdependence logic, Ukraine is furthermore recognized as a European partner, evident primarily in the area of energy and foreign and security policy, but tentatively also regarding migration (see further below).

Ukrainian recognition of the EU

Ukrainian perception of the EU falls into a larger spectrum of a pro-European and pro-Euro-Atlantic orientation among the main centres of the Ukrainian political elite. Ukraine seeks closer integration with the EU, and seeks an active role in European issues. In a significant speech to the Ukrainian Rada in September 2006, Prime Minister Viktor Yanukovych established the future course of relations to the EU, stating:

> [C]onsidering the European integration as a strategic goal of Ukraine, the new Government sees its task in becoming a player which is strong, self-sufficient and therefore interesting to Brussels instead of a role played by Ukraine until now – the role of a "beggar" in the EU negotiations. We should also do everything to harmonize the legislation of Ukraine with the EU legislation as soon as possible.
>
> (Yanukovych 2006a)

The following month – October 2006 – Yanukovych reiterated his country's pro-Western orientation, for instance stating that 'Ukraine has made a choice for Europe and will pursue closer relations with all European and Euro-Atlantic institutions – there should be no doubting our nation's European direction' (Yanukovych 2006b).

These public declarations can fruitfully be understood against the background of the so-called 'Borjomi Declaration', issued by Ukrainian President Viktor Yushchenko and Georgian President Mikheil Saakashvili in the summer of 2005 upon the establishment of the Community of Democratic Choice. In that context, the two presidents acknowledged:

> [O]ur strong belief that the strengthening of democracy and civil society is one of the main tasks of and prerequisites for the economic development of our countries and our region.... We express our firm conviction that our region, if based and developed on the right principles of democracy, freedom and prosperity, represents today in Europe one of the major areas of opportunities.... We pledge to conduct our policies in our respective countries ... based on those principles, as members of the European family, sharing European values and history. As members of the Community of Democracies ... we are considering the creation of a community of democracies in our part of Europe: the Community of Democratic Choice.
>
> (Community of Democratic Choice 2005)

The two presidents invited all the leaders of the Baltic–Black–Caspian Sea region to a summit in Ukraine in the autumn of 2005, 'to put a final end to the history of division in Europe, of restricted freedoms and domination by force and by fear, and mark a new beginning in neighbourly relations based on mutual respect, confidence, transparency and equality'. The summit took place in Kiev in December 2005, and while not explicitly mentioning the European Union as a frame of reference, the contents of the creation of the Community of Democratic Choice is more or less synonymous with EU values and norms (Community of Democratic Choice 2005).

Also President Yushchenko's address to the European Parliament in the spring of 2005 signals Ukraine's adoption and consolidation of core EU values: 'Democracy is a value which unites us all. It is the cornerstone of our prosperity.... We have chosen Europe: it is not just a question of geography, but a matter of shared spiritual and moral values' (CEPS 2005a: 1).

The EU is recognized as so attractive by the Ukrainian leaders that they regularly return to the issue of Ukrainian EU membership. President Yushchenko, for one, noted already in 2005: 'The neighbourhood policy has already been overtaken by events. We hope that at the end of the Action Plan, in 2007, we will be in a position to begin EU membership negotiations' (CEPS 2005a). In the same vein, Deputy Prime Minister Oleg Rybachuk has argued that

> Our goal is Ukraine in the European Union. History, economic prospects, interests of the people show clearly that the Ukrainian way to the future is together with the United Europe.... Ukraine has agreed to consider the neighbourhood policy as a temporary modus vivendi in its relations with the EU.... The ideals and values promoted by the EU are close and dear to Ukraine.
>
> (CEPS 2005b)

It should be noted, however, that the government's Western orientation is not completely without critics in Ukraine. There have been recurrent splits within the government and in parliament, between pro-Western and pro-Russian attitudes (former Prime Minister Yanukovych, for one, has publicly expressed hesitation about Western integration). It is striking however, that this goes significantly more for NATO accession and pro-Russian policy than the issue of EU accession ((RFE/RL 2006a).

There is thus also what we could call the Russian factor. Russian energy supply was cut off in the winter and spring of 2006 (technically executed through Gazprom, but fully supported by the Russian government, see further analysis in CEPS 2006: 2–6). This action, together with Russia imposing trade sanctions against exports from Georgia, Moldova and Ukraine (CEPS 2006: 13–14) can be assumed to further increase the desire to turn to the EU among pro-Western groups, potentially creating a more competitive domestic political situation. Already before the crisis, President Yushchenko said: 'Ukraine's membership of the EU and NATO is not against Russian interests – on the contrary, a stable Ukraine could help bring Russia closer to Europe' (CEPS 2005a: 1).

Conditionality and socialization at work

There are two issue-areas where the logic of conditionality and socialization is very evident. One concerns the field of energy, especially energy security, the other cooperation on external security matters. In both areas, Ukraine is invited to further cooperation against the background of achieving general progress in the ENP framework, and specifically signalling its commitment to European values.

On the topic of energy cooperation, throughout the period it has been evident that one of the most important issues that brings the EU and Ukraine together is energy, which is principally significant both in terms of security interdependence on strategic resources and regarding the relationship to Russia. A Memorandum of Understanding was signed between the EU and Ukraine in December 2005, aiming at the long-term prospect of integrated energy markets. It was noted with satisfaction at the EU–Ukraine summit in October 2006 that progress was made; the EU side specifically welcomed Ukraine's intention of acceding to the Energy Community Treaty (EU–Ukraine Summit 2006). The Commission has noted that 'Ukraine contributes, as a key transit country, to the EU's energy security, notably as regards transit of Russian gas and oil supplies' (Commission 2006c: 14). The European Parliament, moreover, has stressed Ukraine's 'critical role in ensuring the energy security of the EU' and has therefore supported Ukraine's accession to the Energy Community Treaty (European Parliament 2007b). Interestingly enough, the dispute between Gazprom and Ukraine made Ukraine's strategic importance clear, and also reinforced EU–Ukrainian relations.

Second, of central significance regarding values and identity is also the specific observation on 'increasingly close cooperation' on security issues, especially regarding crisis management and regional stability. Ukraine has participated in the police missions of the EU (EUPM) in Bosnia and Herzegovina as well as in Macedonia, has been praised by the EU for its contribution to regional stability and crisis management and has aligned itself with a very significant number of EU statements concerning external security issues (EU–Ukraine summit 2006). In the Commission progress report of December 2006 it was noted the

> Good cooperation between the EU and Ukraine on foreign policy, with Ukraine aligning with the EU positions on issues of regional and international relevance.... In particular, enhanced co-operation regarding the settlement of the Transnistria issue and the launch and successful work of the EU Border Assistance Mission have provided positive momentum.
> (Commission 2006c: 2)

As of July 2006, Ukraine had aligned itself with 549 out of 589 CFSP declarations (Commission 2006c: 5).

At the EU–Ukraine Joint Summit in September 2007, note was again taken of the increasing convergence of the parties' positions regarding regional and international issues 'through mechanisms of regular policy consultations, alignment of Ukraine with EU foreign policy positions and participation of Ukraine in EU crisis management efforts. EU leaders expressed their high appreciation of Ukraine's role in EU-led crisis management operations' (EU–Ukraine Summit 2007).

Making a new assessment in early 2008, the Commission repeats the picture that Ukraine has aligned itself with nearly all of the EU CFSP declarations open for alignment. Moreover, formal and informal contacts were taken regarding foreign policy planning, and an agreement for security procedures for exchange of classified information was made (Commission 2008k: 6).

It is evident that Ukraine has sought to play an important role together with the EU in a sub-regional context. For instance, Ukraine (and Moldova) aligned themselves with EU presidency statements on the recognition of Montenegrine independence in May 2006 (Council 2006h), on the sentencing of Belarusian presidential candidate Aleksandr Kozulin in July 2006 (Council 2006g), and regarding the status of the Transnistrian referendum in September 2006 (Council 2006d). In the Georgian crisis in the autumn of 2006, Ukraine and EU members Lithuania and Poland in an official statement called for all parties to show restraint and calm, but importantly, stressed the sovereignty and territorial integrity of Georgia (Ministry of Foreign Affairs of Ukraine 2006). And in July 2007, Georgia, Moldova and Ukraine aligned themselves with the EU Presidency declaration on the illegitimacy of the so-called presidential elections in Nagorno-Karabakh, explicitly also underlining that the independence of the region is not recognized (Council 2007g).

Concluding remarks: EU–Ukraine interface

The EU–Ukraine interface is an extreme case in ENP comparison. It is best described as an *inclusion* interface, involving the mutual recognition of the other as friendly in nature, obvious value compatibility against the background of a clear Ukrainian commitment to EU values, and an obvious power asymmetry in favour of the EU (although much less pronounced than in the Moldovan case). In short, Ukraine is highly motivated to move in the direction of the EU, has received substantial amounts of economic aid and is entertaining a political dialogue to consolidate human rights and democracy. At the same time, Ukraine is seen by the EU as a strategically important country that is firmly set on the road towards close EU cooperation, reaping the benefits of previous efforts. In this interface, conditionality and socialization clearly seem to work. It is significant that Ukraine (and Morocco) were the first recipients of allocations made under the new ENP Governance Facility, which provides additional support to partner countries that have made most progress in implementing governance reforms (€22 million for Ukraine, €28 million for Morocco) (Commission 2007a).

Regarding EU power superiority, agenda-setting, financial and expert assistance all point to the use of productive, institutional and structural power. Agenda-setting by the EU is inherently built into the ENP framework, but is also evident in how Ukraine and other countries develop their own frameworks around EU norms, such as with the Community of Democratic Choice in 2005. Financial assistance amounted to €100 million in 2006 and the new ENPI financial mechanism increases this further (the National Indicative Programme for 2007–2010 amounts to €494 million). The €22 million support from the Governance Facility – 'which resulted from Ukraine's good performance in Governance' – comes on top of this (Commission 2008k: 19). As for expert assistance, this has in part dealt with human rights issues, border protection and elimination of landmines and old ammunition. In addition, the Commission itself underlines that 'twinning and TAIEX strengthens the EC's ability to provide expert advice' (Commission 2006c: 17).

Having said that, however, it is obvious that Ukraine has some leverage on its own. In a sign of productive power, Ukraine policy choices actually reinforce the regional profile (and impact) of the EU in the security field, energy included. Moreover, the European Parliament has recognized 'Ukraine's potential as a key partner in management of migration flows and borders' (European Parliament 2007b). Hence, readmission and visa facilitation agreements are not only in the interest of Ukraine but also of the EU.

Finally, a note on Ukrainian EU membership. As has been shown above, Ukrainian leaders have repeatedly stressed the goal of a Ukrainian membership and the public is in large shares positive to EU membership (some estimates show that more than 70 per cent of the population is in favour of EU membership, while only 22–25 per cent favours a NATO membership (*Dagens Nyheter* 2008). The EU has responded with an ambiguous message: membership discussions are not in the agenda, there is no link between the ENP and membership, but at the same time the ENP does not limit future forms of interaction with the EU. EU representatives continually underline that they welcome Ukraine's aspirations of closer relations. Regarding a new enhanced agreement, for instance, the Council concludes: 'the European Union aims to build an increasingly close relationship with Ukraine, aimed at gradual economic integration and deepening of political co-operation' (Council 2007a). Negotiations for an enhanced agreement started in March 2007. The European Parliament (historically proactive in enlargement discussions) subsequently repeated its call on the Council and the Commission of giving Ukraine a 'clear European perspective', and in the meantime, further engaged in negotiations regarding an enhanced agreement (European Parliament 2007b). In a later statement, the Parliament even opens up for the possibility of membership (conditioned on democracy and the rule of law and with explicit reference to the Copenhagen criteria) (European Parliament 2007a).

The membership issue may in the end turn out to be problematic. If not a paradox, it is at least a dilemma that, due the very fact that four years after the Orange Revolution, conditionality and socialization works so successfully in the EU–Ukrainian interface that the Ukrainian quest for membership may be expected to grow more intense. So would disappointment if continually rejected. It is illuminating that Commissioner Ferrero-Waldner said already in 2005 that the EU would be willing to go substantially beyond what was originally offered if Ukraine is willing to implement necessary actions and changes (referred to in Kelley 2006). Immediately after the completion of the Action Plan, President Yushchenko publicly described it as a precursor to membership negotiations (CEPS 2005a: 2). As Ukraine subsequently has made reforms in the direction of the EU, calls for closer association are natural. The current negotiations for a new enhanced agreement are to be seen in this light. It may be relevant here to recall the similarity with the situation regarding the Central European countries in the 1990s – the EU made more and more ambitious agreements to avoid the membership issue, but the Central European countries were not at all content with that and pressed even harder for membership. In that perspective, the decision in the autumn of 2008 to engage in negotiation for an Association Agreement is principally important – will such an agreement eventually satisfy Ukrainian ambitions and dreams, or will it merely spur the further quest for membership?

South Caucasus interfaces

As in the case of the Wider Europe group of interfaces, a few points need to be mentioned before the individual analyses. One is, in parallel to the previous grouping, to refer to the GUAM regional forum as an indication both of the importance of such sub-regional initiatives and of the general direction of transition from communism to democracy and market economy. Although the GUAM format includes only Georgia and Azerbaijan, this general remark goes also for Armenia. Second, regarding EU engagement, it is worth noting that the EU appointed a Special Representative to the South Caucasus already in 2003, which implies EU involvement prior to the launch of the ENP process.

The EU–Armenia interface

The institutional context of the EU–Armenia interface is made up of a Partnership and Cooperation Agreement dating back to 1999, on which the ENP Action Plan of November 2006 rests. The general outlook of the Armenian government is pro-EU, as it has declared EU membership a long-term goal. The neighbourhood policy is thus a means for linking closer to the EU, of interest also in the context of the sensitive relationship to Turkey (by working with the EU, Armenia may induce, perhaps pressure, Turkey to contribute to resolving outstanding conflicts – for instance, opening borders and railway connections with Armenia). Simultaneously, such a pro-European policy also opens up for EU influence over Armenia to solve the Nagorno-Karabakh conflict.

In terms of EU recognition of Armenia, it is worthwhile to look at the Commission evaluation of Armenia as a prelude to setting up the ENP Action Plan. The Commission generally praised Armenia's good macro-economic progress in the years leading up to the evaluation and also pointed to some signs of aligning legislation with that of the EU (with a special mentioning of the anti-corruption strategy). 'However', the Commission concluded, 'major challenges remain for Armenia, particularly in the field of democracy and human rights and in implementing its obligations as a member of the Council of Europe and the OSCE' (Commission 2005a). More precisely, implementation of fundamental freedoms and reform of the law enforcement sector were deemed necessary for assuring human rights. Moreover, developing civil society was deemed important. Above all, it was argued, the conflict over Nagorno-Karabakh with Azerbaijan overshadows all aspects of public life, and needs to be solved peacefully. The focal point of Commission logic is that the 'Armenian government has declared its determination to address these challenges, to develop relations with the EU and to integrate further in European structures'. In establishing a position in favour of an ENP Action Plan for Armenia, the Commission relies on an internationalist idea along the lines that ENP cooperation could promote implementation of necessary reforms. It was stressed that if progress is made regarding the implementation of the Action Plan, a new enhanced agreement could replace the PCA upon expiry (Commission 2005a). The EU has subsequently recognized the democratic progress made in Armenia, for instance in relation to the parliamentary elections in May 2007, which where, on the whole, deemed fair and free by international observers (Council 2007h).

However, the political situation in Armenia has thereafter displayed instability, which led the EU Presidency to express deep concern about the situation after the presidential elections of 1 March 2008, specifically calling 'upon the Armenian authorities to release any citizens detained for exercising their right to peaceful assembly and to lift the state of emergency, which imposes restrictions on media freedom, the freedom of assembly, and on political parties' (Council 2008c).

In its progress report of April 2008, the Commission returned to the positive perception of Armenia, recognizing progress in several important areas, such as reform of the judiciary, election administration and establishing the Ombudsman Institution. Also human rights were mentioned in this context, but here, the Commission underscored, is room for further improvement (Commission 2008c: 2).

Regarding Armenian recognition of the EU, it is clear that the ENP and other institutional means promoted by the EU are seen by the Armenian authorities as the basis for interaction. In terms of Armenian commitment to EU core values, Armenian President Serzh Sargsyan's statement 'Armenians themselves feel profoundly European' (*EuroNews* 2008) succinctly summarizes the orientation of government policy. Addressing the nation on its seventeenth anniversary of independence, the President talked about the substance of that policy in terms of 'values for which the generations have thought, values we cherish: freedom, democracy and equally before the law. We will stand by those values' (Sargsyan 2008). As far as concrete displays of adopting the EU logic go, Armenia has been very active in cooperating on CFSP-related issues and has 'widely aligned with CFSP declarations' (invited on a case by case basis) (Commission 2008c: 2). Moreover, Armenia has engaged in cooperation with the UN and

NATO on exchanging terrorism information, fully in line with EU standpoints (Commission 2008c: 6). In this context could also be mentioned the rapprochement between Turkey and Armenia, clearly taking place within the overall context of European integration and welcomed not least by the EU (*EuroNews* 2008, EC Delegation in Armenia 2008, Council 2008j).

Based on the review above, it is a rather straightforward conclusion that the EU is clearly the more powerful actor, in institutional as well as productive terms. Also in a structural sense is the EU superior, as seen in the financial assistance offered to Armenia (€98 million for the period 2007–2010 (Commission 2008c: 16)). The political mechanisms used by the EU to induce change in a pro-democratic direction seem to work, although there is still a long way to go and disturbances – largely beyond the control of the EU – appear along the road (Nagorno-Karabakh being the obvious example here). In conclusion, it seems reasonable to label the EU–Armenian interface an *adaptation* interface.

The EU–Azerbaijan interface

Many of the elements in the analysis above can be found also in the EU–Azerbaijan interface. In parallel to the Armenian case, a Partnership and Cooperation Agreement was established in 1999, providing for regular political dialogue, and the ENP Action Plan was adopted in November 2006. As in the Armenian case, the institutional framework of EU–Azerbaijani interaction may be thought to also help serve other interests – in the Azerbaijan case to preserve close links to Ukraine and balance against Russia.

In preparation for the ENP Action Plan, the Commission pointed to the lack of democratic consolidation as the primary problem: 'The overriding challenge still facing Azerbaijan is the need to strengthen the rule of law, democratic checks and balances (including free and fair elections), the fight against corruption and fraud and the protection of human rights' (Commission 2005a). Resolving the Nagorno-Karabakh conflict would, the Commission underlined, have a regional impact on economic and political development. Special note was also taken of the government's desire to address the democratic weaknesses and to integrate further into European organizational structures, and, argued the Commission, the interdependence logic of the ENP could promote the implementation of necessary reforms. As part of such positive strategic interaction, the Commission moreover announced its intention – later realized – to open an EC Delegation in Azerbaijan in 2005 (Commission 2005a).

All in all, it is a parallel recognition to that of Armenia, with democratic insufficiencies at centre stage – expressed in terms of 'major challenges remain for Armenia' to be contrasted with 'overriding challenges still facing' Azerbaijan and Georgia (Commission 2005a) – but a fundamental belief in the logic of interdependence for changing both material and ideational conditions through processes of conditionality and socialization.

Subsequent developments do not appear completely parallel, however. States the Commission in its progress report in April of 2008:

There has been limited tangible progress towards meeting the Action Plan objectives in the area of democratic governance.... The Azerbaijani government has not exploited the opportunities offered by the ENP Action Plan to carry out political and economic reforms in the country, in areas such as democracy, rule of law..., human rights and fundamental freedoms.... Of particular importance ... is the further reform of the electoral code.

(Commission 2008b: 2)

Moreover, the report points to serious problems regarding freedom of assembly, freedom of expression and media and regarding minority protection (Commission 2008b: 4). This standpoint mirrors the observations of the Freedom House analyses (Freedom House 2008).

In terms of Azerbaijani recognition of the EU, the following statement by Foreign Minister Elmar Mammadyarov in September 2007 is illuminating: 'The Government of Azerbaijan considers the integration process *to* the European Union as a matter of priority' (Mammadyarov 2007, emphasis added). This picture of EU superiority is complemented by a declaration of value similarity in terms of peace and security, democracy, protection of human rights and the rule of law and with reference to the notion of a 'European code of conduct' to which Azerbaijan ascribes (Mammadyarov 2007). In this context could also be mentioned that Azerbaijan is a signatory of the Community of Democratic Choice and a GUAM founding member, together with Ukraine, Moldova and Georgia. Relations with Georgia – itself a pro-EU country, see further below – have been singled out by Azerbaijan President Ilham Aliyev as of special significance, being based on democratic values and advanced common interests in terms of trade, regional security, and, most importantly, energy (Aliyev 2008). Of interest regarding value similarity, by the end of 2007, Azerbaijan aligned itself with more than half of the CFSP declarations (invited on a case by case basis) (Commission 2008b: 6). Moreover, Azerbaijan's cooperation with EU institutions and member-states regarding hydrocarbon energy (production and diversification of transport routes), specifically in linking the Baltic–Black–Caspian seas in a so-called energy transit space, signals Azerbaijan's deliberate European policy orientation (Baku Summit 2008).

In conclusion, in parallel to the EU–Armenian interface, the EU–Azerbaijan interface is of the *adaptation* kind, but not set on the exact same parameters. Azerbaijan is somewhat less proactive in terms of formal EU–ENP engagement, and has not advanced as far on it democratic reform path, but if judging by official EU reactions, this is not primarily due to lack of commitment to core values. Such a conclusion seems reasonable also against the background of Azerbaijan's active involvement in regional cooperation aiming at democratic consolidation. The EU is clearly the more powerful actor, in terms of institutional power (the ENP framework and logic), productive power (EU ideas/values adopted by Azerbaijan) and structural power, in the form of financial assistance. Regarding this latter point, the ENPI National Indicative Programme for 2007–2010 amounts to €92 million (Commission 2008b: 17). It should be underlined, to balance the picture, that Azerbaijan has made explicit use of some of the leverage granted by its European engagement, notably in the energy sector.

The EU–Georgia interface

By way of a background note, the PCA currently forming the legal basis for EU–Georgian interaction came into effect in 1999. As a prelude to the ENP Action Plan, the Commission issued its Country Report in March 2005. It was somewhat less critical to Georgia than to the two other South Caucasus states, a difference that has remained throughout the ENP process thus far. For Georgia, which has declared EU membership a long-term goal, the ENP is instrumental in preserving close links to Ukraine and balancing Russia, an interest that is as acute as ever upon the culmination of the Russian–Georgian crisis into armed conflict in August 2008.

In essence, the EU recognizes Georgia as a reform-oriented country on its way to adopting the core values of the EU. EU recognition of Georgia relates back to the Rose Revolution in November 2003. The subsequent holding of relatively free and fair presidential and parliamentary elections and the introduction of an extensive reform package were deemed positive signals in the Commission report of 2005. The Commission highlighted seven different reform achievements, including tackling corruption, curbing smuggling, good macro-economic performance and renewed donor confidence (a successful donor conference took place in Brussels in June 2004). Among the overriding challenges still facing Georgia was mentioned the strengthening of the rule of law (including public sector reform and reform of the judiciary, and strengthening democratic checks and balances – developments in these areas 'should help cement Georgia's fight against corruption in a law-based framework'). The Commission pointed out at the time that improving relations with Russia and settling of internal conflicts (regarding South Ossetia and Abkhazia) will be needed for long-term security and prosperity. In conclusion the Commission recognized that the government is committed to address challenges and that an ENP Action Plan will promote implementation of necessary reforms (Commission 2005a). Generally speaking, the 2005 assessment is parallel to that on Armenia and Azerbaijan – interdependence at work, but major challenges remaining for Georgia. To be true, there were some hints in the direction that Georgia had advanced somewhat further than the other two countries, but the general direction and institutional path are the same for all three countries.

EU institutions and member-states have since then become increasingly content with Georgian developments, evident for instance in the so-called 'New Group of Friends of Georgia' (consisting of Estonia, Bulgaria, Czech Republic, Latvia, Lithuania, Poland, Romania, and Sweden, and with the EU Special Representative for South Caucasus as an observer), meeting in Vilnius in September 2007. At the meeting, it was noted that 'Georgia is a true success story in making' and explicit support for Georgia's integration to the EU and NATO was offered. Moreover, it was urged that outstanding issues, such as detrimental visa rules, should be dealt with promptly (Ministry of Foreign Affairs of Georgia 2007).

In its progress report of April 2008, the Commission repeated its general positive recognition of Georgia. 'Georgian authorities have been pursuing an ambitious agenda of political and economic reforms', the Commission noted, but

> [T]he implementation of the Action Plan has revealed the difficulties in reconciling the government's drive for a radical reduction of the role of the government in the economy and the EU regulatory approach reflected in the Action Plan... Some important legislative improvements were achieved in the area of democracy, the functioning of state and local administrative bodies, human rights and fundamental freedoms. However, events in the latter part of the reporting period demonstrate the need for a proper implementation of this legislation.
>
> (Commission 2008d: 2)

Moreover, the Commission took note of Georgia's concrete behaviour in terms of publicly embracing EU values: 'Georgia has widely aligned with CFSP declarations and participates actively in regional cooperation projects' (Commission 2008d: 2). Among issues deemed important by the EU was mentioned border management (an indication, the Commission states, of Georgia taking issues such as illegal arms exports and prohibiting the spread of weapons of mass destruction seriously) and Georgia's strong regional engagement in the Baltic–Black–Caspian Sea efforts to create a European energy corridor together with Azerbaijan, Lithuania, Ukraine and Poland (Commission 2008d: 6). The positive impression of Georgia's political development was reiterated by the External Relations Council in May 2008 as it deemed the parliamentary elections free and fair (with only limited problems) in accordance with reports from international monitors and repeated the support for Georgian independence and territorial integrity (Council 2008e).

Interestingly enough, the long process of increasingly hostile relations with Russia – culminating in the short war of August 2008 – has made the EU perceive Georgia's European orientation in an even clearer fashion (see also analysis in Chapter 6 on the EU–Russia interface). On the issue of South Ossetia, EU representatives clearly view Georgia as a pro-Western state with which interdependence logic may work – while urging Georgian authorities to apply moderation, Russia is clearly singled out as the greater problem (Ferrero-Waldner 2006l, European Parliament 2006b). Moreover, the EU reacted in support of Georgia upon the Russian decision to initiate formal relations with institutions of the de facto authorities of South Ossetia and Abkhazia without the consent of the Georgian government: 'The EU reiterates its firm commitment to the sovereignty and territorial integrity of Georgia' (Council 2008d). This statement was issued the day after a Russian MiG 29 shot down a Georgian reconnaissance drone. A large volume of reactions in the international community followed, among which the Ukraine and Azerbaijan aligned themselves with the EU declaration.

EU reactions to the military confrontation between Georgia and Russia in August 2008 are also illuminating in this regard (this issue is analysed further in

Chapter 6, here focus is strictly on perceptions of Georgia). The Extraordinary European Council on 1 September stressed the respect for Georgian sovereignty and territorial integrity, harshly condemned Russia's 'disproportionate reaction' and 'strongly condemns Russia's unilateral decision to recognise the independence of Abkhazia and South Ossetia. That decision is unacceptable' (European Council 2008c). At this meeting, and more concretely in the weeks that followed, EU commitment to play a decisive role in conflict management in Georgia was vigorously repeated, as EU mediated a peace plan agreed to by the parties on 8 September, decided to send a civilian observer mission, appointed a Special Representative for the crisis in Georgia, and set up a donor conference. Of importance from our perspective is also the repeated commitment to EU (Commission) financial aid and the deemed need to strengthening the EU–Georgia relationship, in particular by finalizing the preparatory work on visa facilitation and readmission, as well as on free trade (European Council 2008c, Council 2008f, 2008k).

In essence, the Georgian government recognizes the EU as a proponent and anchor of values to which Georgia aspires. Argued President Saakashvili early in 2008:

> We are joined by a common and unbreakable bond – one based on culture, on our shared history and identity, and on a common set of values that has at its heart the celebration of peace and the establishment of fair and prosperous societies. Together with our partners in the European Union we will continue to strengthen these historic ties.
>
> (Saakashvili 2008a)

The 'National Security Concept' is perhaps the most authoritative source on the fundamental variables determining Georgia's foreign policy. In the opening paragraph, it is stated that Georgia's 'fundamental national values are rooted in European values and traditions' and that Georgia 'aspires to return to its European tradition and remain an integral part of Europe'. The values referred to are independence (based on sovereignty and territorial integrity), freedom (specified as universally recognized human rights and freedoms of all individuals), democracy and rule of law (application of universal democratic value and principles and subsequent state authority defined by law), prosperity (based on market economy), peace (resolving all disputes by peaceful means, with the specific mentioning of the neighbourhood) and security (protecting state, institutions and individuals under the norms of international law) (Ministry of Foreign Affairs of Georgia 2006a). In strategic terms, the National Security Concept points to the importance of achieving 'full-fledged integration into … the European Union (EU) '(Ministry of Foreign Affairs of Georgia 2006a). The concept continues:

> Georgia views the EU as a community of nations that ensures the peace and prosperity in Europe.… Values and objectives shared by the EU are common to Georgia, which considers EU membership an important guarantee for its economic and political development.

It is, moreover, explicitly stated that Georgia fully subscribes to the European Security Strategy and is ready to participate in its implementation and that EU assistance in the form of technical assistance (TACIS) and the EU Rule of Law Mission to Georgia (EUJUST THEMIS) 'has been instrumental in fostering Georgia's reforms in a variety of spheres' (Ministry of Foreign Affairs 2006a).

The long-term goal of Georgia's European orientation is thus EU membership, but the government is aware that Georgia is currently not ready – says Giorgi Baramidze, Minister for European and Euro-Atlantic integration: 'We don't want to be anybody's headache. We want to be good neighbours and good partners of Europe' (RFE/RL 2006b). In the meantime, a free trade agreement with the EU is a top priority, as is energy cooperation, often noted as an interdependence means for including Georgia in regional political frameworks (Ministry of Foreign Affairs 2006a).

Georgia is, moreover, a founding and central member of GUAM and of the Community of Democratic Choice, which in a practical way shows Georgian preferences regarding the fundamental principles of the EU and its member-states.

In parallel, Georgia is seeking closer relations with NATO, and is ultimately aiming for membership (Ministry of Foreign Affairs of Georgia 2006a). In an act of reciprocity against the background of Georgian reforms regarding democracy, rule of law and civil–military relations, NATO offered Georgia a so-called Intensified Dialogue in September 2006, the same arrangement that was offered to Ukraine earlier the same year. The government's pro-active approach regarding Euro-Atlantic integration was widely supported in a plebiscite in early 2008, in which 77 per cent turned out in favour of Georgia's goal of NATO membership (Saakashvili 2008a).

The conflict with Russia has also proven an opportunity for Georgia to display its European orientation. Addressing the Georgian population in front of the Parliament building at the peak of the August war, President Saakashvili attached fundamental importance to the presence and solidarity of European leaders when proclaiming: 'Together with us here today are six leaders of European countries and leaders of different governments. I can say that this is the biggest worry which our enemies could see here' (Saakashvili 2008b). It could be added that it was a significant non-coincidence, that in addition to the EU presidency, represented by the French president, the leaders present were the Prime Minister of Latvia and the presidents of Poland, Estonia, Lithuania, and Ukraine, all countries with which Georgia's (and Ukraine's) European project is intimately related. The European linkage formed an important part also in President Saakashvili's annual address in September 2008, the occasion at which he expressed: 'Today Russia is not a winner. The victory of Russia would be defeat of the Georgian democracy.... Our final aim is to transform Georgia into a successful European country and to solve the conflicts in a peaceful way' (Saakashvili 2008c). This is in line with the 2007 address to the nation (in the midst of a state of emergency), in which the main message concerned Georgia as a democratic country (Saakashvili 2007).

In conclusion, Georgia is positively buying into the interdependence logic proposed by the EU. This goes for the institutional mechanisms offered, evident for instance in the so-called 'Tblisi Declaration' in which the presidents of Georgia and Azerbaijan and the Prime Minister of Turkey stressed the importance of the ENP framework for Georgia's and Azerbaijan's closer association to the EU (Tblisi Declaration 2007). It can also be seen in choices regarding foreign and security policy, in which Georgia aligns itself heavily with EU rhetoric and practice. It is evident that the EU is in a superior power position based on institutional and productive power bases. In addition, the EU offers substantial financial assistance to Georgia, both within the regular ENP framework (the National Indicative Programme for 2007–2010 encompasses €120 million (Commission 2008d: 19) and together with EU member-states as a result of the EU-led donor conference in the autumn of 2008 in the aftermath of the August war. The power asymmetry forms the basis for, indeed is partly a result of, Georgia's active search for recognition by the EU. Georgia publicly communicates its value similarity to and its ambition to achieve more advanced forms of relationship with the EU. It displays a clear understanding and acceptance of the positive conditionality laid out by the EU. In conclusion the EU–Georgia interface is best described as an *inclusion* interface.

Post-Soviet interface fundamentals

Judging by the analyses above, a pattern in terms of interface character appears (see Table 4.1). A number of conclusions can thus be made regarding the post-Soviet interfaces:

- Europeanization seems to work, except for the case of Belarus. The other five countries are heavily involved with the EU (and other European organizations) and publicly declare their ambition to move closer to the EU against the background of a reform approach proposed by the EU. It is evident that the conditionality/socialization logic works with this group of countries.
- The EU is the superior power in the different interfaces, which is evident both in terms of how the EU sets the rules of engagement (not least through the institutions and mechanism of the ENP) and how it is in a position to provide the lexicon for interaction. It, moreover, financially supports the different societies, which signals the dependence of the post-Soviet states on the EU regarding their development.

Table 4.1 Post-Soviet interfaces

Hostility	Resistance
	Belarus
Convergence	Adaptation
	Armenia, Azerbaijan, Moldova
Community	Inclusion
	Georgia, Ukraine

- The intriguing exception is Belarus. Also in the EU–Belarus interface can the EU be claimed to be the stronger party, in all traditional/aggregate ways of looking at the relationship and also in the bilateral sense that the EU can impose sanctions and other forms of punishment with much greater effect than a potential contrary situation would imply. Nonetheless, the EU logic of socialization and conditionality does not work – the EU has thus far not been successful in inducing change in a direction desired by the EU, and it is not strong enough to force Belarus in a compulsory sense.
- Geographical proximity does not equal similarity in interface logic. The Wider Europe area is the obvious case in point here, where the three countries are involved in three different interface types with the EU. In the South Caucasus, differences in interface terms are not as great, but there is still a significant difference between Georgia, on the one hand, and Armenia and Azerbaijan, on the other hand. In conclusion, then, conventional geographical distinctions do not work in the case of EU interaction, and policy conclusions based on geographic logic may therefore be misdirected.
- Again with the exception of Belarus, there is an obvious similarity in terms of how the post-Soviet states align themselves with CFSP actions. This is one of the strongest signs of Europeanization at work. Against such a background, some countries – notably Ukraine, but also Georgia – have been more active than the others in playing a constructive role with the EU.
- Energy is a key policy area in the interfaces analysed here. Energy production, transit and transport bring some leverage to the post-Soviet states, and thus fit into the picture of EU dependence vis-à-vis the neighbourhood. Energy is also one of, if not the strongest, common instrumental interest of the post-Soviet states under analysis here and provides a leading rationale for sub-regional cooperation.
- Russia figures importantly in all interfaces analysed here. The most obvious cases are Belarus and Georgia, but – naturally – for dramatically different reasons. Whereas the Belarusian ambition is to move closer to Russia on the basis of shared history, culture and identity in aggressive opposition to the EU, Georgia seeks an even more intense linkage to the EU as a result of the war with Russia. But also for the rest of the group is the presence of the great power in the post-Soviet complex a constant factor to have in mind. It is deemed problematic either from a general security point of view, as in the case of Ukraine, or in relation to specific disputes such as the Transnistria issues involving Moldova and Ukraine. Moreover, its energy dominance makes all countries sensitive to Russian policy choices. At the same time, most evident in the cases of Armenia and Azerbaijan, Russia is also considered a neighbour with which one needs to engage in order to achieve stability and security in the future. From an IR theory point of view, it could be added that the variance in interfaces leads us to conclude that great power presence, while possibly influencing the regional logic, is not decisive enough to produce similar relationships to the outside (in this case the EU).

5 Mediterranean interfaces

Introduction

In this chapter, interfaces between the EU and the countries in the eastern and southern Mediterranean are analysed. All in all, ten countries are in focus here, initially divided into two groups of cultural and political significance – the Maghreb and the Levant. The Maghreb countries are Algeria, Libya, Morocco and Tunisia, whereas the Levant countries are Israel, Jordan, Lebanon, the Palestinian Authority and Syria. Egypt traditionally has occupied an ambiguous position between these two groups, but is here considered part of the Levant – Egypt has at times in history belonged to the Levant and is currently intrinsically involved in Middle East politics. In parallel to the previous chapter, these geographical groupings carry no a priori weight for the issue of interface character, but serve as practical tools for analysis. They, moreover, correspond to the subcomplex groups that Barry Buzan and Ole Wæver use in their analysis. As we will see, however, the groups are not internally consistent regarding EU interfaces; instead, there is great variation within each group in this respect.

A couple of general points need to be addressed at this early point of the chapter. First, we need to keep in mind that we are focusing here on countries – with the exception of Israel – that are not liberal democracies (if judging, for instance, by the Freedom House (2008) democracy ratings, where Morocco, Jordan and Lebanon are viewed 'partly free' and the rest of the countries 'not free'). Moreover, these countries display weak human as well as economic development, as pointed out, for instance, by the Arab Human Development Report of the United Nations Developments Programme (UNDP 2005). These fundamentals create challenges for, and to a large extent determine, the agenda for EU interaction. Importantly, ENP Commissioner Benita Ferrero-Waldner referred to the Arab Human Development Report when describing the general picture of the situation in the Arab countries in terms of three deficits – a freedom deficit, a knowledge deficit, a gender deficit (Ferrero-Waldner 2006g). Poor governance structures also imply that while contractual relations between the EU and many of these countries are quite long-standing they may be limited in scope and only partly implemented. In comparison, then, the political conditions are not the same as in the post-Soviet cases – the Mediterranean cases are not cases of transition, but rather cases of (under-) development in the traditional sense.

Second, the military conflicts in the Levant, indeed in the Middle East generally, naturally make normal political life difficult, at times simply impossible. This in consequence also goes for international engagements. Hence, the Commission's conclusion regarding ENP cooperation is of relevance also for our analysis of interfaces: 'In the case of Lebanon and the occupied Palestinian territory, the political context has as yet not allowed Action Plan objectives to be meaningfully addressed, despite noticeable efforts' (Commission 2008a: 3). The tragic developments in the winter of 2008–2009, not least in Gaza, probably render that conclusion valid for a long time to come.

In what follows, EU interfaces with first the Maghreb and then the Levant countries are analysed. First, however, we will take a quick look at regional political processes.

Regional frameworks of interaction: the Euro-Mediterranean Partnership

The Euro-Mediterranean Partnership (EMP), often referred to as the Barcelona process, is a multilateral framework set up in the mid-1990s for cooperation among the EU and Mediterranean countries (Algeria, Egypt, Israel, Jordan, Lebanon, Morocco, the Palestinian Authority, Syria, Tunisia and Turkey). In organizational terms, the EMP draws inspiration from the Conference on Security and Cooperation in Europe (OSCE) and was initially designed around three so-called baskets or areas of cooperation. One concerns security and involves confidence-building measures around principles such as democracy, rule of law, human rights, peaceful resolution of disputes etc. Another concerns economic integration to promote mutual prosperity; in concrete terms, the most ambitious goal so far is the creation of a free trade area by the year 2010. The third area concerns the promotion of people-to-people contacts and the construction of a Mediterranean civil society. At the 2005 Barcelona Summit, recognizing the tenth anniversary of the EMP, a fourth chapter – on 'Migration, Social Integration, Justice and Security' – was introduced.

In conceptual terms, the EMP is interesting since it represents a deliberate attempt – led by the EU – to *create* a Mediterranean region. As such, it relates to issues of regionalism, security interdependence, social construction of identities, and peaceful conflict resolution. Argue Adler and Crawford (2006: 19): The Barcelona process concerns

> [T]he invention of a region that does not yet exist and ... the social engineering of a regional identity that rests, neither on blood nor on religion, but on civil society voluntary networks and civic beliefs. The long-term aim of this experiment is to construct in the Mediterranean region a pluralistic security community whose practices are synonyms of peace.

The Barcelona process has experienced severe problems that have to do with lack of political commitments, setbacks in the Middle East peace process, lack of not least human development in partner countries, the Schengen border regime, and the political conclusions for the EU (and also the United States) of the events of 11September 2001 and the subsequent tensions between European and American liberal projection, on the one hand, and Muslim states, on the other. Having said that, there are signs of the Barcelona process gaining momentum again. A rather advanced work programme is in place and also an agreement on a common code of conduct on countering terrorism. Moreover, the last few years have seen a renewed interest in the Mediterranean dimension, not least spurred by France in the prelude to, and during, the French EU Council Presidency of 2008 regarding a 'Mediterranean Union' (for initial ideas, see Sarkozy 2007). Although not as advanced as the French ambition, in part due to German criticism (Merkel 2007a), the idea of a Mediterranean Union has gained acceptance and is now part of official EU policy. Importantly, it has not replaced but is complementary to the Euro-Mediterranean Partnership, as seen in the formal labelling 'Barcelona Process: Union for the Mediterranean' (Commission 2008a, 2008n; European Council 2008a).

Regarding the relationship between the neighbourhood policy and the Barcelona process, a few points deserve mentioning here. First, it is important to note that whereas the Barcelona process is a truly regional approach, the ENP in reality is a bilateral approach under the heading of a regional arrangement. As such, there are inherent tensions both within the ENP and between the ENP and EMP projects for those states that are involved in both projects. Second, for reasons of scope and against the background of the limited success of the EMP, although officially presented as a complement to the Barcelona process, the ENP currently carries the leading role regarding EU cooperation/integration with its neighbours. Third, the ambitions of the ENP (most evident regarding the potential access to the internal market) as well as the financial possibilities are more far-reaching regarding the neighbourhood policy.

Maghreb interfaces

As it is of interest for the analyses below, here should be mentioned that in addition to the individual forms of engagement with the EU in terms of neighbourhood policy and Barcelona process – described in more detail in the following pages – the Maghreb countries (including Mauritania) cooperate among themselves on a sub-regional basis in the form of the Arab Maghreb Union (established in 1989, primarily an organization devoted to regional economic cooperation and trade). The Maghreb countries are furthermore part of the African Union (AU) – with the exception of Morocco as a consequence of the AU's recognition of the Sahrawi government of West Sahara – and of the Arab League.

The EU–Algeria interface

EU–Algerian interaction formally rests on an Association Agreement in place since 2005. Against the background of this rather recent origin, the Algerian government under President Bouteflika has decided to not negotiate an ENP Action Plan but instead focus on implementing the current agreement. This does not keep the EU from covering Algeria in the financial instrument of the ENP, but it means that there is not the same contractual basis as in most other neighbourhood cases. In its own policy for Algeria, the Commission observes that the political turmoil in recent decades – not least in the 1990s – makes reform take time, in turn explaining the lagging behind regarding EU interaction. The Algerian government seeks to promote reform of the justice system, economic growth and employment and improvements in basic public services (Commission 2006k), which are elements broadly in line with the value base of the EU, but by necessity promoted in a rather diffuse and weak way. Importantly, the EU recognizes Algeria as a strategic partner of the EU, and wishes to establish a 'genuine partnership' with the country (Council 2008n). According to EU sources, although much remains to be done, the government has made considerable efforts to reform and reconcile the country, especially regarding the economy (which is now in comparative terms rather healthy, not least as a result of hydrocarbon exports). Moreover, the government is seen as willing to implement the Association Agreement and strengthen relations to the EU. Of significance is the Commission's recognition of Algeria as a trustworthy partner in combating international terrorism in view of its '10-year experience of confrontation with armed Islamic groups' (Commission 2006k: 7). Algeria furthermore cooperates actively against the spread of weapons of mass destruction and has eliminated its complete stockpile of anti-personnel mines (Commission 2006k: 7).

In conclusion, the interface can be considered a weak form of an *adaptation interface*. The EU is naturally the stronger party in a structural fashion, but cannot make full use of its institutional and productive power as long as Algeria does not participate fully in the neighbourhood policy. But – importantly – the Algerian government is not actively resisting EU engagement, but has simply chosen a cautious – some would say passive – position. Furthermore, the general direction of development is towards increasing interaction and adaptation. In the bilateral context the EU has developed a Country Report regarding Algeria (the major initial step towards an ENP Action Plan, see Commission 2009a) as the Algerian government has begun and continues to implement the Association Agreement (Council 2008w). President Bouteflika has furthermore made constitutional changes in the direction of human rights and gender equality (Bouteflika 2008). In a multilateral context, Algeria is seeking WTO membership and engaging actively in the Arab Maghreb Union (for instance hosting the first-ever Maghreb economic fair in late 2008, see AMU 2008).

The EU–Libya interface

The relationship between Libya and the EU is limited in scope and has only recently displayed some small steps of intensification. The parties have not agreed on any contractual relationship – no Association Agreement or the equivalent is in place, and Libya is merely an observer to the Barcelona process on

Euro-Mediterranean cooperation. It is, furthermore, not participating in the neighbourhood policy programme. Being a founding member of the Arab Maghreb Union, and participating in the African Union as well as the League of Arab States, the Libyan government is not pursuing a policy of complete isolation, but rather one of consciously not interacting with the West in general and the EU in particular. This concrete behaviour has in the past been accompanied by rather harsh rhetoric against the West, which has been reciprocated both in rhetorical form and by means of economic sanctions (arms embargo and trade sanctions by the EU). As is well-known, Libya was implicated in a number of terrorist attacks (most importantly the Lockerbie explosion) and the United States bombed several targets in Libya.

There are important signs of this conflict-ridden relationship changing in the last few years. As a result of 'significant developments' (Commission 2005b) in 2004 (Libya for the first time signalling that it would like to become engaged with the EU in Euro-Mediterranean cooperation and Libyan leader Muammar Khadafi visiting the Commission in Brussels), the EU decided to cautiously change its policy towards Libya. (The background also contains Khadafi accepting responsibility for terrorist attacks in the past and cooperating with Western authorities to extradite the Lockerbie bombers and compensate the families of the victims.) The first-ever high-level visit by an EU representative took place in May 2005, when Commissioner Ferrero-Waldner visited Tripoli and Benghazi, expressing deep sympathy for the victims of the much-publicized AIDS tragedy, but simultaneously requesting that Bulgarian and Palestinian medial workers sentenced to death in connection to the AIDS tragedy be released (Commission 2005b): The medical workers were released in 2007 (Freedom House 2008). In a significant decision in July 2008, the Council decided to authorize the Commission to negotiate an open-ended framework agreement with Libya (Council 2008p). At the start of negotiations in November 2008, Commissioner Ferrero-Waldner referred to the incremental process of building trust, when she argued:

> This was a long awaited moment since the 2004 EU's decision to lift the sanctions against Libya and to start a policy of engagement with this country. I am pleased that we can finally launch these negotiations. Libya is the last south-Mediterranean country with which the EU has no contractual relations and we are keen to establish a clear, long-lasting legal framework in order to strengthen dialogue and cooperation with Libya.
>
> (Commission 2008p)

In a display of productive power, it is furthermore stated: 'Fundamental principles underpinning the Agreement shall be the respect for human rights and democracy' Commission 2008p). This stands, however, in sharp contrast to the constantly non-democratic form of government not recognizing human rights and fundamental freedoms – as an indication, Freedom House (2008) assigns the lowest possible scores for Libya in its freedom index. While there are signs of minor improvements, these cannot readily be related to EU interaction and influence, but, according to Freedom House (2008), most likely to Khadafi's own son pressing for reforms. The aims of the framework agreement were argued to be both contributing to Libya's political and economic development (hence an indication of EU self-image as superior) and treating common problems, for instance related to migration and development (in essence, encompassing an interdependence logic) (Commission 2008p, see also Commission 2005b).

In conclusion, based on the limited materials available from public sources, the EU–Libyan interface is currently best described as a *resistance interface*, in which the EU in the past has made use of compulsory means of power (economic sanctions) and more recently attempted to influence the Libyan government by productive means, directly by proposing formal engagement and in an indirect fashion by pointing to successful interaction with others, notably Morocco. The EU has largely been ineffective, however, in inducing significant change in Libya. As Libya is, moreover, not part of the financial framework of most of the other ENP countries, institutional and structural means for influence are beyond reach. The recent change in EU policy is potentially important, and may lead to the interface changing in the direction of adaptation. It can be interpreted as an attempt to reduce the distrust between the parties and try to move the relationship in a direction of interdependence and interaction, which, incidentally, would increase EU leverage on Libya. The concrete outcome of the new policy of engagement remains to be seen, however.

The EU–Morocco interface

EU–Morocco interaction is dramatically different from the two Maghreb cases considered thus far. The formal basis of engagement is made up of the Association Agreement dating back to 2000. In contrast to many other Mediterranean cases, where agreements have been merely superficial frameworks, in the Moroccan case, deeper cooperation and quicker pace in the past has led to separate sectoral arrangements, for instance regarding fisheries and transport, and twinning arrangements, allowing for transfer of know-how, legislative principles etc. (Lavenex and Schimmelfennig 2006: 150). There are also signs of Morocco changing certain laws after direct input by the EU (Kelley 2006: 45). Morocco is furthermore an active participant of the Barcelona process. As regards the ENP, the Action Plan between the EU and Morocco was adopted in July 2005 for a period of five years.

The EU clearly recognizes Morocco as a reliable partner interested in closer cooperation on the basis of EU core values. The Commission progress report of December 2006 is very illuminating it this regard:

> Over the past two years relations between the EU and Morocco have been significantly strengthened across the board, mainly because Morocco has shown real interest in the European Neighbourhood Policy (ENP), in which it sees the way forward to the 'advanced status' it has always called for. For the Moroccan authorities, securing the country to Europe is a strategic choice.
>
> (Commission 2006i: 2)

While a partly democratic regime according to international observers (Freedom House 2008), numerous reforms initiatives introduced by King Mohamed VI (who ascended the throne in 1999) aimed at modernizing the state, democratization, national reconciliation, human development, status of women, fight against poverty, laws against torture and for political liberty point to a markedly better democracy and human rights situation than in most Arab countries (Freedom House 2008). 'These initiatives', the Commission notes, 'are already reflected as tangible commitments in the Action Plan and place Morocco firmly on the path to reform' (2006i: 2). Cooperation has been especially fruitful regarding economic issues and in the area of migration, and the political debate between the parties is increasingly open and intense (2006i: 2). Moreover, Morocco is actively involved in the discussions on the external security and defence policy (ESDP) – for instance, it was the first ENP country to designate a contact point with the Council (Commission 2006i: 4).

This logic of positive conditionality and socialization also appears in later developments, such as in conjunction with the seventh EU–Morocco Association Council in 2008, when a package of elements for closer cooperation was agreed. In short, the strengthening of relations came as a result of – and in an effort to consolidate – achievements already made in the fields of political and economic transition in the direction of democracy and market economy. The package includes harmonization of laws in the economic area, the preparation for a comprehensive and deep free trade area and closer collaboration on security policy issues, such as crisis management. Moreover, the decision includes the initiation of regular EU–Moroccan summits, ministerial-level concertation mechanisms as well as an offer to Morocco to be present in the wings of certain EU Council ministerial or working group meetings (Council 2008q). In its comprehensive overview of EU–Mediterranean relations, the Council made a special note of Morocco's advanced status in terms of EU interaction, pointing to the 'common willingness of the Kingdom of Morocco and the European Union to establish an increasingly close and mutually beneficial partnership, covering all aspects and all levels' (Council 2008w).

Through concrete behaviour, Morocco recognizes the EU not only as an important instrumental partner in terms of common interests and problem-solving, but also as far as core values are concerned – the EU seems to work as the anchor of Moroccan domestic reform. This is illustrated by Morocco's request in 2007 to gain 'Advanced Status' within the ENP, and by the decisions made at the 2008 Association Council (Council 2008q). In a display of common value base, Morocco sought – and gained acceptance for – participation in the ALTHEA military operation of the EU in Bosnia-Herzegovina. Morocco, moreover, has continually cooperated closely with the EU in the fight against terrorism (Council 2006i: 4). In addition, a number of initiatives have been taken regarding migration (MEDA projects regarding migration management) and justice and police cooperation with several member-states and with Europol (Commission 2006i: 10).

Morocco is one of the main beneficiaries of EU financial support; the financial package of the ENPI for the period 2007–2010 amounts to €654 million (the largest single envelope, an increase of 20 per cent compared to the annual average for the previous decade) (Commission 2007b). As regards technical support, Morocco is deemed 'a pioneer' in the use of the twinning, for instance in areas such as migration and maritime safety (Commission 2006i: 13). In a distinct display of the logic of positive conditionality, Morocco (together with Ukraine) was the first recipient of allocations made under the new ENP Governance Facility, which provides additional support (€28 million for Morocco and €22 million for Ukraine) to partner countries that have made most progress in implementing governance reforms (Commission 2007a).

In conclusion, developments in recent years between the EU and Morocco show signs of increasingly close interaction, a process in which the EU as the stronger party is able to make use of a whole array of power resources – productive, institutional and structural – while Morocco simultaneously acquires a number of benefits not open to other countries. The elements under review here warrant the conclusion that a positive interdependence involving aspects of conditionality, socialization and differentiation is at work. The interface can be concluded to be an advanced form of *adaptation*, although recent developments point in the direction of *inclusion* in the light of Morocco's increasing alignment with EU values and practices.

The EU–Tunisia interface

The relationship between the EU and Tunisia rests on an Association Agreement signed in 1995. Tunisia is participating fully in the Barcelona process and is an active ENP partner – Tunisia was among the first Mediterranean countries to sign an Action Plan (which entered into force already in July 2005). Based on Commission evaluations of Tunisia published in 2006 and 2008, it can be concluded that EU recognition rests on a perception of Tunisia as an active partner in social and economic areas – there is a high degree of cohesion between Action Plan priorities and Tunisia's own reform priorities in these areas – but the lack of democratic reforms, gender equality reforms and human rights promotion in Tunisia in essence signal a lack of commitment to core EU values. In operational terms, good progress in cooperation on social and economic reform matters can be noted, and also regarding transport, energy and scientific research. Much less progress is found in political reform areas of relevance for this analysis. Little or no progress is noted regarding freedom of association and freedom of expression, and the democratic process is flawed (Commission 2006h: 3, 2006l: 2–4). As an anecdotal illustration, by December 2006 the sub-committee on human rights and democracy – one of five sub-committees to the Association Council – had not even agreed on its rules of procedure (Commission 2006h: 2)! There are no obvious signs of the democratic/human rights situation improving – on the contrary, Freedom House has lowered its rating of political rights to the lowest possible 'due to credible accusations of rampant corruption among the president's family and close associates' (Freedom House 2008). However, in the security field, more specifically regarding combating international terrorism, Tunisia is recognized as a 'very reliable partner', signalling some value commonality (2006h: 3).

Although the EU clearly has a lead role in the relationship, it is evident that the EU understands the interdependent nature of security. While political reform ultimately would be desired, the strong focus on economic matters (especially regarding increased productivity and moving towards a knowledge-based economy) is viewed in positive terms against the background of EU dependence: '[The economic reform] objective is all the more relevant in view of the challenge that high growth in unemployment among young graduates, and the social unrest and migration it generates, presents to Tunisia *and Europe*' (Commission 2006h: 2, emphasis added).

EU power vis-à-vis Tunisia is principally channelled through institutional and structural means. Tunisia has engaged in all the institutional mechanisms offered and is rather close to the EU in some sectors as a result, but the EU has been unable – so far – to transfer its institutional power into productive power. In consequence, Tunisia's engagement can be thought of in instrumental rather than ideational terms. As far as structural means are concerned, Tunisia is heavily dependent on EU assistance, and although the assistance for the most part relates to economic matters, new programmes are directed at governance issues, for instance regarding media and justice, and these are considered 'important tests of future cooperation' (Commission 2006h: 10). The volume of the assistance is quite substantial – under the ENPI National Indicative programme, Tunisia is offered €300 million for the period 2007–2013 (Commission 2006l: 0). Tunisia has expressed an interest in a stronger relationship, a wish readily acknowledged by the EU (Council 2008w).

In conclusion, the EU–Tunisia interface is a case of *adaptation* – a rather weak case when looking at political aspects, significantly stronger when regarding economic aspects. The decisive point concerns the lack of commitment to EU core values. The interface cannot, however, be labelled a resistance interface – Tunisia is not actively seeking to undermine the EU's value base, quite the contrary. Rather, it is a question of the EU not being strong enough to induce fundamental change (such transition forms one of the cornerstones of the EU strategy for the next few years (Commission 2006l: 16). As a consequence, the relationship rests on instrumental interests of cooperation, and in that perspective, Tunisia is deemed a reliable partner. The EU is the superior power, drawing both on institutional leverage through the ENP framework and structural power as it is in a position to determine aid conditionality. In that light, it is relevant to note the change in conditionality to the effect that a significant share of assistance has the form of budget support (50 per cent of ongoing programmes in 2006). Argues the Commission: 'This change in the nature of aid reflects a high degree of maturity in implementation of cooperation' (2006h: 10, see also 2006l: 12). There are few obvious signs, however, of EU productive power application.

Levant interfaces

Turning to the remaining group of neighbours, the fundamental security parameter is of course the Arab–Israeli confrontation, which generally concerns all of the countries in the group, but in recent years in particular Lebanon, the Palestinian Authority and Israel. Regarding the first two, the military conflict in essence renders sustainable political and economic development impossible and implies, as we shall see, that interaction with the EU takes a very special form. This comes on top of the general problem of low Arab development, as outlined in the introduction to the chapter. Regarding Israel, the military confrontation complicates the relationship to the EU – while Israel is generally recognized as a democracy (see for instance Freedom House 2008), the way it uses its military superiority creates credibility and legitimacy problems in relation to the EU (and many other actors in a global context).

The EU has engaged strongly in various ways in the Arab–Israeli conflict, for instance as part of the Quartet, but also unilaterally through financial assistance, border assistance, mediation and declaratory means (see further below). The EU has, furthermore, repeatedly expressed full support for the Annapolis process and full commitment to a two-state solution (see for instance Council 2008m). Against this background of security interdependence, let us take a brief look at each of the interfaces.

The EU–Egypt interface

As for many other ENP countries, EU–Egyptian interaction rests on an Association Agreement and an ENP Action Plan. The Association Agreement came into force in 2004, whereas the ENP Action Plan was adopted at the third EU–Egypt Association Council in March 2007. Also in parallel to a number of other cases, the non-democratic nature of the Egyptian regime clashes with core EU values and determines in large part – but not completely – the nature of the interface. Competitive presidential elections have been held but restrictions on human rights and fundamental freedoms determine the political situation (as President Mubarak has ruled largely by emergency law for many years). Oppositions groups, such as the *Kifaya* movement, have argued for democratic practices largely in line with EU ideals (El-Din Shahin 2005). Minor changes have been taking place (for instance regarding freedom of the media) but exceptions to international treaties and protocols in the 'rights and freedoms area' abound and there is a general lack of implementation (Commission 2008f: 4–6). The European Parliament heavily criticized the Egyptian government in January 2008, calling for the government

> [T]o end all forms of harassment, including judicial measures, the detention of media professionals and, more generally, human rights defenders and activists calling for reforms and to fully respect freedom of expression ... end to all forms of torture and ill-treatment.
>
> (European Parliament 2008a)

In such a light, the Commission is surprisingly lenient:

> The challenges we both face, reconciling old and new values ... we share – respect for human rights and democracy.... We appreciate that political reform is a particularly complex and sensitive matter, but the EU is a loyal partner, and we will do everything we can to support Egypt's progress.
> (Ferrero-Waldner 2006o)

Regarding progress in relation to the ENP Action Plan, the Commission progress report of April 2008 states: 'On the whole, Egypt has shown commitment to its Action Plan. It has moved cautiously in the early stages while the administration has been developing a greater understanding of and confidence in the institutional and policy mechanisms' (Commission 2008f: 2). Some developments in the direction of political reform/democratization can be seen in 2007, in particular amendments to the constitutions that in effect make possible the end of the state of emergency in place since 1981. Thus far, this has not implied any major changes. The EU presidency urged the Egyptian authorities to investigate allegations of irregularities and acts of violence in connection to the parliamentary elections in June 2007. So far, there is no indication of such an investigation (Commission 2008f: 3).

Simultaneously, Egypt occupies a special place in EU external relations, for a couple of important reasons. First, it can be seen as a bridge between North Africa and the Middle East, and more specifically for our purposes, Egypt is part of the Arab Maghreb Union as well as the African Union, while it is also intrinsically involved in the Arab–Israeli conflict and Middle East politics more generally. Second, Egypt has come to achieve a special relationship to the EU based on security-political cooperation, not least regarding combating international terrorism (Commission 2008f: 6) and is viewed a strategic partner in bringing a lasting solution to the Israel–Palestine conflict (Council 2008o). As an example, Egypt has worked together with the EU in January 2009 to reach a diplomatic settlement regarding the Gaza strip (*Dagens Nyheter* 2009).

In conclusion, the EU recognizes Egypt as a strategic security partner and as interested in closer EU cooperation, but ultimately a partner country that does not share the fundamental values of the EU due to its non-democratic character.

When it comes to Egyptian recognition of the EU, much the same picture applies. In a significant speech at the occasion of the Euro-Mediterranean summit in November 2005, President Hosny Mubarak pointed to the interdependent relationship of the two shores of the Mediterranean, stressing 'common risks and challenges'. Regarding the Middle East peace process, Mubarak publicly declared Egypt's appreciation for a two-state solution (in line with the EU position, as we shall see later in the chapter) and specifically pointed out that 'we appreciate the role played by the European Union ... and look forward to the continuation and intensification of this role'. Furthermore, the President acknowledged earlier periods of EU assistance, and stated that Egypt aspires for enhanced cooperation within the ENP (Mubarak 2005). Prime Minister Ahmed

Nazif has stressed the same point – Egypt intends to engage in the framework offered to it, and has underlined 'the importance of utilizing this cooperation to promote Egypt's reform process' (Office of the Prime Minister of Egypt 2007). In March 2008 a comprehensive agreement on cooperation and financial agreement was reached (see next section). At the same time, Mubarak has put an outer limit in terms of foreign interference in domestic development, taking a stance that partnership must be built on 'equality, mutual respect and ... on recognition of ... societal specificity ... and on refraining from interfering in ... internal affairs' (Mubarak 2005). The Egyptian government has more recently expressed its wish to strengthen its relations with the EU, an ambition readily recognized by the EU (Council 2008w).

In conclusion, the Egyptian government seeks a closer economic relationship with the EU, recognizes the EU's importance in security matters, specifically in the Middle East, and acknowledges EU superiority through economic and institutional means. At the same time, it resists outside/EU interference in the domestic political developments.

Here it may be relevant to point to indications of public opinion about different countries (although not the EU as an entity), as they are portrayed in a public opinion poll conducted by the official polling centre of Egypt. When asked about perceptions of different countries, Saudi Arabia was considered the most friendly country (61 per cent of respondents), followed by Palestine (51 per cent) and Syria (42 per cent). The non-Arab countries getting the highest figures were Iran (23 per cent), China (18 per cent) and France (15 per cent) (Public Opinion Poll Center of Egypt 2006). For reasons of source criticism, these figures need to be interpreted very cautiously; they may, nevertheless, provide an indication of a value gap compared to the EU area.

In concluding, the EU–Egypt interface is a case of *adaptation*, in its logic rather similar to the EU–Tunisian one, but with the significant difference that Egypt is recognized as a strategically important partner to the EU in security matters. The EU has some leverage due to its financial resources and expertise. EU financial support for the period 2007–2010 has been granted in the amount of €558 million (agreement reached in March 2008 and directed at three main areas – political reform and good governance, competitiveness and productivity of the economy, and socio-economic sustainability of the development process, see Commission 2008f: 17–18). In addition, twinning projects have been launched in areas such as maritime safety, postal management and tourism (Commission 2008f: 17–18). Moreover, the EU is providing capacity building and training in human rights law to judges, state prosecutors and law enforcement officers (Commission 2008f: 4).

Interestingly enough, the Commission (Ferrero-Waldner), when endorsing the assistance package, emphasized that it 'will deepen our partnership in a number of key areas including education, transport, energy, trade and agriculture' (Commission 2008o) – but, notably, said nothing about democratic reforms and human rights promotion. The EU has indeed thus far been largely unable to induce fundamental political change in return for greater integration. As in some other cases under review here, then, the democracy dimension paradoxically diminishes EU influence. There are certain signs of political developments in the right direction as seen from an EU perspective, but it would be premature to assign these changes solely to EU policy. In short, the EU has had limited leverage in terms of productive power.

The EU–Israel interface

Israel signed an Association Agreement with the EU in the summer of 2000 and an ENP Action Plan was adopted in early 2005. It has a special standing in the regional context against the background of its democratic form of government, its developed economy and its longstanding bilateral relationship with the EC/EU, dating back to 1975. Having said that, EU–Israeli relations have been rather troubled, in part due to EU support for the Palestinian Authority, in part due to Israel's lack of interest in deepening cooperation with the EU. ENP cooperation seems to partly change this picture.

EU recognition of Israel rests on two partly contradictory elements – the special place of Israel in regional comparison and Israel's regional security policy. Notes the Commission in relation to ENP implementation during 2005 and 2006: 'on account of its high level of economic development, [Israel] should enjoy special status in its relations with the EU on the basis of reciprocity and common interest' (Commission 2006e: 2). Unprecedented levels of cooperation was noted in many areas of cooperation, including political dialogue, promoting trade and investment, justice and security, science and technology including space cooperation, as well as higher education. 'There has been a greater understanding between the EU and Israel of each other's position on a number of issues', notes the Commission, 'and a greater convergence of views on dealing with terrorism, including Israel's legitimate right of self-defence, and threats to regional stability' (Commission 2006e: 2). The same elements of recognition appear in more recent evaluations of EU–Israeli interaction (see below, also Council 2008w). Israel has demonstrated good progress, according to the Commission, in implementing a large number of priorities of the Action Plan, and is a 'front-runner' when it comes to ENP countries participating in community programmes, such as the 'Competitiveness and Innovation Programme' (Commission 2007a, 2008e: 2). In brute contrast to surrounding states, Israel enjoys minimal financial assistance from the EU, which reflects Israel's status as a developed economy. Only €8 million have been allocated in assistance for the period 2007–2010, directed at supporting implementation of twinning activities (Commission 2008e: 15).

The picture becomes more complex when adding the dimension of (EU recognition of) Israel's security perceptions and policies. Again referring to the Commission, it has explicitly observed the important differences that remain concerning aspects related to EU core values, such as respect for international law and human rights in the context of the conflict, difficulties in respecting the principles of the roadmap, and a number of issues affecting the potential to reach a final status agreement between Israel and the Palestinians (Commission 2006e:

2–3). One such issue concerns the building of settlements in the occupied Palestinian territories, viewed 'illegal under international law' and 'an obstacle to peace' (Council 2008l, 2008m, 2008o). A later evaluation of ENP implementation points to no progress being made on issues such as the peace process, the situation of the Arab minority in Israel, restrictions on the movement in the West Bank and the Gaza strip, the construction of the separation barrier, administrative detentions, envisaged expansions of certain Israeli settlements etc. (Commission 2008e: 5). The EU struggles with the tension between Israel's legitimate rights and its policy choices vis-à-vis its neighbours. The Council stated after Hezbollah's attacks on Israel in the summer of 2006: 'The EU recognizes Israel's legitimate right to self-defence, but it urges Israel to exercise utmost restraint and not resort to disproportionate action' (Council 2006b), the same wording was used a year later (Council 2007b). In the same context, the EU urged Israel to release elected members of the Palestinian Government and open border crossings, especially to Gaza to alleviate the humanitarian situation there. Moreover, the Council reiterated EU's long-term goal of a negotiated two-state solution and stressed that it will not recognize any changes to pre-1967 borders unless agreed to by all parties and that it is particularly concerned with the construction of the barrier on Palestinian land (Council 2007b). As 2007 approached its final months, the EU viewed the opportunity for developing peace between Israel and Palestine as greater than in a long time, again underlining the need for a two-state solution and the leading role of the Quartet (Council 2007c).

As far as Israeli recognition of the EU goes, the material under review here suggests that over time, Israel has been attaching more weight to the EU in economic matters than in security matters, a field where the United States is Israel's closest ally. Moreover, as the relationship to the EU has been part of a broader consideration regarding regional security, interaction has at times been rather tense. As an illustration, it took repeated calls from the EU to get its mission to assist the Palestinian police corps (EUPOL COPPS) accredited by Israel (Commission 2008e: 4).

Recent developments indicate, however, a reorientation of Israel's recognition of the EU in the political field. In June 2008, the EU and Israel agreed on a comprehensive deal – initiated by Israel's Foreign Minister Tzipi Livni – to move relations into a qualitatively new level, involving Israel's integration into the European single market, participation in EU programmes and agencies, and increased diplomatic cooperation (Israel Ministry of Foreign Affairs 2008a). Upgrading relations with Israel was the centrepiece as the EU reviewed its policies towards Mediterranean countries in late 2008 (Council 2008w). Foreign Minister Livni characterized the EU decision as a 'significant step in upgrading Israel's relations with the European Union ... which reflects the common values and similar world views' (Israel Ministry of Foreign Affairs 2008b). In line with this, Israel has been invited to align itself with CFSP declarations on a case by case basis, but had as of April 2008 not yet taken up the offer (Commission 2008e: 4). The two sides have, however, expressed a common understanding regarding terrorism (Israel Ministry of Foreign Affairs 2009).

There are indications that this reorientation of the Israeli government is largely in line with public opinion. According to an opinion poll from mid-February 2007, 75 per cent of the Israelis would like their country to become part of the EU (quoted in Ferrero-Waldner 2007c).

In conclusion, the EU–Israel interface is a complex one bearing signs of both *adaptation* and *inclusion*. On the one hand, Israel is by default closer to the EU than its neighbours in terms of value compatibility due to its democratic credentials. It is also interested in – and has capacity for – instrumental cooperation and has adopted the institutional mechanism offered by the EU. Commissioner Ferrero-Waldner, for one, has noted: 'Of the 16 countries participating in the ENP, Israel is among the best placed to reap significant benefits from closer integration with the EU' (Ferrero-Waldner 2007c). On the other hand, Israel's security considerations mean that cooperation with the EU is part of a larger picture, in which the United States remains its closest ally. Moreover, it may be – although this is hard to substantiate – that EU recognition of the Palestinian Authority is perceived as provocative to the Israelis. In addition, the EU has little structural power given that the level of Israel's political and economic development renders it no assistance from the EU. There is, however, an asymmetrical interdependence relationship in trade in favour of the EU (in being Israel's main trading partner). The EU has engaged itself heavily in the Israel–Palestinian issue, in part in joint projects such as the 'Agreement on Movement and Access' involving Israel and the Palestinian Authority and the EU as a 'third party', in setting up the border assistance mission in Rafah – EUBAM Rafah, on standby, however, since June 2007 due to violent events in Gaza – and in financially supporting the Israeli–Palestinian Energy Cooperation Programme (this programme was however suspended in December 2006 in the light of the situation in the region at the time) (Commission 2006e: 10). The EU has, moreover, tried to play a leading role in direct relation to the Palestinian Authority and territories, continually as a member of the Quartet, and in concrete circumstances, such as creating the 'Temporary International Mechanism' established by the EU after a decision by the Quartet in June 2006, aiming at taking care of immediate needs in the Palestinian territories (Commission 2006e: 10). These are all signs of uses of productive power to contribute to getting Israel as well as Palestine into a new normative mode. The long-term impact remains uncertain, however.

The EU–Jordan interface

The EU–Jordan interface revolves around the Association Agreement from 2002 (originally dating back to 1977) and the ENP Action Plan adopted in January 2005 for a period of five years. In essence, EU recognizes Jordan as an enthusiastic and committed ENP partner, albeit democratically underdeveloped and sometimes lacking in implementation capacity. Jordan was among the first Mediterranean countries to sign an Action Plan, and it was furthermore the first ENP partner to hold a sub-committee meeting with the Human Rights and Democracy subcommittee established by the Action Plan, which is significant against the background of its status of partly free (according to Freedom House 2008). This and other subcommittees are an 'efficient tool', says the EU, in being a means of dialogue allowing for Jordan and EU priorities being synchronized and for more effective EU assistance (Commission 2006f: 2).

In its review after the first year of Action Plan implementation, the EU notes the following:

> Overall, Jordan has shown a real commitment to realising the measures of the Action Plan and has made a start with implementation.... Jordan has shown ... that it remains strongly committed to a number of important political and economic reforms, but it is important that these commitments are indeed translated into concrete progress.
>
> (Commission 2006f: 2)

As regards democracy and rule of law, some progress can be noted, for instance in the form of government interaction with civil society (including the *Kulluna al Urdun* – 'We are all Jordan' initiative), initiation of public sector reform within various ministries, equal treatment of women, and transparency (Commission 2006f: 3). Regarding equal treatment of women, there are preliminary signs of improvement in public life (specific proposals for enhancing women's participation in the labour market have been made. But, notes the Commission, there 'is still a lot of room for progress in developing women's rights and tackling highly sensitive issues such as domestic violence and honour crimes' (2006f: 4). Over the years, Jordan has received substantial amounts of financial technical aid. While this on the one hand signals structural power on the part of the EU, it also plays into EU recognition of Jordan as a committed and reliable partner: 'Since 1995, more than €500 million has been allocated to Jordan under the MEDA programme. Its performance in absorbing funds and implementing programmes has been very satisfactory' (Commission 2006f: 12).

Much the same picture is repeated in a later evaluation: 'Jordan is an active and constructive partner in the ENP and ... has shown a strong commitment to a wide range of social and economic reforms and to a lesser extent to political reform' (Commission 2008g: 2). When it comes to gender equality, indications of improvements can be found, for instance in the form of quotas for municipal council seats (at least 20 per cent women) (Commission 2008g: 3). Women now have the right to obtain passports without the authorization of their husbands, and the legal age of marriage is now set at 18 (Commission 2008g: 4). In the political sphere, some developments in the direction of EU ideals can be found, for instance regarding freedom of the media, the right of access to information, and the level of corruption. However, there are still major restrictions regarding the freedom of assembly and there has been no reform of the election law. The Commission moreover made a special note of the fact that Jordan accepted no international electoral observers for its November 2007 parliamentary elections (Commission 2008g: 2–4).

In the foreign policy field, the EU recognizes Jordan as a constructive partner, for instance regarding cooperation and information exchange in the field of anti-terrorism. It is of principal significance in a regional perspective that the EU in 2007 invited Jordan to align itself with EU declarations in the field of Common Foreign and Security Policy on a case by case basis (as of April 2008, Jordan had thus far not participated, however) (Commission 2008g: 5).

This perspective of 'constructive partner' is even clearer when analysing regional security in the Middle East, where the Commission notes that 'Jordan has worked actively to bring peace and stability to the region. Jordan sincerely adheres to the principles of the Road Map and has been very supportive of the Quartet's efforts to implement it' (Commission 2008g: 5). There are a number of concrete actions that make up the foundation of this picture and that furthermore can be seen as signs of Jordan's affinity with certain EU values, at least pertaining to peace. For instance – against the combined background of humanitarianism and national interest, it could be added – Jordan has sent a large number of humanitarian assistance convoys to the West Bank and Gaza. It is, moreover, hosting a significant number of Iraqi refugees, estimated at around 450,000. As further signs of regional responsibility, the Commission underlines first the decision in August 2007 by the Jordanian government to allow all Iraqi children in Jordan – with or without residence permits – to enrol in Jordanian schools (this later rendered Jordan additional financial assistance from the EU), and second, the active role played by Jordan in ministerial meetings of Iraqi neighbours, where Jordan among other things chairs the working group on refugees (Commission 2008g: 5).

Regarding Jordan's recognition of the EU, it is worth noting that in parallel to ENP concretization, in November 2005, Jordan adopted its so-called National Agenda, which is a long-term reform programme in the direction of EU values, albeit starting from a rather modest situation. It is of relevance that Jordan has since expressed an interest in a stronger relationship, a wish readily acknowledged by the EU (Council 2008w).

By way of conclusions, the review above implies that the EU–Jordan interface is a case of *adaptation*. While the non-democratic nature of the Jordanian regime continues to render criticism from the EU, in a number of areas there are signs of Jordan moving closer to EU standards and ideals. The EU is the superior power and is able to utilize a number of power resources to induce positive conditionality. Of obvious significance is its financial support to Jordan, allocated in the amount of €265 million for the period 2007–2010, with priority attached to political reform and good governance, trade and investment development and institution-building and financial stability (Commission 2008g: 15). The introduction of twinning and TAIEX assistance is also of relevance, as it has facilitated 'regulatory approximation ... and institution building' (Commission 2006f: 12). The EU itself points to the ENP framework as a institutional power mechanism in relation to democracy and human rights: 'The mere fact that a dialogue on such issues can now take place within an institutional framework is a progress brought about by the ENP' (Commission 2006f: 4). This also serves as an example of productive power in the sense that conceptual definitions and discourses are dictated by the EU side. The same logic goes for awareness projects funded by the EU.

The EU–Lebanon interface

EU–Lebanese relations have naturally been affected by the political instability in Lebanon, resulting from domestic challenges to the government and the assassination of former Prime Minister Rafiq Hariri in 2005. EU recognition of Lebanon rests on a perception that Lebanon is a fragile state set on a democratic path, and hence in need of support. In the military confrontation between Israel and Hezbollah in the summer of 2006, for instance, the EU expressed its support for the Lebanese Prime Minister Fuad Siniora, but simultaneously called upon the Lebanese government to restore its sovereignty over Lebanese authority, to disarm the militias, and to prevent attacks on Israeli towns and cities (Council 2006b). In the autumn, the EU reiterated its commitment to help the Lebanese government with emergency and humanitarian missions and also strengthen the government, stressing its commitment to the full implementation of United Nations Security Council Resolution (UNSCR) 1701 and the absolute need for respecting Lebanese territorial sovereignty and the legitimate and democratically elected Lebanese government (Council 2006c, 2006e). The Council repeated the same point in 2008, stating that the EU 'continues to stand by its strong support for the Government and institutions of Lebanon' (Council 2008m).

At its ENP evaluation in the spring of 2008, the Commission took positive note of the domestic reform agenda entitled 'recovery, reconstruction and reform' (adopted the same time as the ENP Action Plan). The overriding impression, however, concerned the on-going political turmoil (parliamentary deadlock in the autumn of 2006 and throughout 2007, no president in office for the period November 2007–May 2008 due to the parliamentary failure to elect one) and the Commission concluded that no overall assessment of progress in Action Plan implementation could be made. Slow reforms regarding human rights, judicial reform and social sector reform were noted, however (Commission 2008h: 2). Very limited progress has been seen regarding democracy and rule of law – the EU Election Observation Mission concluded already in 2005 that a fundamental overhaul of Lebanon's electoral legislation was an 'urgent priority', but this has consistently been blocked in the government process. Governance reforms began in small scale, but not much progress has materialized. Further, the ratification of human rights conventions was blocked in 2007 (Commission 2008h: 3). Reports of torture exist and it is reported there is no progress regarding equality (transmission of nationality and marriage rights). There is possible development regarding child labour (Commission 2008g: 4) and foreign and security policy cooperation has been limited to implementation of major UNSC resolutions relevant for and relating to Lebanon (Commission 2008g: 5).

The main conclusion regarding the EU–Lebanon interface is that both sides appear relatively weak in the relationship, although naturally in very different ways. The power of the EU is to be located in formal aspects regarding institutional structure of interaction and in structural assistance terms – Community financial support amounts to €187 million for the period 2007–2010, distributed along two different lines, one concerning reconstruction needs arising from the military conflicts in 2006 and aiming at reinvigorating the economy, while the rest is focused on key policy objectives outlined by the ENP Action Plan (Commission 2008h: 14)). Thus far, however, the EU has been largely unable to change the political instability and the democratic flaws that exist in Lebanon. For its part, Lebanon is a weak partner in terms of lack of administrative and political capacity to stabilize the political situation and engage in reforms desired by the EU. Judged ultimately by expressed intentions rather than outcomes, the interface is a case of *adaptation*, but the weaker side – Lebanon – suffers from an implementation deficiency.

The EU–Palestine interface

The relationship between the EU and the Palestinian Authority is indeed a very complex issue. Although standard institutional frameworks are in place – an Association Agreement (interim agreement, to be correct) was adopted in July 1997, and an ENP Action Plan was adopted in 2005 – EU–Palestine interaction takes place under very special circumstances. First, the Palestinian side is not a sovereign state in the conventional sense, which presents challenges especially in a Mediterranean perspective where, as we have seen, governments control their territories and entertain state capacity to different degrees. Second, since the Hamas victory in the general election of 2006, the Palestinian side is internally split, evident not least in the violent events in June 2007 resulting in a further political divide between the deposed government in Gaza and the newly established and internationally backed government in Ramallah (Commission 2008j: 3). This is in sharp contrast to 2005, when the Action Plan was established, a time when the EU perceived the Palestinian reform programme – aiming at an independent, democratic and viable Palestinian state – as promising and encouraging (Commission 2008j: 2). Third, the Israel–Palestinian conflict renders normal (political) life largely impossible and makes a fundamental imprint on the relationship. As observed by the Commission in the spring of 2008:

> Any consideration of the bilateral EU–PA relations in the context of the ENP Action Plan must take into account the continuing Israeli occupation under which the PA operates, the lack of control by the PA Government of the Gaza Strip, where Hamas enforces its own rule.
>
> (Commission 2008j: 2)

As a further tragic illustration, the massive EU engagement in January 2009 during the Israeli attack on Gaza represents efforts at acute conflict management but has little to do with the long-term prospects of improved governance and adherence to EU core values that for instance the ENP framework aims at.

EU recognition of the Palestinian Authority is all the more interesting in such a context (and does imply that recognition is indeed a political rather than legal concept). In essence, there are two main elements in EU recognition. One concerns the fundamental EU assumption of a negotiated two-state solution embracing democratic norms, which both legitimizes the current leadership of the Palestinian Authority under President Mahmoud Abbas and underscores European (and American) recognition of the Hamas as a terrorist organization. More specifically, the EU entertains the idea that for the Palestinian Authority to be recognized as a legitimate partner, it needs to substantially implement 'the three principles of non-violence, recognition of Israel's right to exist and acceptance of existing agreements and obligations, including the roadmap' (Council 2006b). The EU has repeatedly expressed its support for Palestinian President Abbas to form a government on the basis of the principles of the Quartet (Council 2006e, 2007b, 2007c, 2007e). It has also stated that it is 'gravely concerned by the critical humanitarian situation ... of the population of Gaza, whom it will not abandon' (Council 2007b, 2008l, 2008m, 2008o). While being critical to Israeli actions regarding settlement as well as using military means, the EU also condemns the military actions of the Palestinian side (Council 2008o). In this context, Hamas represents a drastic shift in relation to the previous government.

The other element concerns the weak administrative and governance capacity of the Palestinian Authority, which has called for massive EU support. The victory of Hamas in the January 2006 legislative elections is important in this context, as it led the EU and international donors (except for some Arab donors) to suspend political contacts and financial assistance. Israel stopped transferring tax and customs revenue collected on behalf of PA. The EU has maintained contact more or less only with President Abbas and his office. EU efforts have focused on alleviating the humanitarian crisis in the territories (including setting up the Temporary International Mechanism (TIM) under European Commission leadership), providing substantial amounts of humanitarian and emergency aid without transiting through the PA (Commission 2006g: 2). Also, the EU has engaged heavily in Palestinian administrative development (which at times is perceived by Israel and others as a rather pro-Palestine stance). Among many examples, the EU police mission in Palestine (the EUPOL-COPPS) stands out as particularly important and it is significant that its mandate was expanded in 2008 (Council 2008o). Here could also be mentioned the EU border assistance mission, which, however, is on stand-by since June 2007 following the violent events at the time.

As for progress towards Action Plan goals, the 2006 and 2008 evaluations by the Commission point towards progress in establishing a functioning, independent judiciary, in strengthening the capacity of the presidential office and in reinforcing democracy and governance structures (Commission 2006g: 2–3, 2008k: 2). It should be noted that for 2006 and the first half of 2007, most initiatives were stalled and political interaction kept at a minimum. The EU resumed normal relations with the Palestinian Authority in June 2007, although Hamas still controlled the Gaza Strip.

However, regarding fundamental freedoms and human rights, the Commission notes:

> Human rights in the occupied Palestinian territory suffered further setbacks, in particular as regards the right to life and personal security and the right to

personal freedom and safety... Both Palestinian and Israeli authorities are responsible for human rights violations... Women continue to suffer from the negative impact of the conflict.... The overall situation also contributed to increased family and societal violence...Women's participation in economic life remains low.... The participation of women in PA political life has increased [from a very low level].

(Commission 2008j: 5)

In conclusion, the EU–Palestinian interface is a case of *adaptation*, albeit of fragile and complex nature. EU engages with Palestine in a number of ways, and currently the ENP aspect of it represents only a limited part. Much of the EU effort in conflict management takes place in the context of the Quartet and the United Nations, whereas state-building is more of a bilateral character. In both spheres, there are signs of adaptation in the direction of the EU values by President Abbas and the government under Prime Minister Salam Fayyad, for instance evident in the reforms programmes of the government. The capacity of the government is limited and in consequence the EU impact in terms of productive influence and leadership is limited. In a structural perspective, EU financial assistance to Palestine is a different matter. The European Commission is the largest donor to the Palestinians (the Commission alone provided €550 million in 2007, the bulk of the money directed at emergency assistance). The Commission moreover co-chaired the Paris Donor Conference in December 2007 where it pledged €440 million, the largest amount of any donor to the Palestinians for 2008 (Commission 2008j: 10–11, Council 2008o). A similar picture seems to appear after the January 2009 events in Gaza.

The EU–Syria interface

The EU–Syria interface is characterized by limited interaction and low degree of trust. While Association Agreements have entered into force with all other Mediterranean countries – except Libya, where a framework agreement is now underway – in the case of Syria, an agreement was negotiated and initialled in 2004, but EU member-states have not yet considered the political conditions in Syria good enough for signing the agreement. The Council conclusion from the autumn of 2006 is still valid: 'Signature is a process. So far, political circumstances have not been right' (Ferrero-Waldner 2006m). As a consequence, current relations are governed by the limited Cooperation Agreement from 1977, and ENP cooperation, including financial support under the ENPI, is out of the question. The Commission perspective on Syria was spelled out by Commissioner Ferrero-Waldner in a speech to the European Parliament in 2006, reiterating a logic of much general relevance for EU external policy:

I believe that re-engaging with Syria should be part of our strategy.... However, under the present political circumstances, it is difficult to envisage deepening our relations with Syria. Overcoming the political deadlock depends on the leadership's ability to translate some of its words of good will into deeds.... In the absence of an Association Agreement, we have limited scope to tackle matters of concern.... But it is not by cutting off contacts that we will achieve much progress. With no dialogue, we have no influence.

(Ferrero-Waldner 2006m)

In the absence of an ENP Action Plan, the EU has formulated a Country Strategy Paper within the ENPI, which is telling in terms of EU perspectives on Syria as well as priority areas to work with in the absence of a more advanced relationship. The strategy paper describes EU–Syrian relations as 'difficult' (2006m: 2). If judging by formulations in the strategy, in essence, the main elements of EU recognition of Syria concern the non-democratic nature of the political system (with the Baath Party always in a central position), the poor governance structures and weak economic system, and simultaneously the strategic importance of Syria due to its transit location in the Middle East and its relevance through its hydrocarbon resources. As far as EU priorities go, it comes as no surprise that the EU seeks to promote democratic and human rights reforms, to support Syria's transition to a socialist market economy integrated into the global economy, and work for social reforms, for instance regarding women's empowerment (2006m: 4, 23). Moreover, closer cooperation with the EU is seen as desirable, against the logic of Syria's importance for the security and stability of the EU and its near abroad.

The lack of substantive contractual relations mirrors the EU lack of institutional and productive power in the relationship. Being by far the largest donor, the EU (and its member-states) does, however, have some structural power (€130 million is allocated for the period 2007–2010 in the country strategy); this could increase were the Association Agreement to enter into force and an ENP Action Plan be established. The interface is currently best described as *resistant*. Syria is not perceived to voluntarily adapting to EU core values, and while the EU has the power to withhold the Association Agreement and economic assistance, it has thus far been unable to induce positive change in Syria.

Mediterranean interface fundamentals

Judging by the analyses above, the following pattern in terms of interface character appears (see Table 5.1):

Table 5.1 Mediterranean interfaces

Hostility	Resistance
	Libya, Syria
Convergence	Adaptation
	Algeria, Egypt, Jordan, Lebanon, Palestinian Authority, Tunisia
Community	Inclusion
	Morocco, Israel

A number of conclusions come to the fore after analysing the different interfaces between the EU and Mediterranean countries outside of the membership track:

- The group of interfaces under analysis here display dramatically different characteristics and qualify for all categories of asymmetric interfaces. It is fundamental to note that the regional groupings conventionally referred to as the Middle East and North Africa, respectively – more precisely captured as the Levant and the Maghreb in this analysis – hold radically different interfaces within them. In consequence, there is no ground for assuming that geographically adjacent states entertain proximate political relations with the EU – our constructivist framework highlights great variation in terms of relative value compatibility within each group.
- In the different interfaces, the EU is the undisputed stronger power, and draws heavily on both institutional and structural power (the latter primarily in the form of financial assistance, but also technical assistance is of relevance). Israel has a special position in this regard, as it is not dependent on EU aid. The degree of relevance of productive power varies across interfaces, however, with Algeria, Libya and especially Syria as clear cases where the EU is largely unable to draw on its normative framing.
- The Mediterranean interfaces illustrate a more general issue concerning the EU as a normative – or productive – power trying to promote democracy on a global scale. As the EU attempts to play a greater role on the regional and global stage, it encounters the challenge to strike the right balance between advancing normative ideals regarding human rights and fundamental freedoms and maintaining and promoting international stability and security in the traditional sense (combating terrorism and the spread of weapons of mass destruction being obvious cases in point). What the right balance is, remains by necessity an indefinite and subjective topic. It is clear, however, that the EU runs the risk of lacking or losing credibility if it is perceived to prioritize short-term stability over long-term democratization and development while maintaining, as it does, a strong rhetoric about what are desirable values in combination with the EU's lead role to achieve them. In some of the interfaces – EU–Egypt being just one example – it seems as if such geopolitical considerations have the upper hand.
- The EU seeks to play a greater role in all of the Middle East. Commissioner Ferrero-Waldner made this clear in a significant speech in June 2006, when she stated that 'we are, and must remain, a key actor in the region, a political and economic partner who supports and manages change and who helps reap the opportunities that flow from it' (Ferrero-Waldner 2006g). She made the same point clear to the European Parliament in September 2006:

> It is specifically by mobilising the very considerable resources of the EU – from the political and security to the technical, economic and financial, and by deploying them in close cooperation with the rest of

the international community, that we may be able to pull the Peace Process [here referring specifically to Lebanon] back onto its feet.... At the Gymnich meeting last weekend many voices called for greater EU leadership in the Middle East. I believe they are right: We have to turn the tragic events of this summer into an opportunity for a long term settlement of the still open conflicts in the region. Our credibility – that of the Quartet and that of the UN – is at stake.

(Ferrero-Waldner 2006n)

The challenging question is *how* to play a greater role, in a context extremely complicated in terms of political logic, and moreover, one in which the United States plays a leading military role. An important part of the answer is the neighbourhood policy, which 'builds on our growing role as an anchor of stability and modernization, which is the logical geopolitical consequence of our successful EU enlargement of 2004' (Ferrero-Waldner 2006g). All the same, the analysis of this chapter shows that in a number of interfaces, the incompatibility of core values (specifically democracy and human rights) result in interfaces of resistance character. Notes the European Parliament in its 2007 resolution on the ENP: 'universal human rights are at the core of EU values ... although since the beginning of the Euro-Mediterranean Partnership (EMP), substantial progress has been achieved as regards democracy and human rights, this progress has not been sufficient' (European Parliament 2007a). This calls the (strategies for) influence of the EU into question.

- In conclusion, despite its power superiority, the EU is unable to induce change in a number of the interfaces under review here. The paradox of the matter is that the positive conditionality and socialization that is at the heart of the EU logic seems to presuppose a certain level of democratization and protection of human rights (as well as a functioning market economy) – in such a perspective, it is no coincidence that in the Mediterranean setting, the most advanced cooperative interfaces – EU interfaces with Morocco, Jordan, and Israel – are those where the EU interacts with countries entertaining a certain level of democracy.

Part III
Great power interfaces

This part of the book deals with EU interfaces with Russia and the United States, respectively – two countries conventionally recognized as great powers, in the American case often also referred to as the remaining superpower. Such a point of departure leads us to believe that these interfaces with the EU may follow a different logic than the neighbourhood cases – in relation to Russia and the United States, the EU does not have the same obvious power superiority as in the neighbourhood setting. The EU does, however, aspire to play a global role, not least from a civilian or normative position, and in consequence, it is of relevance to try to establish both American and Russian recognition of such great power status, and the more exact nature of relational power in these relationships. In consequence, an important issue is to investigate how such a power logic plays into the interaction of the parties, another, how this has changed over time, if at all. Moreover, the EU's self-proclaimed ambition to be a global political actor implies that in relation to both Russia and the United States, global security issues can be expected to be an important dimension of the relationship.

The following two chapters employ the same analytical framework as the analyses of the previous two chapters, albeit in a more in-depth fashion. In the process of establishing the mutual recognition of the parties in order to attempt a categorization of each interface, the analysis goes into some detail regarding a few principally important issues for each relationship. In the EU–Russian case, the issues of EU enlargement, the political economy of energy, and the Georgian crisis are studied in some detail, while in the EU–US case, a larger number of topics are used as illustrations. As in the previous cases, the aim is not to present a full-blown analysis of interaction in each of the relationships, but rather to point to indications of recognition in terms of identity and power.

6 The Baltic interface

Introduction

The EU–Russian relationship is often referred to as a 'strategic partnership', both by the parties in question and by outside observers, Such a label suggest that the parties are important not only to each other but also in a broader context, impacting on other actors as well providing an indication of great power status. It is no exaggeration, then, to expect that the EU–Russian interaction to a significant degree determines the security order in Europe. The aim of this chapter is to establish more precisely *how*, by revealing the nature of the interface of this so-called strategic partnership.

The EU–Russian relationship cannot be analysed in isolation from the Cold War legacies that for long have framed the security-political landscape in Europe, not least in the North. As remarked by Alexander Sergounin regarding the post-Cold War era, the 'general trend was from phobia and confrontation to damage limitation and cooperation' (Sergounin 2003). It has to be added against the background of the developments of the last few years that in some regards, the process has reversed, or at least stalled. Not least in the Baltic Sea setting is this issue pertinent – hence the labelling of the interface – where the demarcation between East and West was most obvious during the Cold War, where Russia borders on the EU, and where important processes of cooperation but also confrontation take place.

The EU–Russian interface is a complex one, since the post-Cold War period holds significant processes of transformation, both in terms of Russian economic and political transition and EU enlargement and deepening of integration. Moreover, both Russia and the EU display reorientation in foreign and security policy. Hence, a perspective of change is necessary. To limit the analysis, focus is on developments in the last decade, roughly.

The chapter proceeds as follows. As a background note, the next section highlights the main developments in terms of the formal aspects of the EU–Russian relations. Thereafter, three key policy areas are analysed – EU enlargement, the political economy of energy, and the crisis in Georgia. After this follows analyses of the two sides' recognition of each other, after which conclusions regarding the EU–Russian interface end the chapter.

Common institutions and policies

EU–Russian interaction is relatively institutionalized, and a number of instruments and programmes make up the formal dimensions of engagement. In terms of a short chronology, a Partnership and Cooperation Agreement was adopted in 1997 for a ten-year period in order to formalize and structure the relationship. The PCA is still in place due to negotiations for a new comprehensive agreement not having been completed. The parties meet at least twice per year in summitry format on the highest political level. At the summit in St Petersburg in May 2003, the parties agreed to intensify relations through four so-called Common Spaces for cooperation (economics, internal security, external security, and people-to-people contacts). Implementation of cooperation in these follows four roadmaps established at the EU–Russia Summit in May 2005. In general terms, cooperation on a broad number of areas has been initialized. In relation to the roadmap on the Common Space of Freedom, Security and Justice, a number of successful starts regarding cooperation on issues such as counter-terrorism, border issues, visa facilitation, and fighting money laundering can be noted (PPC 2006; EU–Russia Summit 2006). Other tangible results regard cooperation on energy and cross-border cooperation and exchange. Moreover, the EU and Russia have been involved in numerous joint efforts on international issues. A primary example concerns their mutual engagement in the UN Quartet for peace in the Middle East. A subsequent Commission progress report (from April 2008) takes note of a number of achievements, most not of major significance, but rather, concerning initiation and procedural aspects of cooperation. Some earlier agreements, such as charges on Siberian overflows and energy early warning mechanisms, still awaited implementation in practice. But the signature and ratification of the Russia–Latvia Border Agreement and the lifting of a Russian ban on Polish meat exports through bilateral implementation of an agreement on meat inspections make up principally important decisions (Commission 2008q).

In addition to this bilateral formula, EU and Russia also interact in a number of other institutional forms. One is the so-called Northern Dimension, an EU-led programme for functional cooperation around the Baltic Sea. After the EU enlargement of 2004, the Northern Dimension is in effect a practical aspect of EU–Russia cooperation. Two different actions plans for the Northern Dimension have been adopted, and functional cooperation has been largely directed at environmental and health issues. There are also a number of sub-regional Baltic Sea forums of which Russia and the EU (through the Commission) as well as individual EU member-states are members. One example is the Council of Baltic Sea States (CBSS), an intergovernmental organization for the littoral states of the Baltic Sea (and Norway and Iceland), engaged in soft security areas, transport, energy, education etc. Here is also the place to note Russia's membership in Black Sea Synergy.

It should be observed, however, that Russia is not part of the EU's neighbourhood policy (but is covered by the same financial assistance framework as the ENP partners). Regarding the ENP, Russian Deputy Foreign Minister V.A.

Chizhov (2003) has argued that Russia has a neighbourhood doctrine of its own, and moreover, that the ENP is built on an 'inherent conceptual deficiency' in placing very different countries under the same umbrella. Here it becomes obvious that with reference to the strategic partnership, Russia–EU interaction is assumed to follow a different logic compared to other relationships.

Negotiations for a new agreement

Regarding the negotiation of a new comprehensive agreement, the European Commission approved the draft negotiating directive for a new EU–Russia agreement in July 2006, underlining that the new agreement ought to be based on recognition of common values such as democracy, human rights and the rule of law, hoping that negotiations should start early in 2007. Argued President Vladimir Putin in October 2006:

> We are very determined to build up a solid and mutually beneficial relationship rooted in common values, common interests. In the near future, we are going to develop a new basic document.... Given the new level of our relations and its prospect, we have suggested to call the new agreement a Strategic Partnership Agreement.
>
> (Putin 2006a)

By the summer of 2007, negotiations had not begun, however. Putin himself noted at the nineteenth Russia–EU summit, Samara, in mid-May 2007 that issues regarding the legal framework were sensitive and complicated. He, moreover, alluded to the complex nature of the EU polity by saying that 'before the EU can engage in talks, it must resolve its internal problems' (Putin 2007c). In 2008, further developments took place in the direction of initiation of talks: On 26 May 2008, the EU General Affairs Council finally approved negotiating directives for a new agreement with Russia. This provided the foundation for an agreement between Russia and the EU at the summit in Khanty-Mansiysk on 27 June to launch negotiations for a new agreement:

> We agreed that the aim is to conclude a strategic agreement that will provide a comprehensive framework for EU–Russia relations for the foreseeable future and help to develop the potential of our relationship. It should provide for a strengthened legal basis and legally binding commitments.
>
> (EU–Russia Summit 2008)

President Dmitry Medvedev went at length to elaborate the Russian perspective:

> The future agreement will be an instrument for genuine rapprochement between Russia and the European Union. It should be built on the principles of equality, pragmatism, mutual respect for each other's interests and, of course, common approaches to key security issues. It will lay the long-term

foundation for the strategic partnership between Russia and the European Union.... We continue to be concerned about the situation with the rights of our compatriots in Latvia and Estonia... We are worried in general by the tendency to take a selective approach to our common history. We should not forget that Europe's prosperity and in some cases the very existence of individual countries were made possible only through the enormous sacrifices of the peoples of the Soviet Union and other European peoples.... Russia and the European Union share the same basic approaches to security issues. Our approach is based on our commitment to international law, the use of political methods rather than force to resolve international conflicts, and strengthening multilateralism... [and an] abundant experience in foreign policy cooperation.
(Medvedev 2008b)

It may here be interesting to contrast this with Commissioner Ferrero-Waldner's account in preparation of the summit:

The hallmarks [of the agreement] should be: results-oriented political cooperation, deep economic integration, a level playing field for our energy relations ... and ever closer relations in the field of freedom, security, and justice, as well as progressive opening of our educational and scientific systems to each other... *while we pursue our common interests with Russia, we must nevertheless remain clear and firm on democracy and human rights*.... We are often close partners with Russia in tackling international challenges, for example as members of the Middle East Quartet.
(Ferrero-Waldner 2008b, emphasis added)

The first round of negotiations on a new agreement took take place in Brussels on 4 July, but negotiations never reached any substantial point, due to the crisis in Georgia and the decision of the EU to withdraw from negotiations as an effect of Russian military intervention in Georgia in August. At the EU–Russia summit in November 2008, however, the EU side proposed resuming negotiations on a new partnership agreement with Russia (Council 2008v, see further analysis of the Georgian crisis below).

EU enlargement

The enlargement of the European Union is one of the key issue areas that have significantly impacted on the relationship between Russia and the EU. Enlargement poses a complex issue-area for Russia. Russian perceptions about EU enlargement include both a rational calculus on outcomes and a psychological process along the inclusion/exclusion dimension – 'immediate gains and losses' versus the long-term effects of 'Russia remaining outside the "core area" of Europe', to use Baranovsky's terminology (Baranovsky 2002).

Regarding material effects of enlargement, one may objectively observe positive effects in the fields of trade and societal contacts. The EU was already, prior to the 2004–2007 enlargement, Russia's largest trading partner and a key provider of investments and credit opportunities; after enlargement, the EU accounts for more than half of Russia's trade. Moreover, Russia benefits from a single set of trade rules, a single tariff, and a single set of administrative procedures. Needless to say, Russia is also physically closer to the EU after enlargement, with a number of new member-states bordering Russia. This, in turn, holds the potential of increasing societal contacts between the two sides, and realizing a number of common interests. The enhanced Northern Dimension initiative is a relevant case in point. In addition, inclusion of the Baltic states in the EU means that there are substantial numbers of 'Euro-Russians', which may facilitate closer contacts between Russia and the EU (Medvedev 2000: 69, see also Trenin 2000: 18, 38–39 and Baranovsky 2002: 133).

On the other hand, there are numerous references in official documents and speeches to the fear of isolation or exclusion to the effect that the EU will become more inward-looking after enlargement, or that the strong demarcation between inside and outside will move much closer to Russia. This is consistent with notions of increasing territorialization resulting from the Schengen arrangement. The Russian leadership has repeatedly made the point that EU enlargement must not lead to negative effects for Russia. Foreign Minister Ivanov, for example, stated early in 2003: 'The EU enlargement, in our view ... should not lead to a drawing in Europe of new dividing lines. On the contrary, it should facilitate the development of a unified Europe' (Ivanov 2003c, see also Ivanov 2003b)

At the 2006 EU–Russia Summit, Putin referred to the Luxembourg Joint Declaration in 2004, recalling that enlargement may not impinge negatively on Russia's situation: 'Issues concerning the expansion of the European Union remain topical as ever. We once again drew our colleagues' attention to the necessity of respecting the provisions of the Joint Declaration' (EU–Russia Summit 2006).

Russian official perception thus in part hinges on the obvious risk that Russia becomes isolated when the EU enlarges – as President Putin has noted, EU enlargement includes 'certain things which, undoubtedly, worry us', not least in terms of changing the relationship between Russia and the countries now on the verge of membership (Ministry of Foreign Affairs of Russia 2003). Foreign Minister Ivanov has explained the Russian view in the following way:

> We see that the enlargement of the Schengen zone by taking in new EU members, the tightening of the regime of its external borders objectively create additional barriers, in the near term, for free movement, especially free communication of people on the continent. And that is a human rights issue.
>
> (Ivanov 2003b)

The EU has for its part continually stressed the liberal logic of interdependence rather than that of differentiation – enlargement facilitates more common interests. Moreover, the EU has repeatedly assured that borders will not become barriers, as seen in the ENP logic spelled out in previous chapters. Dmitri Trenin notes further: 'It is only slowly dawning on the Russians that the dividing lines in Europe, which they dread, are more likely to appear in the form of the EU's eastern limit of enlargement' (Trenin 2000: 35, see also Goodby *et al.* 2002). Such a limit or border has both material and symbolic faces, relating to trade effects of the Baltic states turning to the EU and to the Schengen implications (not least in the Kaliningrad case), on the one hand, and to the feeling of exclusion as the new Europe evolves, on the other. Renée Nyberg points to the normative and institutionalizing effects of enlargement in noting: 'The border between the expanding EU and Russia is quickly turning into a *normative fault line* as the Baltic States and Poland adopt EU standards and legislation' (Nyberg quoted in Leshukov 2001, emphasis in original). This obviously goes for economic activities as well as Schengen-related matters. It is interesting, in this perspective, to take note of the obvious Russian conclusion at the time that the way to advance beyond such formal and mental divisions is to increase interaction rather than to refrain from it. That conclusion has been partly revised in more recent times.

Political meetings at the highest level have addressed these matters on a number of occasions. This is perhaps most evident in relation to the Kaliningrad issue. The status of Kaliningrad became a very sensitive issue in the prelude to the 2004 enlargement, as the Russian enclave – isolated from the Russian mainland through the dissolution of the Soviet Union – in effect became encapsulated within EU territory through enlargement. Lo argues that it is 'indicative of [the Russian] mentality that the main agenda item in the relationship should be visa-free access for inhabitants of Kaliningrad ... transiting Lithuania, and not how Russia can benefit economically from EU enlargement' (Lo 2003: 70, also 56). At the Moscow summit in May 2002, the parties jointly stated:

> This [mutually acceptable solutions for the Kaliningrad region] will be of key importance for the development of a strategic partnership between the Russian Federation and the European Union and for strengthening the atmosphere of good-neighbourliness and mutual understanding.
>
> (EU–Russia Summit 2002)

And continuing, at the Rome summit of 2003, the implementation of 'the package on Kaliningrad' was pointed out to be of special importance. More recent indications show that the overall implementation of the mutually agreed treatment of the passenger transit issue has worked out satisfactorily. Efforts have henceforth been made by President Putin for the further handling of the Kaliningrad question, especially regarding visas (Bengtsson 2004).

Despite the worries explained above, EU enlargement has been perceived in a more positive light than NATO enlargement, to the effect that whereas EU enlargement may bring a more balanced political setting in Europe, NATO enlargement will further reinforce the difference between the security guarantees for those on the inside at the expense of those left outside. This is evident in recent years' development (see the section on Georgia in Chapter 4). It is relevant, however, to show that the early Russian perception was one of equating the two enlargements. Over time, President Putin took the lead to install a spirit of positive cooperation regarding EU enlargement rather than the suspicion of the early days, hence drawing on a differentiation of the two enlargements of NATO and EU. As Nadia Arbatova argues:

> In contrast to many people in the West who see the expansion of NATO and EU as complementary processes, paving the avenue for stability, prosperity and security of post-Cold War Europe, most people in Russia see the two developments as contradictory and leading to very different, even opposite consequences.
>
> (Arbatova 2002)

President Medvedev argues from the perspective of potential critics that 'the left and the nationalist politicians in Russia do not harbour such negative views of the Union, as they do of NATO' (Medvedev 2000). Trenin follows the same logic of reasoning when stating that 'Russia's neutral to positive attitude toward EU enlargement was explained by the contrast it offered to NATO's expansion. Moscow liked the EU for the two things it lacked – America's presence and an integrated military force' (Trenin 2000: 35). Furthermore, EU enlargement may actually mean that Russia's place in Europe may become elevated; as Baranovsky (2002: 126) notes, 'the enlargement of the EU could fit into the broader picture of building a "greater Europe" where Russia could also get a prominent place'.

In conclusion, EU enlargement represents a process formally determined by the EU but with cognitive effects both for Russian recognition of the EU (as potentially inward-looking, raising the barrier to outsiders, but simultaneously changing the security order in a multilateral direction desired by Russia) and EU recognition of Russia (as preoccupied with traditional security considerations rather than functional problem-solving).

The political economy of energy

The energy issue is another central issue for the current state of EU–Russian perceptions. As is well-known, Russia is a key energy supplier to the EU, especially to newer member-states – Russia supplies more than 25 per cent of all energy consumption in the EU (Commission 2006o). At the same time, in the general logic of interdependence, Russia is dependent on persistent energy demand from the EU as well as secure transit routes to the EU. As the Commission observed in its review of external energy relations:

> EU–Russia energy cooperation is crucial in ensuring energy security on the European continent. The EU and Russia should see mutual long term benefits from a new energy partnership, which would seek a balance between expectations and interests on both sides.... Russia seeks ways to secure

energy demand presented by the EU market. The EU needs Russian resources for its energy security. There is a clear interdependence.

(Commission 2006o)

The European Parliament underlined in a resolution after the EU–Russia summit in Sochi in May 2006 the 'strategic importance of cooperation on energy and the need to enhance EU–Russia energy relations' (European Parliament 2006c). As the Sochi summit had failed to produce a formal treaty on energy supply, the European Council in June 2006 called for an Energy Policy for Europe and turned to the Commission and the Council to take measures to establish an Action Plan by the spring of 2007. At the summit, Commission President Barroso stressed the mutual dependence of the two sides – 'recognition of the principle of interdependence' (EU–Russia Summit 2006). In the same context, Russian President Putin remarked:

> [I]t is quite clear that the EU and Russia are natural partners in this [energy] field. And our mutual dependence only contributes to the overall energy security on the European continent and creates good premises to get closer in other areas.
>
> (Putin 2006a)

Putin also explained:

> I drew the attention of our colleagues that whereas in terms of gas, European Union covers 44 per cent of its demand through Russian supplies, in the Russian export structure 67 per cent are supplied to the EU. So, that goes to show that Russia is more dependent on the EU today than the other way around.
>
> (Putin 2006a)

Herein lies at least part of the explanation for Russia's subsequent resistance to ratify the Energy Charter Treaty. Noted Ferrero-Waldner (2006p) about Putin at the EU–Russia summit in November 2006: 'He called for reciprocity'. All in all, the conclusions in 'An Energy Policy for Europe' are quite expected – the Commission points out among the priorities the one of

> [E]nhancing relations with Russia through the negotiation of a new robust, comprehensive framework agreement, including a fully-fledged energy partnership benefiting both sides and that creates the conditions necessary for new investments. This should emphasize the mutual long-term benefits to both Russia and the EU.
>
> (Commission 2007c)

While recognizing each other's importance in the energy area, both sides have simultaneously attempted to reduce dependence in different ways, and in the process politicized the energy issue further. Hence, the remark by Wolfgang Schüssel, President of the European Council at the time of the Sochi summit – 'let's make one thing very clear: buying and selling oil and gas is a purely commercial activity; it is not politics' (EU–Russia Summit 2006) – does not completely correspond to subsequent developments.

On the Russian side, the Nordstream gas pipeline in the Baltic Sea is a way to get around the dependence on transit through Ukraine and other post-Soviet states, and reach the European market directly, through Germany. This has not passed unnoticed by neighbouring countries, however, who perceive the issue as an environmental threat or as a sign of Russian assertiveness. Moreover, Russia and Serbia have concluded an agreement making Serbia a transit hub for supply of Russian energy to southern Europe (technically through Gazprom's acquisition of 51 per cent of the shares in Nfatna Industrija Srbije). Noted Putin in relation to the agreement:

> Let me stress once again that the Serbian people can be certain of having a reliable friend and partner in Russia ... we reiterated that Russia is categorically against any unilateral declaration of independence by Kosovo. This would risk doing serious damage to the whole system of international law, and have negative consequences for the Balkans and for stability in other regions of the world.
>
> (Putin 2008a)

On its side, the EU has adopted a policy of supply diversification (for instance aiming at increasing Algerian gas supply), and, importantly, facilitated the Nabucco gas pipeline, established through a ministerial statement among the energy ministers of Austria, Bulgaria, Hungary, Romania and Turkey as well as the EU energy commissioner. The project will contribute to the diversification of the EU's supplies, reduce dependence on Russia, end Gazprom's monopoly in Hungary and turn Turkey into even more of a key strategic actor for the EU.

The two gas crises between Russia and Ukraine in 2006 and 2009 are also telling in this regard. While on the surface naturally a supply issue between a number of mutually interdependent actors, there was also an EU-based preoccupation with Russian demonstration of power, in effect using its energy resources to sustain its great power status. Russian governments have consistently pointed to economic rationale. Argued Putin in 2007: 'we have no obligation to provide huge subsidies to other countries' economies, subsidies as big as their own national budgets. No one else does this, and so why are we expected to do it?' (Putin 2007a). Putin went on to argue that there had been no transit problems during Soviet times, so why now? Because, he argued,

> [T]he transit countries have realized their importance and want to receive the corresponding financial means for transport. But we already pay 4.2 billion dollars to transit countries.... It is for this reason that we are building

a gas pipeline under the Baltic Sea. For this reason we will expand our possibilities to ship, shall we say, oil in the northwest.

(Putin 2007a)

Georgia

Russia's conflict with Georgia concerning the status of South Ossetia and Abkhazia represents yet another key point of relevance for EU–Russian perceptions. While the conflict has a longer history, with hindsight it suffices here to focus on developments since 2006, and in particular in some detail review developments and rhetoric in relation to three distinct periods of Georgia–Russia confrontation (in the autumn of 2006, in the spring of 2008 and in the summer and autumn of 2008). In the first of these time periods, South Ossetia and Abkhazia moved for independence, allegedly supported by Russia. President Putin's statement at the time was one of Russian non-engagement, however:

> The issue is between Georgia, Abkhazia and South Ossetia. And to our great regret, and great concern, that way this situation is developing, is heading for disaster, for bloodshed.... I stress that Russia cannot assume this responsibility [of solving frozen conflicts in the post-Soviet space]. This is the responsibility of these nations themselves, to reach an agreement, to find compromise.
>
> (Putin 2006a)

At the same time, Russia took different forms of actions against Georgians in Russia – according to official Georgian sources, an estimated 2,598 Georgians were deported by Russian authorities in 'a wave of ethnic targeting and xenophobia' beginning on 27 September (Ministry of Foreign Affairs of Georgia 2006).

The EU response clearly entertained a perspective in support of Georgia and against Russia, a picture that has remained ever since. The Council expressed 'its grave concern at the measures adopted by the Russian Federation against Georgia and at their economic, political and humanitarian consequences. The Council urges the Russian Federation not to pursue measures targeting Georgians in the Russian Federation' (Council 2006e). Along similar lines, the European Parliament adopted a resolution on the situation in South Ossetia in late October 2006, stating among other things that it 'strongly condemns' the attempts by movements in the Georgian regions of Abkhazia and South Ossetia to establish independence unilaterally and called upon the Russian government to withhold support for these movements, urging the Russian authorities 'to halt immediately all acts of repression and harassment carried out and all accusations made by representatives of official state institutions against ethnic Georgians living in Russia' (European Parliament 2006b). The immediate crisis calmed, and in early 2007, diplomatic relations were restored as the Russian ambassador handed over his credentials to the President of Georgia in a move which, according to Putin, 'supports the normalization of relations' (Putin 2007a).

Relations deteriorated again in March 2008, when Russia decided to withdraw from the 1996 CIS decision 'On Measures Aimed at Settling the Conflict in Abkhazia, Georgia'. Not unexpectedly, this was perceived as threatening to the Georgian side. The Georgian Ministry of Foreign Affairs expressed 'extreme concern' at the decision, stating that it

> [C]an be assessed in no other terms but as an overt attempt to infringe Georgia's sovereignty and territorial integrity and an extremely dangerous provocation aimed at abetting separatism and escalating tension in the conflict zone.... By withdrawing unilaterally from these obligations, Russia creates a basis for providing the separatist government with military assistance and establishing military presence in Abkhazia.
> (Ministry of Foreign Affairs of Georgia 2008a)

President Putin's instructions to the government as of mid-April 2008 to interact directly with the 'actual bodies of power in Abkhazia and South Ossetia' mark a clearly more assertive stance on the part of Russia. The authorities are to offer 'more substantive, practical assistance to the populations of the unrecognized republics' in order to 'create mechanisms of comprehensive defense of the rights, freedoms and lawful interests of Russian citizens living in Abkhazia and South Ossetia' (Ministry of Foreign Affairs of Russia 2008a). The background is framed in terms of moral obligations: 'Over the years of drawn-out conflicts, the residents of these unrecognized republics have found themselves in a plight. They were actually deprived of the opportunity to realize universal rights to a decent life and sustainable development' (Ministry of Foreign Affairs of Russia 2008a).

Again, the Georgian response was one of great alarm. In a press release the following day, the Georgian Ministry of Foreign Affairs framed Russian actions in terms of violations of sovereignty and territorial integrity, and made an explicit reference to Georgia's closer relationship to NATO:

> The Russian Federation has made yet another very dangerous step.... The steps taken recently by the Russian Federation towards Georgia clearly contradict the universally recognized norms and principles of international law.... These efforts bear a close resemblance to the most notorious developments of the 1930s when a number of sovereign countries were occupied by the totalitarian regimes under the same pretext. Extremely alarming is Russia's decision to recognize the legitimacy of legal entities and documents of these regions. Taking such decision, Russia justifies the ethnic cleansing of hundreds of thousands of peaceful citizens.... It is our deep belief that Russia's actions are motivated by its desire to prevent Georgia's integration with the North Atlantic Alliance.
> (Ministry of Foreign Affairs of Georgia 2008b)

In opposition to the Russian perspective, EU reactions basically entertained the same logic as that of Georgia, stressing sovereignty, territorial integrity and honouring international commitments. The Council statement of 21 April (to which, interestingly enough Ukraine and Azerbaijan aligned themselves) is illuminating:

> The EU is seriously concerned about recent developments in the Georgian conflict areas, particularly regarding the latest decision of the Russian Federation ... to establish official ties with institutions of the de facto authorities in South Ossetia and Abkhazia without the consent of the Government of Georgia. The EU reiterates its firm commitment to the sovereignty and territorial integrity of Georgia within its internationally recognised borders.... The decision of the Russian Federation jeopardises the implementation of these principles. The EU calls on the Russian Federation not to implement its decision.
>
> (Council 2008d)

As is well-known, the situation deteriorated over the summer, culminating in the August war. The aftermath of the military confrontation is telling both in terms of EU–Russian contemporary perspectives and in terms of EU conflict management. Nicolas Sarkozy, as the President of the Council, negotiated a six-point plan with Russian President Medvedev on 12 August, a plan that included the withdrawal within a week of Russian troops to their positions prior to the outbreak of violence, the return of the Georgian troops to their bases and the EU as 'guarantor of the principle of non-use of force', and for that purpose preparing the deployment of an observation mission (Council 2008s). At its extraordinary meeting the following day, the Council reiterated its fundamental commitment to territorial integrity: 'A peaceful and lasting solution to the conflict in Georgia must be based on full respect for the principles of independence, sovereignty and territorial integrity recognised by international law and UN Security Council resolutions' (Council 2008r). Sarkozy also called an extraordinary meeting of the European Council on 1 September, which spelled out the EU perception regarding Russia (and Georgia) in full light:

> The European Council is gravely concerned by the open conflict which has broken out in Georgia, by the resulting violence, and by the disproportionate reactions of Russia.... The European Council strongly condemns Russia's unilateral decision to recognize the independence of Abkhazia and South Ossetia. That decision is unacceptable and the European Union calls on other States not to recognize this proclaimed independence.
>
> (European Council 2008c)

In a display of various power resources, the European Council expressed, first, that the EU could increase emergency aid amounts already delivered, second, that the EU intended to take the initiative of convening an international donor conference, and third, to 'step up its relations with Georgia, including visa facilitation measures and the possible establishment of a full and comprehensive free trade area as soon as the conditions are met'. Conclusions were also drawn on increased regional cooperation, especially the Black Sea Synergy and the Eastern Partnership, the appointment of a Special Representative for the crisis in Georgia, and the intensification of efforts with regard to the security of energy supply (European Council 2008c).

It is worth noting that also other international reactions were in favour of Georgia. The North Atlantic Council, NATO's top organ, issued two statements that were clearly in favour of Georgia and critical towards Russia:

> We remain concerned by Russia's actions during this crisis and remind Russia of its responsibility for maintaining security and order in the areas where it exercises control, especially in light of continuing reports of Russia's deliberate destruction of civilian infrastructure. Russian military action has been disproportionate and inconsistent with its peacekeeping role....We have also agreed today to support Georgia, upon its request, in a number of areas.
>
> (NATO 2008a, see also NATO 2008b)

In much the same way, the G7 stated:

> We condemn the action of our fellow G8 member.... We deplore Russia's excessive use of military force in Georgia and its continued occupation of parts of Georgia.... We reassert our strong and continued support for Georgia's sovereignty within its internationally recognized borders and underline our respect and support for the democratic and legitimate government of Georgia.
>
> (Group of Seven 2008)

The Russian response to the G7 statement is of relevance also for our focus on interaction with the EU and clearly displays a fundamentally different logic:

> The statement of the G7 ... bears a biased character and is directed at the justification of Georgia's aggressive actions. It groundlessly claims that Russia 'violates' the territorial integrity of Georgia. Ignored is Russia's well-argued case for the difficult, but only correct decision to recognize the independence of South Ossetia and Abkhazia.... The assertion that 'Russia has called into question its commitment to peace and security in the Caucasus' does not stand up to criticism. On the contrary, the timely and resolute actions of Russia's leadership have prevented destabilization of the entire Caucasus region.
>
> (Ministry of Foreign Affairs of Russia 2008b)

Subsequent developments include a number of relevant points. Russian troops withdrew by 9 October. The EU monitoring mission (EUMM) – consisting of more than 200 observers – assumed responsibility for the security situation in Georgia. International peace talks were held in Geneva on 15 October, led by the

EU, UN and OSCE. Russia declined to participate in the formal plenary session. On 23 October, the EU and the World Bank hosted a donor conference, at which 28 countries and 15 international organizations pledged a total of €3.4 billion.

At the donor conference, Barroso stated 'We are here today to show solidarity with the people of Georgia. It is a moral imperative to help a neighbour in need'. Ferrero-Waldner added 'We must not let the crisis distract Georgia from its political and economic reform efforts' (World Bank 2008). It is an understatement to say that the Russian side did not share that perspective. When addressing the Russian Duma in early November, President Medvedev argued:

> Refusing a peaceful, political settlement and legal methods, Georgian leadership chose to embark on the most frightful scenario.... The Caucasus crisis has demonstrated once again that the use of force by one of the parties to a conflict cannot result in a viable solution. The reaction to the events of August 8th and Russia's recognition of the independence of South Ossetia and Abkhazia once again showed that we live in a world of double standards. We proceeded responsibly and did so in the interests of restoring international law and justice.
>
> (Medvedev 2008d)

A final note on the aftermath of the conflict displays the apparent gap between the EU and Russia. In spite of reactions from the EU and other actors, on 24 November, President Medvedev ratified treaties between Russia and South Ossetia and Abkhazia, developing all-round cooperation and establishing extensive relations at all levels and in a broad range of areas – political military, economic, social and humanitarian. The EU, on the other hand, received the credit of the Georgian government:

> It was the EU's, as well as other important international actors' response to Russia's August invasion that sent a clear message to Moscow, helped slow Russian aggression, and cleared the way for the EU to broker the ceasefire agreement. Equally effective were the EU's rapid deployment of the EU Monitoring Mission (EUMM), its provision of generous financial and humanitarian assistance to Georgia, and the Union's decision to speed up Georgia's integration with the EU. Only the EU's strong engagement with steady and consistent actions will deter aggressive states from forcefully changing Europe's boundaries, undermining the sovereignty and territorial integrity of European nations, and using ethnic cleansing as a tool for implementing foreign policy goals.
>
> (Ministry of Foreign Affairs of Georgia 2008c)

EU recognition of Russia

What does the general processes of interaction and the three empirical illustrations tell us in terms of mutual recognition? The following statement from the

European Council succinctly demonstrates EU recognition of Russia in the aftermath of the Georgian war:

> With the crisis in Georgia, relations between the EU and Russia have reached a crossroads. The European Council considers that given the interdependence between the European Union and Russia, and the global problems they are facing, there is no desirable alternative to a strong relationship, based on cooperation, trust and dialogue, respect for the rule of law and the principles recognised by the United Nations Charter and by the OSCE. It was for this reason that we launched negotiations for a new framework agreement between the Union and Russia last July. We call on Russia to join us in making this fundamental choice in favour of mutual interest, understanding and cooperation.
> (European Council 2008c)

Three potentially contradictory conclusions can be drawn from this statement:

- The EU perceives Russia to be a decisive partner in European political developments, hence the appropriate label of 'strategic partnership'.
- The two sides are perceived as heavily interdependent, which incidentally creates mutual opportunities for power projection.
- There are aspects of Russian policy – especially regarding the domestic political situation, policy towards the CIS countries and regarding energy – that conflict with a number of EU normative standpoints.

Let us touch briefly upon each of these issues. Regarding the first point, it is evident that EU official perceptions circle around the notion of Russia as a key European player with which the EU needs to collaborate. Noted Barosso in connection to the summit in 2006: 'We must not forget that Russia is a European country, an important global power and our neighbour. We are therefore committed to a very close partnership with Russia' (EU–Russia Summit 2006).

Turning to the second main point on recognition – interdependence – this is intimately related to the issue of energy. Russia is a key energy supplier for the EU, which has received extensive attention in news media and political circles alike, stimulating a lot of European–EU reactions regarding diversification of supply and transit. At the same time, the EU is Russia's most important trading partner, and EU sources make up 80 per cent of foreign direct investment in Russia. Hence, concludes Ferrero-Waldner, 'the relationship is one of interdependence, not dependence' (Ferrero-Waldner 2008c). EU perceptions of interdependence with Russia can also be found in the field of external security – the idea that Russia is a global great power with which the EU needs to interact in order to achieve foreign policy goals, in institutional settings or in specific contexts, such as the Quartet in the Middle East. Concludes Commissioner Ferrero-Waldner: 'Russia is a key geopolitical actor, whose constructive involvement in international affairs is a necessary precondition for an effective international community' (Ferrero-Waldner 2008c).

Recalling the value foundation of the EU elaborated in Chapter 3, it becomes evident that both Russian foreign policy behaviour and domestic political developments are recognized by the EU side as indicating a value gap in relation to the EU. While not isolated to the Georgian crisis, this event very clearly displayed prevailing differences between the EU and Russia. Commissioner Ferrero-Waldner (2008c) explains: 'For us it is clear. Europe upholds values and established norms of international conduct and we stand by these in all circumstances. These include respect of territorial integrity and the peaceful resolution of disputes' (Ferrero-Waldner 2008c). The conclusion of the Council in November 2008 seems logical against this background: 'The conflict in Georgia has affected the trust which is necessary for the partnership between the European Union and Russia' (Council 2008u).

Another such topic concerns the Russian withdrawal in December 2007 from the Treaty on Conventional Forces in Europe (CFE). The treaty, the Russians contended, 'has long since ceased to meet contemporary European realities' (Ministry of Foreign Affairs of Russia 2007). The EU response was that 'the EU considers the CFE Treaty as the cornerstone of security and stability in Europe' (Council 2007f). In the same way, the American decision to place a part of its missile defence system in Poland was interpreted in different terms by Russia and the EU. As President Medvedev considered the American move provocative, he made public a decision to station the Iskander missile system in Kaliningrad (instead of disarming the region) in order to 'be able, if necessary, to neutralise the missile defense system' (Mcdvedev 2008d). The EU, on the contrary, expressed its 'grave concern' over the Russian decision (Council 2008t).

Regarding domestic politics, democratic deficiencies and the apparent de-democratization of Russia (according to Freedom House (2008), for the period 1999–2006, Russian democracy deteriorated from 4.58 to 5.75 on a seven-grade scale) plays into EU recognition. Human rights conditions and freedom of speech and of the media are among values not perceived to be honoured in Russia, and the murder of Anna Politkovskaya and the sentencing of Mikhail Khodorkovskiy attain symbolic value in this context (see for instance Ferrero-Waldner 2006p).

In conclusion, the EU recognizes Russia as a powerful neighbour with which the EU needs to interact intensely, but which – despite rhetoric to the contrary – does not share the fundamental values of the EU in certain key respects. In consequence, the EU's political understanding of Russia is ambiguous – on the one hand the EU wants to acknowledge EU–Russian interdependence, on the other it does not agree with Russian (great power) practices and perspectives. Ferrero-Waldner recently explained this tension:

> The European Union's relationship with Russia is one of the most challenging of our times. On the one hand we see a complex web of joint activities, and interwoven interests. On the other we see the backdrop of events in Georgia ... we cannot share the principles of foreign policy recently articulated in Moscow, including the resurgence of spheres of influence.
>
> (Ferrero-Waldner 2008c)

These elements can also be found in EU public opinion about Russia. According to a poll conducted by the *Financial Times* in the summer of 2006, of the respondents – residents in the UK, France, Germany, Italy and Spain – only 16 per cent described Russia as a democracy (59 per cent responded no, 25 per cent not sure) and only 20 per cent said that the EU can trust Vladimir Putin. Of all the respondents, 63 per cent agree that it is worrisome that Western Europe is heavily dependent on Russia for its energy supplies. Interestingly enough, however, only 1 per cent considered Russia as the greatest threat to global stability (*Financial Times* 2006a).

Where does this leave us in terms of EU policy choice? The chosen perspective on the EU side is obviously one of 'interaction despite value incompatibility', hoping to influence Russia through engagement rather than isolation, in essence a strategy of productive power. As an example it can be noted that although the EU withdrew from negotiations about a new framework agreement due to Russian behaviour in Georgia, the EU was rather quick to resume talks. Ferrero-Waldner argued in October 2008 in favour of resuming negotiations, saying that 'I know of no better way to pursue our own interests, and make our concerns listened to. On the other hand, we must not behave as though nothing has happened' (Ferrero-Waldner 2008c).

The general logic at play here has been spelled out on other occasions as well. Angela Merkel, in her capacity as president of the Council, noted at the EU–Russia summit in May 2007:

> I can speak for the European Union when I say that we have the desire to overcome all ... obstacles ... we have differences on certain accounts but it is good that we can now talk about them openly and honestly.
> (Merkel (2007b)

Commission President Barroso noted at the same occasion: 'Let us be honest. Difficulties exist...we must not allow the difficulties to pollute or contaminate... progress towards good collaboration' (Barroso 2007c). In preparation for the EU–Russia summit in November 2008, finally, the EU leaders publicly declared:

> For the Union, dialogue and negotiation are the best means of pursuing its aims, furthering its principles and values, and resolutely defending its interests with a united front.... Negotiation and dialogue in no way legitimise the status quo in Georgia, or Russian action contrary to our values and principles.
> (Council 2008u)

Russian recognition of the EU

In order to understand Russian recognition of the EU, it is first necessary to briefly discuss relevant aspects of the Russian self-image as it appears in official rhetoric and manifest behaviour. The picture that emanates from a sequence of official documents and statements and interviews with leading politicians comprises two main elements. The first one boils down to Russia as a responsible global great power, with a unique position in the Eurasian context. The second element focuses on Russia's national interests. These are two sides of the same coin, inextricably linked, but the relative weights of the two shift across time and space. As an example, President Putin gave Russian and foreign journalists the following picture after the gas crisis with Ukraine in 2006:

> You should understand that Russia not only gave these republics their independence, but providing for 15 years huge subsidies to these countries' economies Russia helped them strengthen their independence and sovereignty. 15 years is enough and this cannot go on forever.
> (Putin 2007a)

As for being a responsible actor, Russian leaders repeatedly point to its diplomatic or civilian approach to foreign policy. Said Deputy Prime Minister and Minister of Defence Sergei Ivanov early in 2006: 'Everyone knows that when it comes to war and conflict prevention, Russia always goes first for political, diplomatic, economic and other non-military means ... our firm commitment [is] to the principle of pre-emption.... We are not saber-rattlers' (Ivanov 2006). Later statements confirm the same self-perception: 'We never operate in a confrontational way', said President Putin in early 2007 (Putin 2007a), whereas President Medvedev recently stated that 'we should all refrain from taking any unilateral steps that would affect security. Russia has never taken any such steps' (Medvedev 2008e). Medvedev's proposal for a legally binding pan-European security treaty based on territorial integrity and sovereignty (see Medvedev 2008a, 2008c) can fruitfully be interpreted through the lens of the responsible great power.

At the same time, defending national interests sometimes give rise to a more confrontational mode – as President Putin has noted, 'taking pleasure from ... being praised as you betray national interests is very simple, but to construct pragmatic, business-based relations while defending your national interests is not always possible without a certain amount of tensions and problems' (Putin 2007a).

In Russia's approach to the protection of national interests, military means become important. Said Deputy Prime Minister and Minister of Defence Sergei Ivanov early in 2006:

> Maintaining a robust military capability is clearly in our national interest. Cooperation with international institutions helps promote a foreign policy agenda, though unfortunately it does not provide absolute security guarantees. For those, a state needs a highly effective military capability.
> (Ivanov 2006)

This military logic can of course be found in the handling of the Georgian crisis, but also in reactions to the American plans for global missile defense, as elaborated above – as President Medvedev argued in front of the Russian Duma, 'we will deploy the Iskander missile system in the Kaliningrad to be able, if necessary, to neutralise the missile defense system. Naturally, we envisage using the resources of the Russian Navy for these purposes as well' (Medvedev 2008d.

There are clear indications that there is a growing assertiveness in securing national interests in recent years, as all the events discussed above illustrate (although it could, of course, be argued that these are mere reactions to policy choices of others). The assertiveness is also evident in official Russian strategy. In the Foreign Policy Concept of 2000, it was stated that the priority of Russian foreign policy was to 'create favourable external conditions for steady development of Russia, for improving its economy'. In Putin's annual address of 2005, the tone was different: 'certain that Russia should continue its civilising mission on the Eurasian continent' (Popescu 2006). The Russian withdrawal from the Treaty on Conventional Forces in Europe is yet another relevant sign hereof.

Russian uniqueness, finally, relates to the complex question about Russia's European role and legacy. President Putin has asserted that 'Russia is a natural member of the "European family" in spirit, history, and culture' (Putin 2006b), but on other occasions alluding to a dialectic relationship between Russia and Europe. In a statement on the political and philosophical definition of Russia's European mission, Putin cited a passage in Dostoevsky's Pushkin speech – 'Being a true Russian will ultimately mean bringing reconciliation to Europe's contradictions' – and continued:

> The great writer sensed perfectly that Europe would never be itself in the world without Russia and, at the same time, that Russia would never cease its 'longing for Europe'. I strongly believe the full unity of our continent can never be achieved until Russia, as the largest European state, becomes an integral part of the European process.
>
> (Putin 2007b)

Recognition of the EU

Just as EU recognition of Russia is complex, the Russian recognition of the EU is ambiguous, which relates both to the character of the EU and the Russian self-image elaborated above. On the one hand, the Russian perspective is one of the EU as a great power and strategic partner with overlapping interests, which drives bilateral cooperation based on interdependence, common handling of specific international issues based on common interests, and, as a structural consequence, supports Russia's quest for a multilateral world order. At the same time, the Russian leadership perceives the EU as a competitive actor with a clearly normative agenda, at odds with specific Russian national interests and Russian uniqueness in historical perspective. President Putin's remark after the EU–Russia summit in 2006 is indicative of this ambiguous recognition:

> The results of the discussion confirmed that Russia's and the European Union's approaches to resolving the majority of European and global

problems are in harmony or coincide, and this undoubtedly constitutes a good basis for even more effective cooperation in increasing security in Europe and in the world.... If our partners [the EU] hope for some kind of exclusive relations and want us to put in place a resolutely liberal policy regarding access to infrastructure, production and transportation [in energy], then this raises the question on our side of what do we get in return? Perhaps we could also gain access to infrastructure, production and transportation, but of what kind? Where is your production? Which deposits will you give us access to? What mainland pipelines do you have? If you cannot offer us these things, and you cannot, then we have to find another acceptable form of compensation and take steps to respond to each other's interests. This is the message that our colleagues heard and understood today.

(EU–Russia Summit 2006)

Elaborating the Russian perspective further, the strategic partnership theme can be seen as containing both an interdependence logic and a 'compatible great power' logic. As for interdependence, Putin's statement from 2006 is significant: 'In the past few years, the EU and Russia have become important political and economic partners.... I do not see any areas that are not open to equal, strategic co-operation based on common objectives and values' (Putin 2006b). Which these values are is not clear, however. He went on to argue: 'We will not be able to turn a new leaf in the history of our cooperation if we succumb to fear of growing interdependence' (Putin 2006b). At a later point, upon disagreements on specific issues, Putin argued that the 'main thing is that the immutability of the strategic partnership between the European Union and the Russian Federation could be reaffirmed' (Putin 2007d).

In terms of the EU as compatible great power, again sequences of Putin's statements are significant. Putin stressed the commonality in 2006 when stating that 'Russia and the EU stand for strengthening universal regimes, primarily the non-proliferation regime' (Putin 2006b). Commenting on the topic in October 2007, he noted:

Russia and the EU remain united in their basic approaches to security. We favour the primacy of international law, and the use of political means rather than force to resolve conflicts. We also believe that the general and equal security for all is impossible without strengthening the collective origins of world politics.

(Putin 2007d)

Apart from non-proliferation referred to above, there are signs of overlapping and converging interests between Russia and the EU in the Gulf, in the Balkans, in the Middle East (working together in the Quartet) and in combating international terrorism. Said Foreign Minister Ivanov already in 2003: 'Russia and the EU are natural allies in the search for adequate responses to the new threats and challenges' (Ivanov 2003b). President Putin more recently underscored that 'it is important for us to see that the EU is becoming an increasingly authoritative and influential centre of world politics, considerably contributing to regional and global security' (Putin 2007b).

In opposition to this positive picture of common interests bilaterally and joint approaches to international security, there is a second predominant Russian perception of the EU, which in essence has to do with opposing interests in key areas of interaction and, importantly, EU claims for ideological superiority.

Naturally, in any comprehensive relationship, interests diverge from time to time. Of relevance for our analysis is the persistent Russian focus on the Kaliningrad issue (where EU policies, most obviously regarding border issues, inflict on Russian interests and where the cost-free visa arrangement through Lithuania contains an obvious element of Russian dependence) and the treatment of Russian minorities in Estonia and Latvia. Whereas the EU side has dismissed these issues as 'either been already resolved, or ... can be addressed' (Ferrero-Waldner 2006p), the Russian side returns to this 'extremely important issue, namely the violation of the rights of the Russian speaking population in Latvia and Estonia ... we consider that this is unacceptable and unworthy of Europe' (Putin 2007c). More generally, the implications of EU enlargement (related, to be true, to other processes such as NATO enlargement), continue to preoccupy the Russian leadership: 'We should not let bloc mentalities prevail in European politics, nor should we allow new dividing lines to appear on our continent or unilateral projects to be implemented to the detriment of the interests and security of our neighbours' (Putin 2007b).

As for perceptions of EU attempts to ideological or normative superiority, the bottom line is that the EU has no right to impose foreign thinking on Russian developments. Said Putin: 'When speaking of common values, we should also respect the historical diversity of European civilization. It would be useless and wrong to try to force artificial "standards" on each other' (Putin 2006b).

A key issue in this regard, and the one at the heart of the detrimentally opposing reactions to the developments in Georgia, concerns sovereignty. Putin's perspective is this:

> One cannot apply one rule to Kosovo and other rules to other situations. In what way is the Kosovo situation different from the Abkhazia situation or the South Ossetia? In nothing. They are no different. If we start to manipulate the situation we will find problems. People will feel disappointed and disillusioned.
>
> (*Financial Times* 2006b)

This ties in with the issue of great power responsibility. In the Russian mind, its behaviour in Georgia was necessary to maintain regional stability (see Medvedev 2008d). In parallel, the fact that the EU and the United States both supported the Orange revolution in Ukraine is itself described as 'shocking, problematic' by Putin (*Financial Times* 2006b), even more in combination with claims about Russian behaviour, for instance regarding the supply of gas. Said

Putin: 'If you started it, then go ahead and pay (i.e. subsidies to Kiev). You want the long-term benefits, but you want us to pay. (If) you don't want to pay, take a realistic look at the situation' (*Financial Times* 2006b).

Another key element in the negative perception of the EU concerns EU, and generally, Western claims about democracy and democratic standards. As we noted in the previous section, the lack of consolidated liberal democracy is a corner-stone in EU recognition of Russia. Russia's perspective is dramatically different: 'building a sovereign democratic state, we fully share the fundamental values and principles of the vast majority of Europeans' (Putin 200fb) and 'Russia ... has made an enormous contribution to the European concept of democracy' (Putin 2007c).

The key notion in recent years is that of 'sovereign democracy', developed by Putin's deputy chief of the presidential administration, Vladislav Surkov, to grasp core Russian values that make Russia unique on the basis of its size, historical experience and geographical location. Drawing on Defence Minister Sergei Ivanov's logic 'if there is western democracy, there should be an eastern democracy as well', the 'sovereign democracy' concept stands in opposition to the post-revolutionary Ukraine and Georgian democracy, which are perceived as Western-style, ruled from the outside (Popescu 2006).

Also the Orthodox Church has been active in the campaign against Western normative framing. Metropolit Cyril of Smolensk and Kaliningrad (the president of the department for external relations of the Moscow patriarch), gave his view about democracy in connection to the Moscow 2006 World Summit of Religious Leaders, stating that attempts at relating the Russian democracy to the standards of Western democracy are inherently flawed, leading to 'ideological dependence' and resulting in 'the negation of the originality of national life ... the Western model of democracy is incapable of assuming all the positive national experience, and of discerning that which is negative' (Cyril 2006). In conclusion, then, Russia recognizes the EU in this regard as making claims for universality regarding its interpretation of the meaning of democracy and human rights, and simultaneously not understanding or paying enough respect to Russian uniqueness.

Interface fundamentals

Where does this leave us in terms of the character of the EU–Russian interface? The following conclusions show that the current interface approximates one of *hostility*, based on incompatibility on key values such as democracy, fundamental freedoms and international conduct, and symmetrical power configuration, in our case a mutual recognition as great power. Here, it needs to be underlined, we can find a partial shift as compared to the early years of the Putin period, which, at least on surface, held more elements of *convergence*. The main conclusions of the interface analysis above are:

- The relationship is rather institutionalized, as is evident in the Partnership and Cooperation Agreement, the Common Spaces including roadmaps, negotiations for a new comprehensive agreement, and a well-established summitry process. There is no obvious asymmetry in terms of institutional power in the way that the neighbourhood significantly contributes to EU superiority in relation to ENP partners; rather, it is a mutually agreed institutional format and sequence of interaction. The logic becomes somewhat different when taking into account also sub-regional arrangements, such as the Northern Dimension or the Black Sea Synergy, where the EU (Commission or member-states) are in an agenda-setting position.

- Also in other regards is the relationship symmetrical in power terms. The mutual dependence in the economic field contain power resources for both sides – in the Russian case the hydrocarbon supply superiority, in the EU case controlling Russian access to the EU internal market. By way of examples, the gas crises of 2006 and 2009 are in this perspective similar in terms of symbolic value as illustrations of Russian supremacy and European Union strategic dependence on Russian gas. On the other hand, the decision of the European Council (2008c) in connection to the war in Georgia to postpone negotiations on a new comprehensive agreement until Russian troops were withdrawn to the positions held prior to 7 August is an instance of EU superiority.
- In terms of productive power, the competition for normative framing again renders the conclusion that none of the two sides is superior to the other. Instead we find that key concepts in the relationship – democracy, freedom, values, Europe, sovereignty, security etc. – are filled with different meanings by the two parties in a competitive fashion. As an illustration, the following passage, citing President Putin at the EU–Russia summit in Mafra, Portugal, in October 2007 is appropriate:

> Today I also introduced a new initiative to our partners ... the idea is to create a Russian–European Institute for Freedom and Democracy.... The EU assists the development of similar institutes in Russia using grants. I think that it is high time, given our increasing economic and financial capacity, that the Russian Federation can do the same thing in the European Union, can do its bit, including financially, to contribute to the development of such dialogues. We are suggesting a new institute, either in Brussels or in one of the European capitals.
>
> Putin (2007d)

- While there are a number of issues where Russia and the EU entertain similar perspectives and cooperate in a functional manner, especially regarding international security, when it comes to issues internal to the relationship, there is a fundamental, and growing, gap in perspectives and values. This can be observed in issues such as the status of Kosovo, Georgia, political transition in the post-Soviet space, institutionalization of energy exchange, and not least regarding the Russian domestic political situation and EU enlargement. It is indicative that both sides make similar claims – while the European

130 *Great power interfaces*

Parliament urges Russia to 'accept the realities which emerged after the end of the Cold War and abandon outdated thinking about exclusive zones of influence' (European Parliament 2006b), President Putin has urged the EU to 'not let bloc mentalities prevail in European politics, nor ... allow new dividing lines to appear ... or unilateral projects to be implemented' (Putin2007b). President Medvedev's proposal for a pan-European security treaty follows the same logic.

- As a concluding remark, the 'strategic partnership' may have turned into neither 'strategic' nor 'partnership'. From a multi-causal perspective, this could be ascribed to Russian domestic political developments and its assertive foreign policy as well as to the security-political consolidation, militarization and enlargement of the EU. As argued by Commissioner Peter Mandelsohn in April 2007, the EU–Russia relationship now encompasses a 'level of misunderstanding or even mistrust we have not seen since the end of the Cold War' (Mandelsohn (2007). The conclusion is reasonably no less relevant after the Russian war with Georgia.

7 The transatlantic interface

Introduction

This chapter analyses the transatlantic interface between the EU and the United States. In a book presented as dealing with the European security order, the presence of the United States may need some elaboration. The perspective entertained here is that the United States is indeed a European power. This can be justified on theoretical, instrumental as well as ideational grounds. In theoretical terms, if acknowledging that the United States entertains a position approximating that of a superpower, it can be argued that American policy choices are of political significance in all regional orders. This argument, in line with the Buzan and Wæver framework elaborated in the early parts of this book, relates to perspectives on the rationale for and impact of extra-regional involvement in regional processes (see for instance Ayoob 1999, Goh 2008, Miller 2001).

Instrumentally, the high degree of US–European cooperation – economically, politically, and otherwise, both in the bilateral context and in multilateral forums – displays a relationship of intense interdependence and at times joint global leadership. The EU–US link is arguably the most important one in a comprehensive perspective, but naturally NATO holds a unique bond in terms of military security and collective defence. Also in ideational terms can the United States be argued to be a European power, as the shared history of many Europeans and Americans provide for a significant degree of identification. All three factors, along with a number of others elaborated below, help explain the official EU position that the United States is the closest ally of the EU. The points above also help explain the special standing of the EU (and, to be sure, of individual member-states) in the eyes of American policymakers. It comes as no surprise, then, that the EU–American relationship is a close and positive one; the subsequent analysis seeks rather to further develop the finer points of such a proposition.

At the same time, there are numerous issues on the global agenda where it is, or in some cases was, more appropriate to talk about a transatlantic divide than a bridge. In everything from economic sanctions to the role of the United Nations, the EU and the United States has at times ended up on different sides of the fence. To be sure, the global as well as European importance of the United States actually helps explain the divergence within the EU circle of countries, not least in the security sphere (reactions to the American involvement in Iraq is an obvious case in point).

What does this complex background imply in terms of the character of the interface between the European Union and the United States? This chapter seeks to answer this question by analysing perceptions of the two sides, first, by reviewing common and conflicting behaviour in a number of pressing international issues, and second, by assessing perceptions of each other as expressed in officials statements and interviews (that is, for the consumption of the other party, which may play into subsequent development of perceptions). Initially, however, a brief note on the formal framework for interaction.

Common institutions and policies

In comparison to EU interfaces reviewed thus far, EU–US interaction rests on a relatively low degree of institutionalization, especially when taking into account the history and current scope of cooperation. Diplomatic ties between EU predecessors and the United States date back to the 1950s, as the United States sent observers to the European Coal and Steel Community in 1953 and formally opened a US mission in 1956. An EC delegation was set up in Washington in 1954. It lasted until 1990 until cooperation became more formalized, in the form of the so called 'Transatlantic Declaration', facilitating cooperation in areas such as economy, education, science and culture. It, moreover, established political dialogue on various levels, including a summitry system. This arrangement was developed into the 'New Transatlantic Agenda' in 1995, which is the current framework for interaction. The four main themes/objectives singled out in the agenda are: promoting peace, stability, democracy and development on a global scale; responding to global challenges; contributing to the expansion of world trade and closer economic relations; and building bridges across the Atlantic. These themes effectively summarize the general profile of EU–US interaction – although there obviously is an internal dimension to the relationship, in economics as well as in security, interaction is significantly directed at joint efforts in relation to third parties. At the joint declaration of the new agenda, leaders put forth a perspective that, despite the bitter rift over Iraq (see further below), continues to provide the general direction of engagement:

> For over fifty years, the transatlantic partnership has been the leading force for peace and prosperity for ourselves and for the world. Together, we helped transform adversaries into allies and dictatorships into democracies. Together, we built institutions and patterns of cooperation that ensured our security and economic strength. These are epic achievements.
> (United States Mission to the European Union 2009a)

In what appears as a significant step to institutionalize economic cooperation, the Transatlantic Economic Council was created in April 2007, with the aim of promoting regulatory cooperation, eliminating barriers to transatlantic trade, advancing capital markets liberalization and furthering investment in each other's economies. Bilateral cooperation has also developed in dialogue form especially in the economic area through the establishment of the Transatlantic Business Dialogue, the Transatlantic Consumer Dialogue and also the Transatlantic Environmental Dialogue. The Transatlantic Policy Network (a non-governmental grouping of members of the US Congress and the European Parliament, business leaders and think tanks) has also been established (see further the United States Mission to the European Union 2009a).

The character of the joint agenda and framework gives rise to two principally important reflections. First, the common security agenda is primarily externally oriented in dealing with development and security outside of the EU–US relationship proper. To be effective such an approach calls for common perceptions of issues, relationships, and actors. The American side has argued that the key element concerns the quest for freedom (Volker 2006). Second, the bilateral part of the agenda is explicitly transnational rather than intergovernmental in nature. This is especially evident in the economic field, where the magnitude of the mutual investment relationship, the trade exchange and the transatlantic mergers and acquisitions in combination with people-to-people exchanges imply that the two societies, rather than only the political establishments, are connected. This may have an effect on public perceptions of the relationship in terms of common destiny, interdependence and common threats faced (see for instance Transatlantic Trends 2008: 9–12).

Since 1990, the most important political channel for engagement is the annual summit of the American President, the Head of Government of the country holding the EU Presidency, and the President of the European Commission. A number of ministerial meetings (including relevant commissioners) also take place. In that context, the High Representative for the CFSP also participates. In an ambition to introduce popular participation in policy formulation, at each summit, time is allotted for representatives of one or more of the dialogues to deliver opinions to the political leaders.

Cooperation in international security matters

As noted above, apart from these bilateral channels, the EU and the United States also maintain cooperation in a large number of international issues. This section briefly reviews some of the most prevalent issues on the international agenda to establish what patterns, if any, of EU–US interaction in international security may be discerned.

Perhaps the most prominent topic on the transatlantic security agenda in the last decade has been *Iraq*. After well-known disagreements among European countries as well as between the EU and the United States over the American intervention in Iraq, the last few years has seen a shift towards joint work for the democratic development of Iraq. Noted President Bush in February 2005: 'Some European nations joined the fight to liberate Iraq, while others did not. [But] all nations now have an interest in the success of a free and democratic Iraq' (Bush 2005a, see also Volker 2006). Subsequent cooperation displays elements of a division of labour logic. While the United States provides the bulk of the military engagement in Iraq, the EU has primarily provided massive reconstruction assistance, electoral experts and international observers and have also started negotiations on a trade and negotiation agreement. Practical cooperation between the EU and the United States can be found in the co-hosting of the international conference on Iraqi reconstruction in June 2005 (Bush 2005b, Juncker 2005, Volker 2006). As a further prominent example of the EU's civilian efforts, the EUJUST LEX mission began its operation in 2005, aimed at educating Iraqi police officers, judges, prosecutors and prison wardens. By the end of 2008, more than 2,000 individuals had taken part in the programme designed to foster trust, mutual respect and more efficient cooperation among the different sets of actors (Delegation of the European Union to the USA 2009: 7).

Also in the case of *Afghanistan* are there signs of transatlantic cooperation and joint leadership. Although the military deployment has been primarily an American issue in NATO format, by the end of 2008, there were more than 22,000 troops, half of the NATO-led International Security Assistance Force (ISAF) from EU countries (Delegation of the European Union to the USA 2009). The EU has furthermore made significant financial contributions to the restructuring of Afghanistan (Barroso 2009). The EU and the United States together financed the elections in 2005. President Bush stated the same year: 'European governments are helping Afghanistan to succeed, and America appreciates your leadership' (Bush 2005a, for a background on American accounts of EU involvement in Iraq, see also Bush 2005b, Volker 2006, Burns 2007, 2008). The good cooperation between the United States and the EU has been duly recognized also by the EU (Commission 2008r).

Regarding the issue of *combating terrorism*, there is an obvious pattern of sharing the end goals, but disagreeing over the means to reach the desired outcome. Both parties acknowledge each other's importance in combating terrorism – here is an obvious logic of interdependence (see for instance EU–US Summit 2008), but they have had partly different approaches as far as how to deal with the issue. Reactions to the Guantanamo detention centre are a well-known and obvious case in point. In the internal relationship, the quarrel over the transfer of passenger name records is another relevant example. At the same time, there is extensive cooperation between American and European authorities regarding, for instance, border protection and sharing of intelligence (Delegation of the European Union to the USA 2009).

In the Middle East conflict between *Israel and Palestine*, there is a difference in policy balance between the EU and the United States to the effect that the United States is Israel's closest ally, whereas, as we have seen earlier in the book, the EU has been massively supporting the Palestinian side financially, and could be added, through inclusion of the Palestinian Authority in the neighbourhood policy. All the same, the EU and the United States are key partners in the institutional setting of the UN Quartet, consider Hamas a terrorist organization and define the overriding goals for engagement in the conflict in terms of peace, stability and a two-state solution in line with the Annapolis agreement (EU–US Summit 2008).

As for the *Western Balkans*, again there is a background of at least partial disagreements over means (the NATO bombings being obvious cases in point), but a common perspective on the desired outcome. In recent years, there is clearly a joint effort in *Bosnia* and *Macedonia*, and not least regarding *Kosovo*, where the United States and the EU have pursued more or less identical policies (Volker 2006, Burns 2007). As far as EU engagement is concerned, a police mission was launched in Bosnia in 2003, aimed at establishing a professional and up-to-date multi-ethnic police force. Moreover, the EU launched the EUFOR Althea military operation in December 2004 to ensure compliance with the Dayton peace accords and working against organized crime. It is significant in our perspective that the EU took over this task from NATO. Also in Kosovo is there a common EU–US definition of the situation and of the guiding principles to be employed. As in the Bosnian case, a picture of division of labour presents itself, to the effect that NATO was military engaged early in the conflict process (bombings in 1999) and has later assumed leadership of the UN-mandated KFOR peacekeeping force, whereas the EU has maintained a key civilian role throughout the process. Examples of EU engagement include offering assistance and incentives to Kosovo and launching the EULEX Kosovo rule of law mission in 2008 to assist local authorities in constructing an independent and multi-ethnic legal system, police force and customs service. It is to be noted that in October 2008, the United States decided to take part in the EULEX Kosovo mission, reflecting the close value similarity of the EU and the United States. At the same time it should be underlined that EU member-states provide more than 75 per cent of the KFOR troops (by the end of 2008, 15,900 troops) (Delegation of the European Union to the USA 2009).

It must be added that EU recognition of the Western Balkan countries as eligible for future EU membership is a significant signal of EU's engagement in the region. Historically, the membership possibility exercises a very strong pull on most countries, evident in the 2004–2007 round of enlargement, as well as on countries of European direction that have thus far not been formally recognized by the EU, for instance Ukraine and Georgia.

The issue of *Iran and weapons of mass destruction* is another key issue on the joint international security agenda of the European Union and the United States. The parties are equally eager to contain the Iranian threat, but as in other cases, have been split over how and when to act. As in other cases, there is a fundamental similarity regarding the issue of the danger of Iranian acquisition of weapons of mass destruction, but especially some time back, disagreements about policy options regarding how and when to interact in different ways. Noted President Bush in 2005: 'In safeguarding the security of free nations, no option can be taken permanently off the table' (Bush 2005a). In consequence, military intervention has not been ruled out by the United States, whereas the EU has been favouring a diplomatic response. Furthermore, there have been disagreements over the scope and timing of economic sanctions and over European export credits (Burns 2008). In recent years, however, the parties have acquired more of a common view regarding means (consecutive UN sanctions can be seen as a testimony to this), in particular in the so-called P-5+1 (the permanent members of the United Nations Security Council plus Germany) (Burns 2008, see also EU–US Summit 2008).

Finally, the United States and the EU have reacted in more or less identical ways to *Russian de-democratization and foreign policy behaviour*. For instance, the conclusion of Secretary of State Condoleezza Rice – 'The emerging picture is an increasingly authoritarian and aggressive Russia' (Rice 2008, see also Burns 2008) – is completely in line with EU recognition of Russia as displayed in the previous chapter. The same goes for energy: 'We will expand and defend an open global energy economy from abusive practices. There cannot be one set of rules for Russia, Inc. and another for everyone else' (Rice 2008).

In relation to the Russian–Georgian war, there is a joint EU–US understanding of the situation in terms of key international relations principles (such as upholding formal sovereignty and territorial integrity) and Russian violation of Georgian fundamental rights. Referring to such a common transatlantic perspective, and with special reference to Georgian and Ukrainian aspirations, Secretary of State Rice stated 'we will not allow Russia to wield a veto over the future of the Euro-Atlantic community – neither what states we offer membership, nor the choice of those states to accept it' (Rice 2008). As the United States and the EU met on 25 September 2008 to reaffirm commitment to Georgia, Assistant Secretary of State Daniel Fried stated: 'The trans-Atlantic community is not going to accept Russia's recognition of South Ossetia and Abkhazia', adding that the 'solidarity shown was quite striking' (United States Mission to the European Union 2008).

In conclusion, the picture that comes across when reviewing a number of pressing international problems contains four main elements. First, there is large-scale unity between the European Union and the United States as far as overriding goals and normative principles of international security are concerned. Second, there is mutual recognition of the other as a great power exercising leadership on a global scale. Third, a number of empirical illustrations show that there are disagreements about how to achieve the desired goals; the gap in means is diminishing, however. Fourth, there is evidence of a division of labour to the effect that the United States is traditionally the key military actor and the European Union more of a civilian actor (as we have seen in financial terms and regarding missions in the area of rule of law). As has been shown, however, this picture needs to problematized, as the United States clearly is also a civilian actor, and the EU in recent years also a military actor.

These conclusions stand in stark contrast to the picture some years ago in terms of transatlantic rifts and troubles. Numerous voices were heard, both in academic and political circles, to the effect that there were fundamental differences, even competition, in international perspectives of the United States and the EU and its member-states. Under-Secretary of State Nicholas Burns has referred to these conflicts in terms such as 'the great trans-Atlantic wars' (Burns 2007). American policy analyst Robert Kagan argued in the summer of 2002 that it had become evident that

> Europeans and Americans no longer share a common view of the world.... On major strategic and international questions today, Americans are from Mars and Europeans are from Venus; they agree on little and understand one another even less.
> (Kagan quoted in *European Voice* 2002)

In contrast, it was stressed by the American administration at the time that although disagreements and serious rifts had occurred, they represented a minor portion of the overall relationship. Argued a senior administration official in connection to the US–EU summit in June 2003:

> [T]here is a much stronger commonality of views between the United States and Europe than is commonly understood. Specifically, the threats [terrorism, proliferation, adverse effects of globalization] to the Euro-Atlantic community are being seen by Americans and Europeans, the EU, in increasingly similar terms.
> (*European Voice* 2003)

Rockwell Schnabel, the US Ambassador to the EU at the time of the Iraq crisis pointed to similar dimensions, when noting the common links through NATO–EU cooperation, the joint interests in combating terrorism and rebuilding Afghanistan, and the joint efforts at crisis management activities (Schnabel 2002, 2003). Assistant Secretary of State Wayne, finally, noted that the

> [R]eality is that on economic policy as well as on foreign policy, the U.S. and the EU collaborate on far more than we fight. And where we do contend, it is ... not a sign of deteriorating transatlantic political and economic relations.
> (Wayne 2002)

At the same time, it must be acknowledged that the 'relaunch' of the transatlantic partnership by President Bush in 2005 (see further the section on American recognition of the EU below) indeed took place against the background of a number of negative years in which the relationship had deteriorated.

EU recognition of the United States

In essence, the EU recognition of the United States builds on three principal elements: ideological compatibility, advanced transnational interdependence and global leadership. The ideological compatibility is often asserted by EU representatives, and encompasses values that are fundamental to both polities – democracy, rule of law, freedom and liberty, as spelled out in Chapter 3 (see also Juncker 2005, Barroso 2009). This does not preclude, of course, strong differences regarding individual issues. The approach to capital punishment is an often-cited example. As far as international politics goes, EU Commission President Barroso noted in the midst of the financial crisis that the two sides also share important perspectives on the future of the multilateral order. Speaking at the Munich Security Conference in February 2009 (the first time a Commission President has been invited to speak there, interestingly enough), Barroso stated:

> Our indispensable partner in this endeavour to build an effective multilateral system will always be the United States. Not just because of our shared values and deep, historical links. But also because we have traditionally provided the ballast for the UN, the IMF, the World Bank, the WTO, the G8 and other multilateral organisations and partnerships that make up the international system.
>
> (Barroso 2009)

The second element concerns the United States as the closest and most important partner of the EU at the background of advanced forms of interdependence, both bilaterally in trade and security, and internationally, in the need of the EU for US collaboration to achieve desirable outcomes on global issues. While the deep transatlantic interdependence in the economic field is generally acknowledged to be reciprocal, the security dimension may need some further elaboration. The heart of the matter concerning security is that although the United States naturally is the stronger party militarily, EU representatives underline that it is not a relationship of dependence, but of interdependence. This implies that the EU is important to the United States, and conversely, that the EU is dependent on the United States, for instance in external security. Regarding the first point, as the meaning of security is generally acknowledged to change, the EU self-image is that the significance of the EU is increasing. As argued by Commission President Barroso: 'Through its comprehensive approach to security – in particular by addressing the nexus of security and development – the EU plays a key role in meeting ... global security challenges' (Barroso 2009). In relation to the second point, again Barroso's speech in Munich may serve as an illustration:

> The EU is the largest donor in Afghanistan, and has made a long-term commitment, especially focusing at the police sector, public health and agriculture. At the same time, Afghanistan needs a combination of soft and hard security measures, a process in which the EU needs American engagement.
>
> (Barroso 2009)

The third element – global leadership – concerns the EU recognition of American possibility to project power on a global scale. Here, all power dimensions discussed in earlier chapters may be relevant – the potential for the United States to use compulsory power, also of military kind, as well as structural means (development assistance, for instance), institutional power (evident not least in the United Nations Security Council and the Bretton Woods institutions) and productive power in normatively framing topics in particular ways in order to promote desirable outcomes. With reference to the previous section, EU recognition does contain, however, a distinction between means and ends, to the effect that whereas American global leadership is desired by the EU and American ends are coinciding with European ones against the background of value commonality, the means chosen by the Americans are not always readily acknowledged by EU. This goes for the choice of power resources (the military readiness of the United States) and the strategic approach of sometimes promoting unilateralism and working outside institutional frameworks.

This falls back on an EU self-perception of potency to the effect that when acting in concert, the EU and the United States can make a difference. Said President Barroso in the preparations for the EU–US summit in June 2008: 'Over the past four years the EU–US Partnership has proven that it can deliver transatlantic responses to the big challenges of our day' (Commission 2008r). In such a perspective, an American go-it-alone mentality also limits EU leadership.

In conclusion, a passage from Jean Claude Juncker, President of the EU Council at the time, (reciprocating the move by President Bush to reinvigorate the transatlantic relationship, see next section) succinctly summarizes the EU recognition of the United States as 'being not only a strategic partner, but the most important partner we have, not only as far as political strength relations are concerned, but also as far as heart relations are concerned' (Juncker 2005).

American recognition of the EU

The American recognition of the EU largely reciprocates that of the EU as regards the United States. The EU is viewed as an ideologically compatible and globally leading entity with which the United States entertains advanced interdependence. However, regarding global leadership, the picture is a bit more complicated: whereas the EU readily observes the leading American position, the United States has only recently come to recognize the global power of the EU.

As for ideological compatibility, the point needs little elaboration: Consecutive American administrations recognize the fundamental freedoms and democracy as key traits connected to the EU, (Bush 2005a), also bringing a common value base for external actions – as Kurt Volker (a senior State Department officer) has put it: 'For the European Union, the promotion of democratic values comes naturally' (Volker 2006). President Bush spoke at length about the common values of the EU and the United States in the summer of 2005, when EU leaders visited Washington. Bush underlined the fundamental importance of common values – 'human rights, human dignity, rule of law, transparency when it comes to government, decency' – and applied a perspective of universalism to the effect that the EU and the United States also has the obligation to spread these values. He moreover underlined the link between level of freedom and the attainment and quality of peace (Bush 2005b).

Regarding interdependence, two principal points could be made as far as American recognition is concerned. The first one has to do with societal interaction. The deep trade and investment relation is a fundamental parameter in the bilateral relationship, and the development of institutions such as the Transatlantic Economic Council is a testimony to the direction of further integration. The transnational character of interdependence, through communication and exchange, travel and academic cooperation means that societies rather than governments are interacting, of importance also for popular understanding of the relationship (Bush 2005b). This is in stark contrast to the EU–Russia interface, where interdependence much more has a political, or intergovernmental, character. A second principal point concerns security interdependence and the need for the United States to engage the EU in order for American security desires to work. The illustration in the previous section about the transfer of passenger name records is a concrete example of this.

As far as EU's global role is concerned, the United States has explicitly welcomed what we could call the security-political consolidation of the EU which in combination with EU enlargement creates a more potent European actor. Under-Secretary of State Stuart Eizenstat noted already a decade ago: 'European Union is increasingly a positive force joining with us to deal with a variety of global challenges. Repeatedly ... where the United States and the European Union act in concert toward common challenges, those challenges are overcome' (Eizenstat 1999).

The EU has historically been viewed by the United States as weak in capacity and slow in decision-making (Bengtsson 2004, Burns 2008); this seems now to change. President Bush noted in 2005 that the United States 'continues to support a strong European Union as a partner in spreading freedom and democracy' (Bush 2005b). Under-Secretary of State Nicholas Burns has later made the same point, stressing the achievements of the EU first in terms of unifying the European continent – 'a great, great historical accomplishment', (Burns 2007) – and then taking on a global role as 'our natural partner' (Burns 2008).

Having said that, EU developments, while generally perceived as positive, must not turn into competition between the EU and NATO. Hence, President Bush officially conditioned a greater role for the EU in the European security dynamic, if it was 'properly integrated with NATO' (cited in Goodby *et al.* 2002). Developments in terms of EU–NATO relations and in EU actor capacity, displayed for example in Macedonia, Bosnia and the Middle East, have on balance been perceived in positive terms by EU, NATO and American leaders. Solutions regarding EU use of NATO resources mark an interesting turn in the inter-institutional relationship, in providing the EU with actor potential, while also pointing to NATO superiority in specific areas/means. As Vershbow has noted:

> NATO and the EU have had no institutional relationship despite the fact that they are engaged in solving many of the same problems. The United States believes it is now time for these two institutions to promote together what they have sustained so well in their separate spheres.
>
> (Vershbow 2000: 79)

Under-Secretary Wayne has made the same sort of remark regarding the institutional division of labour:

> Our idea is that the three institutions – NATO, the OSCE, and the EU – doing what they do best, should mutually reinforce the others, strengthening the overall transatlantic relationship.
>
> (Wayne 1999: 93–94)

In conclusion. the United States increasingly perceives the EU as an actor with which it can make a division of labour. References are made to successful examples in the Balkans, regarding Iraq and Afghanistan, and for a longer time period regarding the Israel–Palestine conflict. It may further be concluded that the EU is perceived as a civilian/non-military actor, and the United States is repeatedly pointing at the need for the EU to take on a stronger global military commitment. To conclude, against the background of a combination of common values (ideological similarity based on democracy and market economy) and common interests (interdependence), the overriding American perception of the security-political consequences of enlargement and the consolidation of the EU as a security-political actor is a positive one. This holds both in terms of effects on the European continent – EU enlargement as a vehicle for peaceful change in Europe – and when it comes to international engagements and the issue of division of labour with the US.

Interface fundamentals

The analyses above give rise to the following set of conclusions:

- At the summit in Brno in the summer of 2008, the principally important catch-line ran: 'The strategic partnership between the EU and the US is firmly anchored in our common values and increasingly serves as a platform from which we can act in partnership' (Commission 2008r). This perspective is significant – the transatlantic agenda in security is more or less all about external issues. As was noted by Under-Secretary of State Nicholas Burns in March 2007:

  > US–European relations now are all about not Europe but the rest of the world.... Our whole agenda ... is what Europe and America can do to combine our force, our power ... to make the world more peaceful and more stable.
  >
  > (Burns 2007)

  This effectively leads to the conclusion that after the rift over Iraq/war on terror, there are no fundamental disagreements regarding bilateral relations in the security field. In the economic field, to be sure, there is bilateral competition and from time to time trade disputes (as evidenced in numerous

142 *Great power interfaces*

WTO cases), but the parties are in agreement regarding the principles in terms of an open global economy and free trade and investment.
- There is no obvious relational power asymmetry at hand – the United States is obviously the more powerful actor of the two, especially in the military sphere, but the argument here is that neither side claims superiority bilaterally through use of power resources. This falls back on the one hand on the low degree of institutionalization and on the other on the value compatibility of the two sides (which, in essence, implies that neither side seeks to exploit the other). One objection, again referring to the military, could be the structural inequality within NATO as far as member-state deployment of forces go, but as we have seen, the EU has in recent years deployed substantial troops, and at any rate, this does not impinge on the power relationship of the EU and the United States.
- Reflecting on the change from the solidarity expressed in 2001 'standing shoulder to shoulder' to the fundamental disagreement in 2003 (resulting in 'old' and 'new' Europe) to the renewed friendship after the 2005 reorientation of the Bush presidency, it seems that on the surface, the interface changes over time. If judging from the fundamental nature of the relationship, it seems appropriate to conclude that the change has not been really fundamental. As far as popular opinion goes, in 2003 the Transatlantic Trends survey indicated that the public on both sides of the Atlantic perceived a value gap, although they could not specify what the gap was rooted in (Transatlantic Trends 2003: 4). In the 2008 survey, there seems to be a great overlap in perspectives, at least if looking at threats (with climate change being the major exception, where Europeans are far more concerned than Americans, see Transatlantic Trends 2008: 9–12).
- As far as reciprocal global leadership goes, the Bush relaunching of the transatlantic partnership deserves mentioning. Being the first American president to visit the EU headquarters, former President Bush called on European partners in February 2005: 'when Europe and America stand together, no problem can stand against us. As past debates fade, as great duties become clear, let us begin a new era of transatlantic unity' (Bush 2005a). After the rift over Iraq, this step carries significant weight. Bush continued: 'our friendship is essential to peace and prosperity across the globe, and no temporary debate, no passing disagreements of governments, no power on earth will ever divide us' (Bush 2005a). In terms of European developments, the joint statement at the EU–US summit in 2008 read: 'The process of unifying Europe is one of the outstanding historical legacies of our partnership over the past half century' (EU–US Summit 2008). As an illustration of popular opinion, in 2003, there was equally strong support among Americans for the EU and the US to exert a strong leadership in world affairs (Transatlantic Trends 2003: 7, 2008: 8, 10).
- A general conclusion for the interface is that the common value base seems to provide the foundation for agreement on various ends, although there may be – as has been the case in the past – disagreements about the means to be

used. Said British Foreign Secretary David Miliband upon meeting with the new US Secretary of State Hillary Clinton in February 2009: 'We're interested in the means, but in the end, it's the ends that count' (United States Mission to the European Union 2009b). This line of reasoning is mirrored by popular sentiments as expressed in the Transatlantic Trends 2003 survey, where one of the main findings were that 'Americans and Europeans have similar views on threats, but different impulses on how to respond to them' (Transatlantic Trends 2003: 3).

- In conclusion, the transatlantic interface is a case of *community interface*, where an integrationist logic in the bilateral relation, supported by a common projection on external issues, is at play among roughly equal parties, if assessing the power situation internal to the relationship.

Part IV
Conclusions

8 Concluding remarks

This book concerns the European Union and the European security order. More specifically, it sets out to analyse the role and position of the EU in relation to countries that are part of the European security order but are not EU members, recognized candidate states, or voluntary opt-outs. The background rationale is provided by the notion of the regional security complex, as developed by Barry Buzan and Ole Wæver. In their analytical framework, different complexes can attain different character in terms of security relationship. As far as the European complex is concerned, the EU is the undisputed leader and the complex internally holds such a high quality that it approximates Karl Deutsch's notion of a security community, in which the use of military force is no longer considered for conflict resolution. This book is in general agreement with the Buzan and Wæver characterization – here the ambition is to study interaction between the EU and different countries that are adjacent to the EU but belong to other complexes (the post-Soviet and the Middle East and North African ones, and including the United States as a global great power).

In order to study this interaction from a relational point of view, the book develops an analytical framework based in constructivism and rationalism, focusing the notions of interfaces and recognition. The general logic is as follows: An interface consists of the mutual recognition of two or more actors. Recognition denotes the process through which actors establish their dispositions vis-à-vis other actors. The process comprises three analytically different elements: self-image, perception of the other, and of context. In that process, material and ideational resources of actors become decisive. Interfaces vary according to two dimensions, the degree of value compatibility and the character of relational power, distinguishing between symmetrical and asymmetrical power relationships.

A range of different conclusions result from the analyses in the preceding chapters. In what follows, a number of empirical conclusions are discussed, after which a few reflections of theoretical and methodological nature are shared. A summary of the findings is shown in Table 8.1.

A number of reflections and comments can be made at this point. As far as great power interfaces are concerned, two conclusions can be observed. The first concerns the qualitative difference of the two interfaces under study here. The

Table 8.1 European interfaces

Hostility	Resistance
Russia	Belarus, Libya, Syria
Convergence	*Adaptation*
	Algeria, Armenia, Azerbaijan, Egypt, Jordan, Lebanon, Moldova, Palestinian Authority, Tunisia
Community	*Inclusion*
United States	Georgia, Israel, Morocco, Ukraine

EU–US interface can be characterized as a community interface, in which there is a high degree of value compatibility, in terms of democracy, rule of law, human rights, and also as regards conduct in international relations. This in turn explains the close external cooperation in the field of security. Although the means have certainly been, and still remain to some extent, different for the two, the goals and ambitions are mostly the same. In contrast, the EU–Russian interface is a case of a hostility interface, in which value incompatibility leads to instrumental interaction (but not isolation) rather than strengthening the common ground. This difference serves as one possible explanation for the difference in degree of institutionalization of cooperation, to the effect that EU–Russian interaction needs a higher degree of detailed regulation.

The second set of conclusions takes as its point of departure the observation that both interfaces encompass power symmetry in terms of relational power. There is a fundamental difference between the two interfaces, however, to the effect that whereas the EU–US interface is internally symmetrical largely due to a lack of power projection, the EU–Russian interface is symmetrical because both parties try to project power but do not succeed, and furthermore realize the interdependent nature of their relationship.

As a consequence of the power symmetry, it follows that the EU is perceived by both the United States and Russia as a great power in the security sphere. It is significant, however, that in the American perception, the EU is primarily a partner in dealing with external issues, whereas the Russian perception is predominantly about EU ambitions of normative superiority – projecting productive power – in the European security order as well as on a global scale.

As far as the neighbourhood interfaces are concerned, they all share the characteristic that the EU is the markedly stronger power. However, there is variation in the degree to which the EU is able to project power as well as regarding what power resources it possesses. In a few cases – Belarus, Syria, Libya – the EU is fundamentally unable to induce (or force) change, as far as can be seen at this point in time, despite its superiority in financial, technical and normative terms. Moreover, it cannot take advantage of the institutional means it has set up, for instance in the form the ENP. The EU has a hard time realizing its power potential in these cases. In contrast, in most interfaces, the weaker party is adapting to EU values as well as practices, although in different ways partly depending on the capacity of the state in question, which may be linked to the level of democratic development.

In a few principally important cases, the interface is rather of inclusive character, to the effect that the weaker party not only is adopting key EU perspectives, but is recognized by the EU as a close political ally of the EU in relation to third parties and issues beyond the bilateral relationship. In these cases, it ultimately becomes a question of how to define the European security complex. Could it be argued that these states are actually part of the European complex although they are not recognized by the EU as eligible for membership? In the end, the answer will depend on how important the European connection generally and EU relationship specifically is in relation to other political considerations.

There is also great variation in terms of geography, implying that conventional geographical distinctions cannot be use for generalizations about perceptions. Each of the four sub-complexes under study here displays variation, and in three out of four, all the kinds of interfaces are represented. Rather than geography, then, it is question of cognition.

A number of principal points result from the analyses in previous chapters. To begin with, a fundamental point of the book is that political actorness results from a combination of internal and external developments, in concrete terms internal capacity-building and external recognition of means as well as ends. In our empirical case, it means that the perspective of the EU as a potent security actor in the European security order results not only from institutional developments in the EU polity, such as establishing the ESS or developing the ESDP, but just as much from how others perceive these developments. Such logic requires a relational analysis of which this book is an example.

On methodology, it may be noted that the methodological approach chosen – official rhetoric and manifest behaviour as a display of perceptions – appears appropriate against the background of a theoretical assumption that perceptions are mutually constitutive, in which case the public display of disposition may be hypothesized to influence outcomes at later points in time.

Finally a reflection on the EU-internal aspects of EU actorness. The Commission has come to acquire a key role also in the CFSP area, in parallel to the logic displayed in enlargement negotiations. This transfer of competence is more evident in the neighbourhood interfaces than in the great power interfaces, but can certainly be found also there. While it would probably be incorrect to say that the Commission is gaining influence on behalf of the Council, it may rather be expressed as the EU system being involved in external relations in a more complex manner than before. The extent to which this is a problem – for instance in terms of coherence – and the extent to which the Lisbon Treaty solves this problem is too early to say.

In conclusion, it can be noted that the EU has come to play a central role in the European security order, attaining a great power status in a regional perspective (and also global perspective). In terms of security complex character, it goes without saying that EU–Europe is a security community. The results of the analyses above give rise to three different conclusions in this regard. First, given the variation in interface, and the perspective that some interfaces are of inclusive nature (in addition to the EU–US community), we may enter into discussion of the exact boundaries of the European security community. Second, interface variation poses a critical question about policy construction. More precisely, one may ask how effective the ENP can be as an overriding framework. Third and final, the relationship between non-European actors and the EU may appear more complex and challenging than politics at the margins of Europe. This goes not least for non-European great powers such as China.

Notes

1 The Palestinian Authority is not a regular state in the traditional sense, as the corresponding territory is occupied by Israel. Sometimes the label 'occupied Palestinian territory(ies)' is used. For the purposes of this book – recognition of official administrations/regimes – the authority label is the more appropriate one.
2 The analysis in this and subsequent sections of this chapter draws on an article published by the author in *Journal of European Integration* vol. 30, no. 5, December 2008, pp. 597–616, entitled 'Constructing interfaces: the neighbourhood discourse in EU external policy'.

Bibliography

Official documents and speeches

Aliyev, Ilham (2008) 'Statement of H.E. Mr Ilham Aliyev, the President of the Republic of Azerbaijan in joint press conference of heads of states participating in GUAM Batumi Summit', 1 July 2008. Online, available at: www.president.az/print.php?item_id=2008070121056589&sec_id=70.

AMU (2008) 'Algeria to host first Maghreb economic fair'. Online, available at: www.maghrebarabe.org/en/news.cfm?type=2&id=70.

Baku Summit (2008) 'Baku Energy Summit Declaration', 14 November 2008. Online, available at: www.president.az/print.php?item_id=20081115110458909&sec_id=140.

Barroso, José Manuel Durão (2007a) 'Shared challenges, shared futures: taking the neighbourhood policy forward', speech, 3 September 2007. Online, available at: http://europa.eu/rapid/pressReleasesAction.do?reference=SPEECH/07/502&format=HTML&aged=0&language=EN&guiLanguage=en.

Barroso, José Manuel Durão (2007b) 'A message to the people of Belarus from European Commission President José Manuel Barroso – 25 March 2007', MEMO/07/116, 25 March 2007. Online, available at: http://europa.eu/rapid/pressReleasesAction.do?reference=MEMO/07/116&format=HTML&aged=0&language=EN&guiLanguage=en.

Barroso, José Manuel Durão (2007c) 'Joint press conference following the Russia–European Union Summit meeting, Samara, Russia', 18 May 2007. Online, available at: www.kremlin.ru/eng/speeches/2007/05/18/2256_type82914type82915_129617.shtml.

Barroso, José Manuel Durão (2009) 'Managing instability: global challenges and the crisis of global governance', speech/09/44, 7 February 2009. http://europa.eu/rapid/pressReleasesAction.do?refeernce=SPEECH/09/44&format=HTML.

Berlin Declaration (2007). Online, available at: http://europa.eu/50/docs/berlin_declaration_en.pdf.

Black Sea Forum (2006) 'Joint declaration of the Black Sea Forum for Dialogue and Partnership', 5 June 2006. Online, available at: www.blackseaforum.org/joint_declaration.html.

Bouteflika, Abdelaziz (2008) 'Official message on human rights', 10 September 2008. Online, available at: www.el-mouradia.dz/francais/president/activites/PresidentActi.htm.

Burns, Nicholas (2007) 'Challenges and opportunities facing the transatlantic community', speech, 26 March 2007. Online, available at: http://useu.usmission.gov/Dossiers/TransAtlantic/Mar2607_Burns_CEPS.asp.

Burns, Nicholas (2008) 'Interview with Stefan Kornelius, Süddeutsche Zeitung', 30 January 2008. Online, available at: http://useu.umission.gov/Article.asp?ID=D8398EBD-3C77-48BB-9DAB-7B44A590.

Bush, George (2005a) 'Remarks at Concert Noble', 22 November 2005. Online, available at: http://useu.umission.gov/Article.asp?ID=2A17CEE7-C702-45A8-8579-203A49-485.

Bush, George (2005b) 'Remarks by President Bush', 20 June 2005. Online, available at: http://useu.umission.gov/Article.asp?ID=155A6D29-0926-4CFA-80FF-67CF31BC6.

Chizhov, V.A. (2003) Statement at the International Conference on Wider Europe, 11 November 2003. Online, available at: www.ln.mid.ru/bl.nsf/0/bad7fec519a73ec343256ddb0047f328?OpenDocument.

Commission (2003) 'Wider Europe – neighbourhood: a new framework for relations with our eastern and southern neighbours', communication COM(2003) 104 final from the Commission to the Council and the European Parliament, 11 March 2003. Online, available at: http://ec.europa.eu/world/enp/pdf/com03_104_en.pdf.

Commission (2004) 'European Neighbourhood Policy strategy paper', communication COM(2004) 373 final from the Commission, 12 May 2004. Online, available at: http://ec.europa.eu/world/enp/pdf/strategy/strategy_paper_en.pdf.

Commission (2005a) 'European Neighbourhood Policy, recommendations for Armenia, Azerbaijan, Georgia and for Egypt and Lebanon', communication COM(2005) 72 final from the Commission to the Council, Brussels, 2 March 2005.

Commission (2005b) 'Commissioner Ferrero-Waldner's visit to Libya', press release IP/05/605, 25 May 2005. Online, available at: http://europa.eu/rapid/pressReleasesAction.do?reference=IP/05/605&format=HTML&aged=1&language=EN&guiLanguage=en.

Commission (2006a) 'Communication from the Commission to the Council and the European Parliament on strengthening the European Neighbourhood Policy', COM(2006) 726 final, 4 December 2006. Online, available at: http://ec.europa.eu/world/enp/pdf/com06_726_en.pdf.

Commission (2006b) 'Communication from the Commission to the Council and the European Parliament on strengthening the European Neighbourhood Policy: overall assessment', COM(2006) 726 final, 4 December 2006. Online, available at: http://ec.europa.eu/world/enp/pdf/com06_726_en.pdf.

Commission (2006c) 'Communication from the Commission to the Council and the European Parliament on strengthening the European Neighbourhood Policy: ENP progress report Ukraine', COM(2006) 726 final, 4 December 2006. Online, available at: http://ec.europa.eu/world/enp/pdf/com06_726_en.pdf.

Commission (2006d) 'Communication from the Commission to the Council and the European Parliament on strengthening the European Neighbourhood Policy: ENP progress report Moldova', COM(2006) 726 final, 4 December 2006. Online, available at: http://ec.europa.eu/world/enp/pdf/com06_726_en.pdf.

Commission (2006e) 'Communication from the Commission to the Council and the European Parliament on strengthening the European Neighbourhood Policy: ENP progress report Israel', COM(2006) 726 final, 4 December 2006. Online, available at: http://ec.europa.eu/world/enp/pdf/com06_726_en.pdf.

Commission (2006f) 'Communication from the Commission to the Council and the European Parliament on strengthening the European Neighbourhood Policy: ENP progress report Jordan', COM(2006) 726 final, 4 December 2006. Online, available at: http://ec.europa.eu/world/enp/pdf/com06_726_en.pdf.

Commission (2006g) 'Communication from the Commission to the Council and the European Parliament on strengthening the European Neighbourhood Policy: ENP progress report Palestinian Authority', COM(2006) 726 final, 4 December 2006. Online, available at: http://ec.europa.eu/world/enp/pdf/com06_726_en.pdf.

Bibliography

Commission (2006h) 'Communication from the Commission to the Council and the European Parliament on strengthening the European Neighbourhood Policy: ENP progress report Tunisia', COM(2006) 726 final, 4 December 2006. Online, available at: http://ec.europa.eu/world/enp/pdf/com06_726_en.pdf.

Commission (2006i) 'Communication from the Commission to the Council and the European Parliament on strengthening the European Neighbourhood Policy: ENP progress report Morocco', COM(2006) 726 final, 4 December 2006. Online, available at: http://ec.europa.eu/world/enp/pdf/com06_726_en.pdf.

Commission 2006j 'Commission proposes renewed consensus on enlargement', press release IP/06/1523, 8 November 2006. Online, available at: http://europa.eu/rapid/pressReleasesAction.do?reference=IP/06/1523&format=HTML&aged=0&language=EN&guiLanguage=en.

Commission (2006k) 'European Neighbourhood and Partnership Instrument – Algeria: strategy paper 2007–2013'. Online, available at: http://ec.europa.eu/world/enp/pdf/country/enpi_csp_nip_algeria_en.pdf.

Commission (2006l) 'European Neighbourhood and Partnership Instrument – Tunisia: strategy paper 2007–2013'. Online, available at: http://ec.europa.eu/world/enp/pdf/country/enpi_csp_nip_tunisia_summary_en.pdf.

Commission (2006m) 'European Neighbourhood and Partnership Instrument – Syrian Arab Republic: strategy paper 2007–2013'. Online, available at: http://ec.europa.eu/world/enp/pdf/country/enpi_csp_nip_syria_en.pdf.

Commission (2006n) 'EU–Belarus: new message to the people of Belarus', press release IP/06/1593, 21 November 2006. Online, available at: http://europa.eu./rapid/pressReleasesAction.do?reference=IP/06/1593&format=HTML&aged=0&language=EN&guiLanguage=en.

Commission (2006o) 'Communication on external energy relations', 12 October 2006. Online, available at: http://ec.europa.eu/comm/external_relations/energy/docs/com06_590_en.pdf.

Commission (2007a) 'A strong European Neighbourhood Policy', COM(2007) 774 final, 5 December 2007. Online, available at: http://ec.europa.eu/world/enp/pdf/com07_774_en.pdf.

Commission (2007b) 'Morocco: Commission proposes more than €650 million in support of reforms', press release IP/07/274, 2 March 2007. Online, available at: http://europa.eu/rapid/pressReleasesAction.do?reference=IP/07/274&format=HTML&aged=0&language=EN&guiLanguage=en.

Commission (2007c) 'Communication from the Commission to the European Council and the European Parliament – an energy policy for Europe', COM(2007) 1 final, 10 January 2007. Online, available at: http://eur-lex.europa.eu/LexUriServ/LexUriServ.do?uri=COM:2007:0001:FIN:EN:PDF.

Commission (2008a) 'Implementation of the European Neighbourhood Policy in 2007: communication from the Commission to the Parliament and the Council', COM(2008) 164, 3 April 2008.

Commission (2008b) 'Implementation of the European Neighbourhood Policy in 2007: progress report Azerbaijan', SEC(2008) 391, 3 April 2008.

Commission (2008c) 'Implementation of the European Neighbourhood Policy in 2007: progress report Azerbaijan', SEC(2008) 392, 3 April 2008.

Commission (2008d) 'Implementation of the European Neighbourhood Policy in 2007: progress report Georgia', SEC(2008) 393, 3 April 2008.

Commission (2008e) 'Implementation of the European Neighbourhood Policy in 2007: progress report Israel', SEC(2008) 394, 3 April 2008.
Commission (2008f) 'Implementation of the European Neighbourhood Policy in 2007: progress report Egypt', SEC(2008) 395, 3 April 2008.
Commission (2008g) 'Implementation of the European Neighbourhood Policy in 2007: progress report Jordan', SEC(2008) 396, 3 April 2008.
Commission (2008h) 'Implementation of the European Neighbourhood Policy in 2007: progress report Lebanon', SEC(2008) 397, 3 April 2008.
Commission (2008i) 'Implementation of the European Neighbourhood Policy in 2007: progress report Moldova', SEC(2008) 399, 3 April 2008.
Commission (2008j) 'Implementation of the European Neighbourhood Policy in 2007: progress report the occupied Palestinian territory', SEC(2008) 397, 3 April 2008.
Commission (2008k) 'Implementation of the European Neighbourhood Policy in 2007: progress report Ukraine', SEC(2008) 402, 3 April 2008.
Commission (2008l) 'Barcelona Process: Union for the Mediterranean', COM(2008) 319 final, 20 May 2008. Online, available at: http://ec.europa.eu/external_relations/euromed/com08_319_en.pdf.
Commission (2008m) 'Report on the first year of implementation of the Black Sea Synergy', 19 June 2008. Online, available at: http://ec.europa.eu/external_relations/blacksea/doc/com08_391_en.pdf.
Commission (2008n) 'Communication from the Commission to the European Parliament and the Council: Eastern Partnership', COM(2008) 823 final, 3 December 2008.
Commission (2008o) 'Commissioner Ferrero-Waldner and Egyptian Minister of International Cooperation Aboulnaga sign 558 million EUR assistance package', 6 March 2008.
Commission (2008p) 'EU–Libya: negotiations on future Framework Agreement start', press release IP/08/1687, 12 November 2008. Online, available at: http://europa.eu/rapid/pressReleasesAction.do?reference=IP/08/1687&format=HTML&aged=0&language=EN&guiLanguage=en.
Commission (2008q) 'EU–Russia Common Spaces: progress report 2007', 3 April 2008. Online, available at: http://ec.europa.eu/external_relations/russia/russia_docs/commonspaces_prog_report2007.pdf.
Commission (2008r) 'EU–US Summit in Slovenia to discuss further strengthening of strategic relationship', IP/08/903, 9 June 2009. Online, available at: http://europa.eu/rapid/pressReleasesAction.do?reference=IP/08/903&format=HTML.
Commission (2009a) 'The European Neighbourhood Policy'. Online, available at: http://ec.europa.eu/world/enp/policy_en.htm.
Commission (2009b) 'The EU's relations with Russia'. Online, available at: http://ec.europa.eu/external_relations/russia/intro/index.htm.
Commission (2009c) 'The EU's relations with the United States of America'. Online, available at: http://ec.europa.eu/external_relations/us/intro/index.htm.
Community of Democratic Choice (2005) 'Declaration of the Countries of Democratic Choice', Kiev, 2 December 2005. Online, available at: www.mfa.goc.ua/mfa/en/news/detail/1341.htm.
Council (2003a) 'Wider Europe – New Neighbourhood', 6941/03 (presse 63), 18 March 2003. Online, available at: www.consilium.europa.eu/ueDocs/cms_Data/docs/pressData/en/gena/75004.pdf.
Council (2003b) 'Wider Europe/New Neighbourhood', 8220/03 (presse 105), 14 April 2003. Online, available at: www.consilium.europa.eu/ueDocs/cms_Data/docs/pressData/en/gena/75419.pdf.

Council (2003c) 'Wider Europe – New Neighbourhood – Council conclusions', 10369/03 (presse 166), 16 June 2003. Online, available at: www.consilium.europa.eu/ueDocs/cms_Data/docs/pressData/en/gena/76201.pdf.
Council (2004) 'European Neighbourhood Policy – Council conclusions', 10189/04 (presse 195), 14 June 2004. Online, available at: www.consilium.europa.eu/ueDocs/cms_Data/docs/pressData/en/gena/80951.pdf.
Council (2006a) 'Council conclusions on Belarus', 10 April 2006. Online, available at: www.eu2006.at/en/News/Council_Conclusions/1004ConclusionsBelarus.pdf.
Council (2006b) 'General affairs and external relations Council conclusions', IP11575/06 (presse 219), 18 July 2006. Online, available at: www.eu2006.fi/news_and_documents/conclusions/vko29/en_GB/1153166423674/_files/75573921501938591/default/90565.pdf.
Council (2006c) 'Council conclusions on the Middle East peace process', 15 September 2006. Online, available at: www.eu2006.fi/news_and_documents/conclusions/vko37/en_GB/1158333606396/.
Council (2006d) 'Declaration by the Presidency on behalf of the European Union on the "referendum" in the Transnistrian region of the Republic of Moldova 17 September 2006', 18 September 2006. Online, available at: www.eu2006.fi/news_and_documents/cfsp_statements/vko38/en_GB/1158588611562/.
Council (2006e) 'External Relations Council conclusions', 13340/06 (presse 265), 17 October 2006. Online, available at: www.eu2006.fi/news_and_documents/conclusions/vko42/en_GB/1161845830699/_files/76142733215596611/default/ST13340.EN06.pdf.
Council (2006f) 'Presidency statement on the detention and sentencing of Mr Alexander Milinkevich', 27 April 2006. Online, available at: www.eu2006.at/en/News/CFSP_Statements/April/2704Belarus.html.
Council (2006g) 'Declaration by the Presidency on behalf of the European Union on the sentencing of the former presidential candidate Aleksandr Kozulin', 18 July 2006. Online, available at: www.eu2006.fi/news_and_documents/cfsp_statements/vko29/en_GB/1153221178461/.
Council (2006h) 'Declaration by the Presidency on behalf of the European Union regarding the referendum in Montenegro', 23 May 2006. Online, available at: www.eu2006.at/en/News/CFSP_Statements/May/2305montenegro1.html.
Council (2007a) 'Council conclusions concerning the negotiation of a new enhanced agreement between the EU and Ukraine', 22 January 2007. Online, available at: www.eu2007.de/en/News/download_docs/Januar/0122AASteinmeier/Council_Conclusions_on_Ukraine.pdf.
Council (2007b) 'External Relations Council conclusions on the Middle East peace process', 24 July 2007. Online, available at: www.consilium.europa.eu/cms3_applications/applications/search/pics/doc.gif.
Council (2007c) 'External Relations Council conclusions on the Middle East peace process', 15 October 2007. Online, available at: www.consilium.europa.eu/ueDocs/cms_Data/docs/pressData/en/gena/96521.pdf.
Council (2007d) 'Strengthening the ENP – Council conclusions', 11016/07. Online, available at: http://register.consilium.europa.eu/pdf/en/07/st11/st11016.en07.pdf.
Council (2007e) External Relations Council conclusions on the Middle East', 16327/07 (presse 289), 10 December 2007. Online, available at: www.consilium.europa.eu/ueDocs/newsWord/en/gena/98412.doc.
Council (2007f) 'EU Presidency statement – CFE Treaty', 12 December 2007. Online, available at: www.eu2007.pt/UE/vEN/Noticias_Documentos/Declaracoes_PESC/20071212CFE.htm.

Council (2007g) 'Presidency declaration on "presidential elections" in Nagorno-Karabakh on 17 July 2007', 17 July 2007. Online, available at: www.eu2007.pt/UE/vEN/Noticias_Documentos/Declaracoes_PESC/20070719PESCNAG.htm.

Council (2007h) 'EU Presidency statement on the parliamentary elections in Armenia', 13 May 2007. Online, available at: www.eu2007.de/en/News/CFSP_Statements/May/0513Armenien.html.

Council (2008a) 'External Relations Council conclusions on the European Neighbourhood Policy', 18 February 2008. Online, available at: http://consilium.europa.eu/ueDocs/newsWord/en/gena/98790.doc.

Council (2008b) 'Presidency declaration on Belarus', 28 March 2008. Online, available at: www.eu2008.si/en/News_and_Documents/CFSP_Statements/March/0328MZZ_Belorusija.html.

Council (2008c) 'Presidency declaration on the situation after the presidential elections in Armenia', 4 March 2008. Online, available at: www.eu2008.si/en/News_and_Documents/CFSP_Statements/March/0403MZZ_Armenia.html.

Council (2008d) 'EU Presidency declaration on Georgia', 18 April 2008. Online, available at: www.eu2008.si/en/News_and_Documents/CFSP_Statements/April/0418MZZ_Gruzija.html.

Council (2008e) 'EU External Relations Council conclusions on Georgia', 26 May 2008. Online, available at: www.consilium.europa.eu/ueDocs/newsWord/en/gena/100674.doc.

Council (2008f) 'EU External Relations Council conclusions on Georgia', 16 September 2008. Online, available at: www.consilium.europa.eu/ueDocs/newsWord/en/gena/102749.doc.

Council (2008g) 'Council conclusions on relations with the republic of Moldova', 18 February 2008. Online, available at: www.consilium.europa.eu/ueDocs/newsWord/en/gena/98782.doc.

Council (2008h) 'Council conclusions on the Republic of Moldova', 13 October 2008. Online, available at: www.consilium.europa.eu/ueDocs/newsWord/en/gena/103287.doc.

Council (2008i) 'Council conclusions on Belarus', 13 October 2008. Online, available at: www.consilium.europa.eu/ueDocs/newsWord/en/gena/103299.doc.

Council (2008j) 'EU–Armenia Cooperation Council – ninth meeting', 17026/08 (presse 366), 9 December 2008.

Council (2008k) 'EU–Georgia Cooperation Council – ninth meeting', 17030/08 (presse 368), 9 December 2008.

Council (2008l) 'External Relations Council conclusions on the Middle East peace process', 28 January 2008. Online, available at: www.consilium.europa.eu/ueDocs/newsWord/en/gena/98412.doc.

Council (2008m) 'EU Presidency declaration on the Middle East', 7648/08 (presse 72), 14 March 2008. Online, available at: www.consilium.europa.eu/ueDocs/newsWord/en/cfsp/99437.doc.

Council (2008n) 'EU–Algeria Association Council', 10 March 2008.

Council (2008o) 'External Affairs Council conclusions on the Middle East', 9868/08 (presse 141), 26 May 2008. Online, available at: www.consilium.europa.eu/ueDocs/newsWord/en/gena/100674.doc.

Council (2008p) 'EU Justice and Home Affairs Council conclusions on Libya – framework agreement', 11653/08 (presse 205), 25 July 2008. Online, available at: www.consilium.europa.eu/ueDocs/cms_Data/docs/pressData/en/jha/102007.pdf.

Council (2008q) 'The European Union and Morocco strengthen their partnership', press release 08/1488, 13 October 2008. Online, available at: http://europa.eu/rapid/press ReleasesAction.do?reference=IP/08/1488&format=HTML&aged=0&language=EN&guiLanguage=en.

Council (2008r) 'Extraordinary meeting of the EU General Affairs and External Relations Council', 12453/08 (presse 236), 13 August 2008. Online, available at: www.consilium.europa.eu/ueDocs/newsWord/en/gena/102338.doc.

Council (2008s) 'Implementation of the plan of 12 August 2008', presidency press release, 13 August 2008. Online, available at: www.ue2008.fr/webdav/site/PFUE/shared/import/0908_visites_moscou_tbilissi/Implementation_of_the_plan_of_12_August_2008.pd.

Council (2008t) 'EU presidency statement on remarks by President Medvedev to the Russian Federal Assembly', 7 November 2008. Online, available at: www.ue2008.fr/PFUE/lang/en/accueil/PFUE-11_2008/PFUE-07.11.2008/PESC_Russie%20.

Council (2008u) 'Council conclusions on preparation for the EU–Russia summit', 15396/08 (presse 319), 11 November 2008. Online, available at: www.consilium.europa.eu/ueDocs/newsWord/en/gena/104048.doc.

Council (2008v) 'Presidency press release on EU–Russia Summit', 14 November 2008. Online, available at: www.ue2008.fr/PFUE/lang/en/accueil/PFUE-11_2008/PFUE-14.11.2008/CR_Sommet_UE_Russie.

Council (2008w) 'Strengthening of the European Union's bilateral relations with its Mediterranean partners', Council conclusions 16863/08 (presse 360), 9 December 2008. Online, available at: www.consilium.europa.eu/ueDocs/cms_Data/docs/pressData/en/gena/104616.pdf.

Council (2009) 'Sanctions or restrictive measures in force'. Online, available at: http://ec.europa.eu/external_relations/cfsp/sanctions/measures.htm.

Cyril (2006) 'Statement by Metropolit Cyril of Smolensk and Kaliningrad', Brussels, 15 June 2006, reprinted in *European Neighbourhood Watch* issue 18, Brussels: CEPS.

Denisov, Andrey (2003) 'Address by Andrey Denisov at Minister's Plenary Session, Baltic Development Forum', 16 October 2003. Online, available at: www.ln.mid.ru/Brp_4.nsf/arh/C3FF47E9D99D382143256DBA003E9335?OpenDocument.

EC Delegation in Armenia (2008) 'Joint statement by President of the European Commission, José Manuel BARROSO, and President of the Republic of Armenia, Serzh Sargsyan', Yerevan, 7 November 2008. Online, available at: www.delarm.ec.europa.eu/en/press/07_11_2008.htm.

Eizenstat, Stuart (1999) 'The future of our economic partnership with Europe', testimony before the House International Relations Committee, 15 June 1999. Online, available at: http://usembassy-australia.state.gov/hyper/WF990615/epf206.htm.

Eurobarometer (2006) 'Special Eurobarometer 259 – the European Union and its neighbours', October 2006.

Eurobarometer (2007) 'Special Eurobarometer 285 – the EU's relations with its neighbours', November 2007.

Eurobarometer (2008) 'Standard Eurobarometer 69, section 1: values of Europeans', November 2008. Online, available at: http://ec.europa.eu/public_opinion/archives/eb/eb69/eb69_en.htm.

European Council (2003) 'European Security Strategy: a secure Europe in a better world', 12 December 2003. Online, available at: www.consilium.europa.eu/uedocs/cmsUpload/78367.pdf.

European Council (2006) 'Declaration on Belarus', 23–24 March 2006. Online, available at: www.eu2006.at/en/News/Council_Conclusions/2403EuropanCouncil.pdf.

European Council (2008a) 'Presidency conclusions', 7652/08, 14 March 2008. Online, available at: www.eu2008.si/en/News_and_Documents/Council_Conclusions/March/0314ECpresidency_conclusions.pdf.
European Council (2008b) 'Presidency conclusions', 20 June 2008. Online, available at: www.eu2008.si/en/News_and_Documents/Council_Conclusions/June/0619_EC-CON.pdf.
European Council (2008c) 'Extraordinary European Council on the conflict in Georgia', 1 September 2008. Online, available at: www.consilium.europa.eu/ueDocs/newsWord/en/ec/102545.doc.
European Parliament (2003) 'Report on "Wider Europe – neighbourhood: a new framework for relations with our eastern and southern neighbours"', A5–0378/2003 final, 5 November 2003. Online, available at: www.europarl.europa.eu/sides/getDoc.do?language=EN&objRefId=31192.
European Parliament (2005) 'Report on the European Neighbourhood Policy', A6–0399/2005 final, 7 December 2005. Online, available at: www.europarl.europa.eu/sides/getDoc.do?objRefId=106027&language=EN.
European Parliament (2006a) 'Resolution on the parliamentary elections in Ukraine', 6 April 2006. Online, available at: www.europarl.europa.eu/sides/getDoc.do?pubRef=-//EP//TEXT+TA+P6-TA-2006–0138+0+DOC+XML+V0//EN.
European Parliament (2006b) 'Resolution on the situation in South Ossetia', 26 October 2006. Online, available at: www.europarl.europa.eu/sides/getDoc.do?pubRef=-//EP//TEXT+TA+P6-TA-2006–0456+0+DOC+XML+V0//EN&language=EN.
European Parliament (2006c) 'Resolution on the EU–Russia Summit held in Sochi on 25 May 2006'. Online, available at: www.europarl.europa.eu/sides/getDoc.do;jsessionid=8147F8FE6B346135B7CEFC8B6EF3E53D.node1?language=EN&pubRef=-//EP//TEXT+TA+P6-TA-2006–0270+0+DOC+XML+V0//EN.
European Parliament (2007a) 'Resolution on strengthening the European Neighbourhood Policy', 15 November 2007. Online, available at: www.europarl.europa.eu/sides/getDoc.do?pubRef=-//EP//TEXT+TA+P6-TA-2007–0538+0+DOC+XML+V0//EN&language=EN.
European Parliament (2007b) 'Recommendation for negotiation mandate for a new EU–Ukraine enhanced agreement', 12 July 2007. Online, available at: www.europarl.europa.eu/sides/getDoc.do?Type=TA&Reference=P6-TA-2007–0355&language=EN.
European Parliament (2008a) 'Resolution on the situation in Egypt', 28 January 2008. Online, available at: www.europarl.europa.eu/sides/getDoc.do?pubRef=-//EP//TEXT+TA+P6-TA-2008–0023+0+DOC+XML+V0//EN&language=EN.
EU–Russia Summit (2001) 'Joint statement on international terrorism', 3 October 2001. Online, available at: www.eur.ru/eng/neweur/summits/sum41.doc.
EU–Russia Summit (2006) 'Declaration of the 17th EU–Russia Summit', Sochi, 25 May 2006–. Online, available at: www.eu2006.at/en/News/Press_Releases/May/2505Sochi.html.
EU–Russia Summit (2008) 'Joint statement of the EU–Russia summit on the launch of negotiations for a new EU–Russia agreement', 11214/08 (presse 192), 27 June 2008. Online, available at: www.eu2008.si/en/News_and_Documents/download_docs/June/0627_eu_RUS-izjava.pdf.
EU–Ukraine Summit (2005) 'Joint statement', PRES/05/337, 1 December 2005. Online, available at: http://europa.eu/rapid/pressReleasesAction.do?reference=PRES/05/337&format=HTML&aged=0&language=EN&guiLanguage=en.

EU–Ukraine Summit (2006) 'Joint press statement', 27 October 2006. Online, available at: www.eu2006.fi/news_and_documents/press_releases/vko43/en_GB/1161940819448/.

EU–Ukraine Summit (2007) 'Joint press statement', 14 September 2007. Online, available at: www.eu2007.pt/UE/vEN/Noticias_Documentos/20070914UKRAINE.htm

EU–US Summit (2008) '2008 EU–US Summit declaration', 10562/08 (presse 168), 10 June 2008.

Ferrero-Waldner, Benita (2005a) 'Europe's neighbours – towards closer integration', speech, 22 April 2005. Online, available at: http://ec.europa.eu/external_relations/news/ferrero/2005/sp05_253.htm.

Ferrero-Waldner, Benita (2005b) 'The European Neighbourhood Policy: helping ourselves through helping our neighbours', speech, 31 October 2005. Online, available at: http://ec.europa.eu/external_relations/news/ferrero/2005/sp05_31-10-05.htm.

Ferrero-Waldner, Benita (2005c) 'Quo vadis Europa?', speech, 14 December 2005. Online, available at: http://europa.eu/rapid/pressReleasesAction.do?reference=SPEECH/05/797&format=HTML&aged=0&language=EN&guiLanguage=en.

Ferrero-Waldner, Benita (2006a) 'European strategies for promoting democracy in post-Communist countries', speech, 20 January 2006. Online, available at: http://europa.eu/rapid/pressReleasesAction.do?reference=SPEECH/06/35&format=HTML&aged=0&language=EN&guiLanguage=en.

Ferrero-Waldner, Benita (2006b) 'The essential role of community conditionality in the triumph of democracy and market economy', speech, 21 January 2006. Online, available at: http://europa.eu/rapid/pressReleasesAction.do?reference=SPEECH/06/27&format=HTML&aged=0&language=EN&guiLanguage=en.

Ferrero-Waldner, Benita (2006c) 'Migration, external relations and the European Neighbourhood Policy', speech, 24 January 2006. Online, available at: http://europa.eu/rapid/pressReleasesAction.do?reference=SPEECH/06/30&type=HTML&aged=0&language=EN&guiLanguage=en.

Ferrero-Waldner, Benita (2006d) 'The EU in the world', speech, 2 February 2006. Online, available at: http://europa.eu/rapid/pressReleasesAction.do?reference=SPEECH/06/59&format=HTML&aged=0&language=EN&guiLanguage=en.

Ferrero-Waldner, Benita (2006e) 'European Neighbourhood Policy', speech, 7 March 2006. Online, available at: http://europa.eu/rapid/pressReleasesAction.do?reference=SPEECH/06/149&format=HTML&aged=0&language=EN&guiLanguage=en.

Ferrero-Waldner, Benita (2006f) 'Clash of civilisations or dialogue of cultures: building bridges across the Mediterranean', speech, 6 June 2006. Online, available at: http://europa.eu/rapid/pressReleasesAction.do?reference=SPEECH/06/279&format=HTML&aged=0&language=EN&guiLanguage=en.

Ferrero-Waldner, Benita (2006g) 'The EU, the Mediterranean and the Middle East: a partnership for reform', speech, 2 February 2006. Online, available at: http://europa.eu/rapid/pressReleasesAction.do?reference=SPEECH/06/341&type=HTML&aged=0&language=EN&guiLanguage=en.

Ferrero-Waldner, Benita (2006h) 'The European Neighbourhood Policy: bringing our neighbours closer', speech, 6 June 2006. Online, available at: http://europa.eu/rapid/pressReleasesAction.do?reference=SPEECH/06/346&format=HTML&aged=0&language=EN&guiLanguage=en.

Ferrero-Waldner, Benita (2006i) 'Political reform and sustainable development in the South Caucasus: the EU's approach', speech, 28 August 2006. Online, available at: http://europa.eu/rapid/pressReleasesAction.do?reference=SPEECH/06/477&format=HTML&aged=0&language=EN&guiLanguage=en.

Ferrero-Waldner, Benita (2006j) 'Opening address: towards an EU external energy policy to assure a high level of supply security', speech, 20 November 2006. Online, available at: http://europa.eu/rapid/pressReleasesAction.do?reference=SPEECH/06/710&format=HTML&aged=0&language=EN.

Ferrero-Waldner, Benita (2006k) 'Democracy promotion: the European way', speech, 17 December 2006. Online, available at: http://europa.eu/rapid/pressReleasesAction.do?reference=SPEECH/06/790&format=HTML&aged=0&language=EN.

Ferrero-Waldner, Benita (2006l) '"Frozen conflicts": Transnistria, South Ossetia, and the Russian–Georgian Dispute', Speech/06/629, 25 October 2006. Online, available at: http://europa.eu/rapid/pressReleasesAction.do?reference=SPEECH/06/629&format=HTML&aged=0&language=EN&guiLanguage=en.

Ferrero-Waldner, Benita (2006m) 'EU–Syria Association Agreement', Speech/06/630, 25 October 2006. Online, available at: http://europa.eu/rapid/pressReleasesAction.do?reference=SPEECH/06/630&format=HTML&aged=0&language=EN.

Ferrero-Waldner, Benita (2006n) 'Statement on the situation in the Middle East', Speech/06/483, 6 September 2006. Online, available at: http://europa.eu/rapid/pressReleasesAction.do?reference=SPEECH/06/483&format=HTML&aged=0&language=EN.

Ferrero-Waldner, Benita (2006o) 'Egypt–European Union relations in the age of reform', Speech/06/281, 7 May 2006. Online, available at: http://europa.eu/rapid/pressReleasesAction.do?reference=SPEECH/06/281&format=HTML&aged=0&language=EN.

Ferrero-Waldner, Benita (2006p) 'Statement on EU–Russia summit of 24 November 2006', Speech/06/758, 29 November 2006. Online, available at: http://europa.eu/rapid/pressReleasesAction.do?reference=SPEECH/06/758&format=HTML&aged=0&language=EN&guiLanguage=en.

Ferrero-Waldner, Benita (2007a) 'The Middle East in the EU's external relations', speech, 11 January 2007. Online, available at: http://europa.eu/rapid/pressReleasesAction.do?reference=SPEECH/07/7&format=HTML&aged=0&language=EN.

Ferrero-Waldner, Benita (2007b) 'Opening speech: European Neighbourhood Policy conference', speech, 3 September 2007. Online, available at: http://europa.eu/rapid/pressReleasesAction.do?reference=SPEECH/07/500&format=HTML&aged=0&language=EN&guiLanguage=en.

Ferrero-Waldner, Benita (2007c) 'Bilateral relations between Israel and the European Union', speech/07/108, 27 February 2007. Online, available at: http://europa.eu/rapid/pressReleasesAction.do?reference=SPEECH/07/108&format=HTML&aged=0&language=EN.

Ferrero-Waldner, Benita (2008a) 'Signature of an EU–Belarus Memorandum of Understanding on the establishment of an EC Delegation in Minsk', 3 March 2008. Online, available at: www.delblr.ec.europa.eu/page2328.html?id=4710.

Ferrero-Waldner, Benita (2008b) 'EU/Russia Summit preparation', speech at the European Parliament, Speech/08/344, 18 June 2008. Online, available at: http://europa.eu/rapid/pressReleasesAction.do?reference=SPEECH/08/344&type=HTML&aged=0&language=EN&guiLanguage=en.

Ferrero-Waldner, Benita (2008c) 'EU/Russia: a challenging partnership, but one of the most important of our times', speech at the EP Plenary Debate on EU/Russia, Speech/08/545, 21 October 2008.

Financial Times (2006a) 'Harris Interactive Poll on Russia', perceived by the public in France, Germany, Great Britain, Italy, and Spain, conducted 6–12 July 2006.

Financial Times (2006b) 'Interview with Vladimir Putin', Novo-Ogaryovo, 9 September 2006.

Freedom House (2008) *Freedom in the World 2008*, Washington, DC: Freedom House. Online, available at: available at www.freedomhouse.org/template.cfm?page=363&year=2008.

Group of Seven (2008) 'Statement on Georgia of G7 foreign ministers', 27 August 2008. Online, available at: www.ceps.eu/files/NW/Canada, France, Germany, Italy, Japan, the United States and the United Kingdom.

GUAM (2006) 'Kyiv declaration on the establishment of the Organization for Democracy and Economic Development – GUAM', 23 May 2006. Online, available at: www.guam.org.ua/en/node/468.

Israel Ministry of Foreign Affairs (2008a) 'The European Union upgrades its relations with Israel', 18 June 2008. Online, available at: www.mfa.gov.il/MFA/About+the+Ministry/MFA+Spokesman/2008/.

Israel Ministry of Foreign Affairs (2008b) 'EU ministers vote to upgrade diplomatic dialogue with Israel', 19 December 2008. Online, available at: www.mfa.gov.il/MFA/About+the+Ministry/MFA+Spokesman/2008/.

Israel Ministry of Foreign Affairs (2009) 'Joint press conference with FM Livni and EU representatives', 5 January 2009. Online, available at: www.mfa.gov.il/MFA/Governemnt/Speeches+by+Israeli +leaders/2009/.

Ivanov, Igor (2003a) 'Speech by Russian Minister of Foreign Affairs Igor Ivanov at the twelfth ministerial session of the Council of the Baltic Sea States', Pori, 11 June 2003. Online, available at: www.ln.mid.ru/Brp_4.nsf/arh/41EEE2C6596354AB43256D42005864EF?OpenDocument.

Ivanov, Igor (2003b) 'Article by Russian Foreign Minister Igor Ivanov published by the newspaper Izvestia under the title "association or dissociation? will new barriers appear in a united Europe?"', 11 January 2003. Online, available at: www.ln.mid.ru/Brp_4.nsf/arh/439168B181D7F9D443256CAD0046BA9C?OpenDocument.

Ivanov, Igor (2003c) 'Replies by Russian Minister of Foreign Affairs Igor Ivanov to questions from the Greek newspaper Katimerini', 24 January 2003.

Ivanov, Sergei (2006) 'The new Russian doctrine', *Wall Street Journal Europe*, 11 January 2006.

Juncker, Jean-Claude (2005) 'Remarks by President Juncker', 20 June 2005. Online, available at: http://useu.umission.gov/Article.asp?ID=155A6D29-0926-4CFA-80FF-67CF31BC6.

Landaburu, Eneko (2006) 'From neighbourhood to integration policy: are there concrete alternatives to enlargement?', speech, 23 January 2006. Online, available at: http://ec.europa.eu/world/enp/pdf/060223_el_ceps_en.pdf.

Mammadyarov, Elmar (2007) 'Speech at the ENP conference on "working together – strengthening the European neighbourhood"', 3 September 2007. Online, available at: http://ec.europa.eu/world/enp/pdf/conference2007/enp_conference_azerbaijan_en.pdf.

Mandelsohn, Peter (2007) 'The EU and Russia: our joint political challenge', speech, 20 April 2007. Online, available at: http://ec.europa.eu/commission_barroso/mandelson/speeches_articles/sppm147_en.htm.

Medvedev, Dmitry (2008a) 'Speech at the meeting with German political, parliamentary and civic leaders', 5 June 2008. Online, available at: www.kremlin.ru/eng/speeches/2008/06/05/2203_type82912type82914type84779_202153.shtml.

Medvedev, Dmitry (2008b) 'Press statement by Russian President Dmitry Medvedev following the EU–Russia Summit', 27 June 2008. Online, available at: www.kremlin.ru/eng/text/speeches/2008/06/27/2114_type82914type82915_203194.shtml.

Medvedev, Dmitry (2008c) 'Speech at the World Policy Conference on a new European security treaty', 8 October 2008. Online, available at: www.kremlin.ru/eng/speeches/2008/10/08/2159_type82912type82914_207457.shtml.

Medvedev, Dmitry (2008d) 'Address to the Federal Assembly of the Russian Federation', 5 November 2008. Online, available at: www.kremlin.ru/eng/speeches/2008/11/05/2144_type70029type82917type127286_208836.shtml.

Medvedev, Dmitry (2008e) 'President Medvedev's statement after the 22 Russia–EU Summit', 14 November 2008. Online, available at: www.kremlin.ru/eng/speeches/2008/11/14/2126_type82914type82915_209207.shtml.

Merkel, Angela (2007a) 'Speech at the convention for Germany', 5 December 2007, unofficial translation reprinted in *European Neighbourhood Watch* issue 31, Brussels: CEPS. Online, available at: www.ceps.be.

Merkel, Angela (2007b) 'Joint press conference following the Russia–European Union Summit meeting, Samara, Russia', 18 May 2007. Online, available at: www.kremlin.ru/eng/speeches/2007/05/18/2256_type82914type82915_129617.shtml.

Ministry of Foreign Affairs of Georgia (2006a) 'National security concept of Georgia'. Online, available at: http://mfa.gov.ge/print.php?gg=1&sec_id=24&info_id=37&lang_id=ENG.

Ministry of Foreign Affairs of Georgia (2006b) 'Ethnic targeting and deportations continue across the Russian Federation', non-paper, 8 December 2006, reprinted in *European Neighbourhood Watch* issue 22, Brussels: CEPS.

Ministry of Foreign Affairs of Georgia (2007) 'Chairman's summary of the meeting of the foreign ministers of 'new group of friends of Georgia', 14 September 2007. Online, available at: www.mfa.gov.ge/index.php?lang_id=ENG&sec_id=459&info_id=5073%20.

Ministry of Foreign Affairs of Georgia (2008a) 'Statement on the Russian Federation's withdrawal from the 19 January 1996 decision of the CIS Council of the Heads of State on "measures aimed at settling the conflict in Abkhazia"', Georgia, 7 March 2008. Online, available at: http://embassy.mfa.gov.ge/index.php?lang_id=ENG&sec_id=972&info_id=4479.

Ministry of Foreign Affairs of Georgia (2008b) 'Statement on the Russian President's instructions with regard to Abkhazia and South Ossetia', press release 17 April 2008, reprinted in *European Neighbourhood Watch* issue 37, Brussels: CEPS.

Ministry of Foreign Affairs of Georgia (2008c) 'Statement on EU conclusions on EU–Russia Relations', 11 November 2008, reprinted in *European Neighbourhood Watch* issue 43, Brussels: CEPS.

Ministry of Foreign Affairs of Russia (2000) 'The medium-term strategy for development of relations between the Russian Federation and the European Union 2000–2010'. Online, available at: www.eur.ru/eng/neweur/user_eng.php?func=apage&id=53.

Ministry of Foreign Affairs of Russia (2003) 'Interview with Russian President Vladimir Putin, granted to Bulgarian national television and the newspaper Trud', 27 February 2003.

Ministry of Foreign Affairs of Russia (2007) 'Statement regarding suspension by Russian Federation of the CFE Treaty', 12 December 2007. Online, available at: www.mid.ru/brp_4.nsf/e78a48070f128a7b43256999005bcbb3/10da6dd509e4d164c32573af004cc4be?OpenDocument.

Ministry of Foreign Affairs of Russia (2008a) 'The Russian President's instructions to the Russian Federation Government with regard to Abkhazia and South Ossetia', press release 16 April 2008. Online, available at: www.mid.ru/brp_4.nsf/e78a48070f128a7b-43256999005bcbb3/b75734bac2796efbc325742d005a6f7c?OpenDocument.

Ministry of Foreign Affairs of Russia (2008b) 'Commentary on G7 statement', 29 August 2008. Online, available at: www.mid.ru/brp_4.nsf/e78a48070f128a7b43256999005bcbb3/d296c73b1bd9c4c5c32574b4004bb07d?OpenDocument.

Ministry of Foreign Affairs of Ukraine (2006) 'Statement of the presidents of Lithuania, Poland and Ukraine', 5 October 2006. Online, available at: www.mfa.gov.ua/mfa/en/publication/content/7022.htm.

Mubarak, Hosny (2005) 'Address by H.E. President Mohammed Hosny Mubarak to the plenary session of the Euro-Mediterranean Summit', 28 November 2005.

NATO (2007) 'Statement on the Russian Federation's "suspension" of its CFE obligations', 12 December 2007. Online, available at: www.nato.int/docu/pr/2007/p07–139e.html.

NATO (2008a) 'Meeting of the North Atlantic Council', 19 August 2008. Online, available at: www.nato.int/docu/pr/2008/p08–104e.html.

NATO (2008b) 'Statement by the North Atlantic Council on the Russian recognition of South Ossetia and Abkhazia regions of Georgia', 27 August 2008. Online, available at: www.nato.int/docu/pr/2008/p08–108e.html.

Office of the Prime Minister of Egypt (2007) 'PM probes activation of Egypt's ENP Action Plan', 18 March 2007. Online, available at: www.egyptiancabinet.gov.eg/News/News_Details.asp.

OSCE (2006) 'Preliminary conclusions of the international election observation mission in Ukraine', 26 March 2006. Online, available at: www.osce.org/documents/odihr/2006/03.

Patten, Chris and Solana, Javier (2002) 'Wider Europe', letter to the Council, 7 August 2002. Online, available at: http://ec.europa.eu/world/enp/pdf/_0130163334_001_en.pdf.

PPC (2006) 'Declaration of the Permanent Partnership Council (PPC) on freedom, security and justice cooperation', 22 March 2006. Online, available at: www.eu2006.at/includes/Download_Dokumente/Background_Information/EU-Russia_PPC_declaration_English.pdf

Prodi, Romano (2002) 'A Wider Europe – a proximity policy as the key to stability', speech, 6 December 2002. Online, available at: http://europa.eu/rapid/pressReleasesAction.do?reference=SPEECH/02/619&format=HTML&aged=0&language=EN&guiLanguage=en.

Public Opinion Poll Center of Egypt (2006) 'An opinion poll measuring citizens' attitudes towards different countries'. Online, available at: www.pollcenter.gov.eg/view_poll details.aspx?ws_poll_id=1022.

Putin, Vladimir (2006a) 'Remarks at the informal meeting of EU heads of state or government', 21 October 2006. Online, available at: www.eu2006.fi/news_and_documents/other_documents/vko42/en_GB/1161383205709.

Putin, Vladimir (2006b) 'Europe has nothing to fear from Russia', *Financial Times*, 21 November 2006. Online, available at: www.ft.com/cms/s/ddc234d6–7994–11db-90a6–0000779e2340.html.

Putin, Vladimir (2007a) 'President Putin's annual press conference with the Russian and foreign media', 1 February 2007, reprinted in *European Neighbourhood Watch* issue 24, Brussels: CEPS.

Putin, Vladimir (2007b) '50 Years of the European integration and Russia', *Sunday Times, Frankfurter Allgemeine Sonntagszeitung, Le Monde*, 25 March 2007, reprinted in *European Neighbourhood Watch* issue 25, Brussels: CEPS.

Putin, Vladimir (2007c) 'Joint press conference following the Russia–European Union Summit meeting, Samara, Russia, 18 May 2007. Online, available at: www.kremlin.ru/eng/speeches/2007/05/18/2256_type82914type82915_129617.shtml.

Putin, Vladimir (2007d) 'Press statement and answers to questions following the 20th Russia–European Union Summit', Mafra, Portugal, 27 October 2007. Online, available at: www.kremlin.ru/eng/speeches/2007/10/26/1918_type82914type82915_149706.shtml.

Putin, Vladimir (2008a) 'Press statement following Russian–Serbian talks, 25 January 2008. Online, available at: www.kremlin.ru/eng/speeches/2008/01/25/1330_type-82914type82915_158129.shtml.

Rice, Condoleezza (2008) 'Transatlantic unity on Russia', article in multiple European newspapers, 29 September 2008. Online, available at: http://useu.usmission.gov/Article.asp?ID=A75B2367.

Saakashvili, Mikheil (2007) 'Address to the nation', 8 November 2007. Online, available at: www.president.gov.ge/?l=E&m=0&sm=3&st=0&id=2394.

Saakashvili, Mikheil (2008a) 'Remarks to the Parliamentary Assembly of the Council of Europe', Strasbourg, 24 January 2008. Online, available at: www.presdient.giv.ge/print_txt.php?id=2495&l=E.

Saakashvili, Mikheil (2008b) 'The president of Georgia Mikheil Saakashvili addressed Georgian population in front of the parliament building together with the European leaders', 12 August 2008. Online, available at: http://president.gov.ge/print_txt.php?id=2707&l=E.

Saakashvili, Mikheil (2008c) 'The President of Georgia Mikheil Saakashvili's annual speech presented in the Parliament of Georgia', 16 September 2008. Online, available at: www.president.gov.ge/print_txt.php?id=2740&l=E.

Sargsyan, Serzh (2008) 'Address by President Serzh Sargsyan on the occasion of the 17th anniversary of independence'. Online, available at: www.president.am/addons/tasks/print/?sub=statements&id=16.

Sarkozy, Nicolas (2007) 'Speech on the Mediterranean Union', Tangier, 23 October 2007, unofficial translation reprinted in *European Neighbourhood Watch* issue 31, Brussels: CEPS. Online, available at: www.ceps.be.

Schnabel, Rockwell (2002) 'U.S.–EU relations: drift or common destiny', remarks at the American Hellenic Chamber of Commerce, 15 October 2002. Online, available at: www.state.gov/p/eur/rls/rm/2002/14755pf.htm.

Schnabel, Rockwell (2003) 'Making the U.S.–EU partnership work better', address to the Cercle Royal Gaulois, 16 January 2003. Online, available at: www.state.gov/p/eur/rls/rm/2003/16681pf.htm.

Tblisi Declaration (2007) '"The Tblisi Declaration" on common vision for regional cooperation', 7 February 2007. Online, available at: www.president.gov.ge/print_txt.php?id=2133&l=E.

Transatlantic Trends (2003) *Transatlantic Trends 2003*, German Marshall Fund of the United States. Online, available at: www.transatlantictrends.org.

Transatlantic Trends (2008) *Transatlantic Trends 2003: Key Findings*, German Marshall Fund of the United States. Online, available at: www.transatlantictrends.org.

UNDP (2005) *Arab Human Development Report*, New York: United Nations Development Programme. Online, available at: http://arabstates.undp.org/subpage.php?spid=14.

United States Mission to the European Union (2008) 'Trans-Atlantic unity stabilizing situation in Georgia', 25 September 2008. Online, available at: http://useu.usmission.gov/Article.asp?ID=98592795.

United States Mission to the European Union (2009a) 'Transatlantic relations: the U.S.–EU partnership'. Online, available at: http://useu.usmission.gov/Dossiers/TransAtlantic/default.asp#summits.

United States Mission to the European Union (2009b) 'Remarks by Secretary Clinton, British Foreign Secretary Miliband', 3 February 2009. Online, available at: http://useu.usmission.gov/Article.asp?ID=4A06EC81.

Verheugen, Günter (2003) 'EU enlargement and the Union's neighbourhood policy', speech, 27 October 2003. Online, available at: http://ec.europa.eu/world/enp/pdf/verheugen-russia-eu_enlargement_and_the_union_en.pdf.

Verheugen, Günter (2004) 'Towards a Wider Europe: the new agenda', speech, 19 March 2004. Online, available at: http://europa.eu/rapid/pressReleasesAction.do?reference=SPEECH/04/141&format=HTML&aged=0&language=EN&guiLanguage=en.

Vershbow, A. (2002) 'European defense: European and American perceptions', speech, 18 May 2000, reprinted in Sidabras, V.A., Peterson, K.E. and Fahraeus, A.W.E., *Baltic Brief 2000: A Collection of U.S. Speeches and Statements on Northern Europe and Russia*, Stockholm: Embassy of the United States of America.

Volker, Kurt (2006) 'The United States and the European Union: a renewed partnership delivering results', 11 May 2006. Online, available at: http://useu.usmission.gov/Dossiers/TransAtlantic/May110g_Volker_Partnership.

Wayne, E.A. (1999) 'U.S. perspectives on the European Union', speech, 8 November 1999, reprinted in Sidabras, V.A, Peterson, K.E. and Fahraeus, A.W.E., *Baltic Brief 2000: A Collection of U.S. Speeches and Statements on Northern Europe and Russia*, Stockholm: Embassy of the United States of America, 2000.

Wayne, E.A. (2002) 'The U.S. and the EU today: trade and economic issues in the trans-Atlantic relationship', remarks in Athens, 9 December 2002. Online, available at: www.state.gov/e/eb/rls/rm/2002/16079pf.htm.

World Bank (2008) 'International donor conference', press release, 23 October 2008. Online, available at: http://web.worldbank.org/WBSITE/EXTERNAL/NEWS/0,,contentMDK:21949175~menuPK:34463~pagePK:34370~piPK:34424~theSitePK:4607,00.html.

Yanukovych, Viktor (2006a) 'Speech at the Verkhovna Rada of Ukraine', 5 September 2006. Online, available at: www.ya2008.com.ua/eng/press-center/news/44fd2b468dfa1/.

Yanukovych, Viktor (2006b) 'Ukraine's choice: toward Europe', 5 October 2006. Online, available at: www.ya2008.com.ua/eng/press-center/digest/4524d5f40f5e1/.

Books, articles and other secondary sources

Adler, E. (1997) 'Imagined (security) communities', *Millennium* vol. 26, no. 2, pp. 249–277.

Adler, E. (2002) 'Constructivism and international relations' in Carlsnaes, W, Risse, T. and Simmons, B.A. (eds), *Handbook of International Relations*, London: SAGE.

Adler, E. and Barnett, M. (eds) (1998a) *Security Communities*, Cambridge: Cambridge University Press.

Adler, E. and Barnett, M. (1998b) 'A framework for the study of security communities' in Adler, E. and Barnett, M. (eds), *Security Communities*, Cambridge: Cambridge University Press.

Adler, E. and Crawford, B. (2006) 'Normative power: the European practice of region-building and the case of the Euro-Mediterranean partnership' in Adler, E., Bicchi, F., Crawford, B. and Sarto, R.A. del (eds), *The Convergence of Civilizations: Constructing a Mediterranean Region*, Toronto: University of Toronto Press.

Adler, E., Bicchi, F., Crawford, B. and Sarto, R.A. del (eds) (2006) *The Convergence of Civilizations: Constructing a Mediterranean Region*, Toronto: Toronto University Press.

Bibliography

Anderson, J. (2002) 'Borders after 11 September 2001', *Space and Polity* vol. 6, no. 2, pp. 227–232.

Arbatova, Nadia (2002) 'Persistent obstacles to mutual understanding: security paradoxes in the Baltic Sea region' in Knudsen, O.F. (ed.), *Cooperation or Competition? A Juxtaposition of Research Problems Regarding Security in the Baltic Sea Region*, Stockholm: Södertörn University College.

Ayoob, Mohammed (1999) 'From regional system to regional society: exploring key variables in the construction of regional order', *Australian Journal of International Affairs* vol. 53, no 3, pp. 247–260.

Baranovsky, Vladimir (2002) *Russia's Attitudes towards the EU: Political Aspects*, Helsinki and Bonn: Ulkopoliittinen instituutti and Institut für Europäische Politik.

Barnett, M. and Duvall, R. (eds) (2005) *Power in Global Governance*, Cambridge: Cambridge University Press.

Bellamy, A.J. (2004) *Security Communities and their Neighbours: Regional Fortresses or Global Integrators*, Houndmills: Palgrave Macmillan.

Benford, R.D. and Snow, D.A. (2000) 'Framing processes and social movements: an overview and assessment', *Annual Review of Sociology* vol. 26, pp. 611–639.

Bengtsson, R. (2000a) *Trust, Threat, and Stable Peace: Swedish Great Power Perceptions 1905–1939*, Doctoral dissertation, Lund: Department of Political Science.

Bengtsson, R (2000b) 'The cognitive discussion of stable peace' in Kacowicz, A.M., Bar-Siman-Tov, Y., Elgström, O. and Jerneck, Magnus (eds) *Stable Peace among Nations*, Lanham, MD: Rowman and Littlefield.

Bengtsson, R. (2004) *The EU as a Security Policy Actor: Russian and US Perceptions* (research report 36), Stockholm: Swedish Institute of International Affairs.

Bengtsson, Rikard (2008) 'Constructing interfaces: the neighbourhood discourse in EU external policy', *Journal of European Integration* vol. 30, no. 5.

Bengtsson, R. (2009a) 'Den internationella fredens anatomi [The anatomy of international peace]' in Jerneck, M. (ed.), *Fred i realpolitikens skugga [Peace in the Shadow of Power Politics]*, Lund: Studentlitteratur.

Bengtsson, R. (2009b) 'I den stabila fredens gränsland: EU: s utvidgning och den europeiska grannskapspolitiken [In the borderlands of stable peace: EU enlargement and the European Neighbourhood Policy]', in Jerneck, M. (ed.), *Fred i realpolitikens skugga [Peace in the Shadow of Power Politics]*, Lund: Studentlitteratur.

Bretherton, C. and Vogler, J. (2006) *The European Union as a Global Actor*, second edition, London: Routledge.

Buzan, B. (1991) *People, States and Fear: An Agenda for International Security Studies in the post-Cold War Era*, Hemel Hempstead: Harvester Wheatsheaf.

Buzan, B. and Wæver, O. (2003) *Regions and Powers: The Structure of International Security*, Cambridge: Cambridge University Press.

CEPS (2005a) Reprint of President Viktor Yushchenko's speech 'Ukraine's future is in the EU' in the European Parliament, 23 February 2005, *CEPS Neighbourhood Watch* issue 1, Brussels: CEPS, p. 1.

CEPS (2005b) Reprint of Deputy Prime Minister Oleg Rybachuk's speech 'Ukraine and the EU: how close? how soon?' at EPC, Brussels, 21 April 2005, *CEPS Neighbourhood Watch* issue 3, Brussels: CEPS, pp. 4–10.

CEPS (2006) *CEPS Neighbourhood Watch* issue 12, January 2006, Brussels: CEPS, pp. 2–6.

CEPS (2008a) 'Results of the national opinion poll conducted in Belarus on March 3–13, 2008', *European Neighbourhood Watch* issue 37, April 2008, Brussels: CEPS, p. 11.

Bibliography

CEPS (2008b) 'Polish–Swedish proposal: "Eastern partnership"', *European Neighbourhood Watch* issue 38, May 2008, Brussels: CEPS, pp. 6–7.

Christiansen, T., Jørgensen, K.E., and Wiener, A. (eds) (2001) *The Social Construction of Europe*, London: Sage.

Clark, E. and Petersson, B. (2003) 'Boundary dynamics and the construction of identities' in Petersson, B. and Clark, E. (eds), *Identity Dynamics and the Construction of Boundaries*, Lund: Nordic Academic Press.

Dagens Nyheter (2008) 'Vi vill närma oss EU [We want to get closer to the EU]', *Dagens Nyheter*, 22 November 2008. Online, available at: www.dn.se.

Dagens Nyheter (2009) 'Spänt lugn i Gaza', *Dagens Nyheter*, 19 January 2009. Online, available at: www.dn.se.

Delegation of the European Union to the USA (2009) 'EU focus', March 2009. Online, available at: www.eurunion.org/eufocus.

Deutsch K. (1957) *Political Community and the North Atlantic Area: International Organization in the Light of Historical Experience*, Princeton, NJ: Princeton University Press.

Die Welt (2007) 'Interview with Alexander Lukashenko', 25 January 2007, reprinted in *European Neighbourhood Watch* issue 23, January 2007, Brussels: CEPS, pp. 4–6.

El-Din Shahin, Emad (2005) 'Egypt's moment of reform: reality or an illusion?', *CEPS Policy Brief* no. 78, July 2005.

Emerson, Michael (2005) 'The Black Sea as epicentre of the after-shocks of the EU's earthquake', *CEPS Policy Brief* no. 79, July 2005.

EuroNews (2008) 'President Serzh Sargsyan's exclusive interview to EuroNews'. Online, available at: www.president.am/addons/tasks/print/?sub=press&id=17.

European Voice (2001) 'War and peace in the European borderlands', 20 December 2001, p. 8.

European Voice (2002) 'Time to face reality: Americans come from Mars, Europeans are from Venus', 27 June 2002, p. 22.

European Voice (2003) 'EU–US relations boosted by 'reinvigorating' summit ', 26 June 2003, p. 1.

Financial Times (2001) 'Intense suspicion gives way to support', survey on Russia, 9 April 2001, p. 3.

Ginsberg, R.H. (2001) *The European Union in International Politics: Baptism by Fire*, Lanham: Rowman and Littlefield.

Goh, Evelyn (2008) 'Great powers and hierarchical order in Southeast Asia: analyzing regional security strategies', *International Security* vol. 32, no 3, pp. 113–157.

Goodby, J., Buwalda, P. and Trenin, D. (2002) *A Strategy for Stable Peace: Towards a Euroatlantic Security Community*, Washington, DC: United States Institute of Peace Press.

Gourevitch, P (2002) 'Domestic politics and international relations' in Carlsnaes, W, Risse, T. and Simmons, B.A. (eds), *Handbook of International Relations*, London: SAGE.

Hassner, P. (2002) 'Fixed borders or moving borderlands?: a new type of border for a new type of entity', in J. Zielonka (ed.) *Europe Unbound: Enlarging and Reshaping the Boundaries of the European Union*, London: Routledge.

Herrmann, R. (2002) 'Linking theory to evidence in international relations' in Carlsnaes, W, Risse, T. and Simmons, B.A. (eds), *Handbook of International Relations*, London: SAGE.

Hill, C. (1993) 'The capability–expectations gap, or conceptualising Europe's international role', *Journal of Common Market Studies* vol. 31, no. 3, pp. 305–325.

Hollis, M. and Smith, S. (1991) *Explaining and Understanding International Relations*, Oxford: Clarendon Paperbacks.

Houtum, H. van and Strüver, A. (2002) 'Borders, strangers, doors and bridges', *Space and Polity* vol. 6, no. 2, pp. 141–146.
Hurrell, A. (2005) 'The regional dimension in international relations theory' in Farrell, M., Hettne, B. and van Langenhove, L., *Global Politics of Regionalism: Theory and Practice*, London: Pluto Press.
Hyde-Price, A. (2006) '"Normative" power Europe: a realist critique', *Journal of European Public Policy* vol. 13, no. 2, pp. 217–234.
International Herald Tribune (2007) 'Iran and Belarus forge "strategic partnership"', 21 May 2007. Online, available at: www.iht.com/articles/2007/05/21/europe/belarus.php%20.
Jepperson, R., Wendt, A. and Katzenstein, P. (1996) 'Norms, identity, and culture in national security', in Katzenstein, P. (ed.), *The Culture of National Security*, New York: Columbia University Press.
Kacowicz, A.M., Bar-Siman-Tov, Y., Elgström, O. and Jerneck, Magnus (eds) (2000) *Stable Peace among Nations*, Lanham, MD: Rowman and Littlefield.
Kagan, R. (2003) *Of Paradise and Power: America and Europe in the New World Order*, New York: Alfred Knopf.
Kelley, Judith (2006) 'New wine in old wineskins: promoting political reforms through the new European Neighbourhood Policy', *Journal of Common Market Studies* vol. 44, no. 1, pp. 29–55.
Kelsen, Hans (1941) 'Recognition in international law: theoretical observations', *American Journal of International Law* vol. 35, no. 4, pp. 605–617.
Kirchner, E.J. (2006) 'The challenge of European Union security governance', *Journal of Common Market Studies* vol. 44, no. 5, pp. 947–968.
Kupchan, Charles A. (1997) 'Regionalizing Europe's security' in Mansfield, Edward D. and Milner, Helen E. (eds), *The Political Economy of Regionalism*, New York, NY: Columbia University Press.
Lavenex, Sandra and Schimmelfennig, Frank (2006) 'Relations with the Wider Europe', *Journal of Common Market Studies* vol. 44, annual review, pp. 137–154.
Leshukov, Igor (2001) 'Can the northern dimension break the vicious circle of Russia–EU relations?' in Ojanen, H. (ed.), *The Northern Dimension: Fuel for the EU?*, Helsinki and Bonn: Ulkopoliittinen instituutti and Institut für Europäische Politik.
Lo, Bobo (2003) *Vladimir Putin and the Evolution of Russian Foreign Policy*, London: Royal Institute of International Affairs/Blackwell Publishing.
Manners, I. (2002) 'Normative power Europe: a contradiction in terms?', *Journal of Common Market Studies* vol. 40, no. 2, pp. 235–258.
Manners, I. (2006) 'Normative power Europe reconsidered: beyond the crossroads', *Journal of European Public Policy* vol. 13, no. 2, pp. 182–199.
Manners, I. and Whitman, R. (2003) 'The "difference engine": constructing and representing the international identity of the EU', *Journal of European Public Policy*, vol. 10, no. 3, pp. 380–404.
Medvedev, Sergei (2000) *Russia's Futures: Implications for the EU, the North and the Baltic Sea Region*, Helsinki and Bonn: Ulkopoliittinen instituutti and Institut für Europäische Politik.
Miller, Benjamin (2001) 'The global sources of regional transitions from war to peace', *Journal of Peace Research* vol. 38, no 2, pp. 199–225.
Moldpres (2008) 'President Voronin: Commission for European Integration's 2009 goal is to monitor implementation of laws', 3 December 2008. Online, available at: www.moldpres.md/default.asp?Lang=en&ID=99840.

Moses, J.W. and Knutsen, T.L. (2007) *Ways of Knowing: Competing Methodologies in Social and Political Research*, Houndmills: Palgrave Macmillan.

Møller, B. (2005) *The EU as a Security Actor: 'Security by Being' and 'Security by Doing'*, DIIS Report 2005: 12. Copenhagen: Danish Institute of International Studies.

Nye, Joseph (2005) *Soft Power: The Means to Success in World Politics*, New York: PublicAffairs.

Payne, R. (2001) 'Persuasion, norms and frame construction', *European Journal of International Relations* vol. 7, no. 1, pp. 37–61.

Peterson, M.J. (1982) 'Political uses of recognition: the influence of the international system', *World Politics* vol. 34, no. 3, pp. 324–352.

Popescu, Nicu (2005) 'The revolutionary evolution in Moldova', *CEPS Neighbourhood Watch* issue 3, April 2005, Brussels: CEPS, pp. 1–3.

Popescu, Nicu (2006) 'Russia's soft power ambitions', *CEPS Policy Brief* 115, October 2006.

Radio Free Europe/Radio Liberty (RFE/RL) (2006a) 'Ukraine: Yanukovych blows hot and cold in Brussels', 14 September 2006. Online, available at: www.rferl.org/content/article/1071342.html.

Radio Free Europe/Radio Liberty (RFE/RL) (2006b) 'Georgia: Integration Minister says "we try to be patient"', 21 September 2006. Online, available at: www.rferl.org/content/article/1071538.html.

Ringmar, E. (2002) 'The recognition game: Soviet Russia against the West', *Cooperation and Conflict* vol. 37, no. 2, pp. 115–136.

Sergounin, Alexander (2003) 'Russia's security policies in the Baltic Sea region: changing priorities'. Online, available at: www.cirp.ru/publications/sergounin/cont_e.htm.

Sjursen, H. (2006) 'What kind of power?', *Journal of European Public Policy* vol. 13, no. 2, pp. 169–181.

Stadtmüller, Elzbieta (2005) 'Regional dimensions of security' in Farrell, M., Hettne, B. and van Langenhove, L., *Global Politics of Regionalism: Theory and Practice*, London: Pluto Press.

Strömvik, M. (2005) *To Act as a Union*, Doctoral dissertation, Department of Political Science, Lund University, Sweden.

Tonra, B. and Christiansen, T. (eds) (2004) *Rethinking European Union Foreign Policy*, Manchester: Manchester University Press.

Trenin, Dmitri (2000) 'Security cooperation in north-eastern Europe: a Russian perspective' in Trenin, Dmitri and van Ham, Peter (eds), *Russia and the United States in Northern European Security*, Helsinki and Bonn: Ulkopoliittinen instituutti and Institut für Europäische Politik.

Yu, George T. and Longenecker, David J. (1994) 'The Beijing–Taipei struggle for international recognition: from the Niger affair to the UN', *Asian Survey* vol. 34, no. 5, pp. 475–488.

Wæver, O. (1998) chapter in Adler, E. and Barnett, M. (eds) *Security Communities*, Cambridge: Cambridge University Press.

Wendt, A. (1999) *Social Theory of International Politics*, Cambridge: Cambridge University Press.

Index

Abbas, Mahmoud 99–100
Abkhazia 28, 75–6, 116–20, 127, 136
actorness 4–5, 18, 29–32, 46, 149
Afghanistan 134, 137–8, 141
African Union (AU) 82, 84, 90
alignment: CFSP 62–3, 67–8, 70–1, 73, 75, 78–9, 87, 93, 96, 118
Aliyev, Ilham 73
anarchy 20, 24
Annapolis 89, 135
Arab Maghreb Union (AMU) 82–4, 90

Balkans 13, 23, 41, 60, 115, 126, 135, 141
Barcelona Process *see* Euro-Mediterranean Partnership
Barroso, José Manuel 48–9, 52, 59, 114, 120, 123, 138–9
Black Sea Forum 56, 62
Black Sea Synergy 12, 42, 56, 108, 119, 129
Borjomi Declaration 65; *see also* Community of Democratic Choice
Bosnia and Herzegovina 67, 86, 135, 140
Bush, George 133–5, 137, 139–40, 142

Cold War 15, 107
Common Foreign and Security Policy (CFSP) 5, 96, 131, 133, 149; *see also* alignment; High Representative
Common Spaces 15, 43, 108, 128
Commonwealth of Independent States (CIS) 11, 117, 121
Community of Democratic Choice 62, 65–6, 69, 73, 77
conditionality 13, 33, 43, 45, 51, 53, 60, 63, 67–9, 72, 78–9, 86–8, 96, 115
constructivism 9, 34, 147
Council of Baltic Sea States (CBSS) 15, 108
Council of Europe 3, 55, 71

democracy: EU core value 43, 45–7, 51, 58–9, 69, 81, 84, 90, 102–3, 109–10, 128–9, 132, 137, 139, 141, 148
differentiation: ENP 43, 51–2, 87, 111, 113

Eastern Partnership (EaP) 56
energy: politics of 8, 41, 48, 53, 57, 59–60, 66–7, 73, 75, 77, 79, 108, 110, 113–15, 119, 121, 123, 126, 136
enlargement: 2004–2007 5, 42, 108, 135; as foreign policy 13–14, 16, 45, 56, 110–13, 127, 130, 140–1; relation to ENP 10, 14, 43–4, 49, 51–3, 103
EU Border Assistance Mission (EUBAM) 57, 61–2, 64, 94
EU core values 45, 66, 103, 122, 148; *see also* democracy; human rights; rule of law
EU Monitoring Mission (EUMM) 107–8
EU special representative 74
Euro-Mediterranean Partnership (EMP) 12, 15, 81–3, 85, 87
Europe: conceptualization 3, 21, 38, 46, 65–6, 110–13, 122, 125, 129, 142, 149
European Neighbourhood and Partnership Instrument (ENPI) 15, 43, 52
European Neighbourhood Policy (ENP) 5, 12, 14–16, 39, 42–6, 48–56, 68–9, 82, 103, 109
European Security and Defence Policy (ESDP) 5, 31, 86, 149
European Security Strategy (ESS) 46, 77, 149
Europeanization 55, 78–9

Ferrero-Waldner, Benita 45–51, 53, 58–9, 69, 80, 84, 94, 100, 102, 114, 120–3
framing 30, 33, 51, 53, 63, 102, 128–9, 139

Index

Freedom House 73, 80, 84–7, 122

G7 119
Gaza 81–90, 93–4, 96, 98–100
Gazprom 66–7, 115
GUAM (Organization for Democracy and Economic Development) 42, 57, 62, 70, 73, 77

Hamas 98–9, 134
Hezbollah 93, 97
High Representative (of the CFSP) 4, 42, 133
human rights 43, 45–6, 48, 51, 102–3, 110, 139, 148

identity 3, 8, 12–13, 17–19, 21, 25–8, 31–7, 35–6, 46
implementation capacity 61, 94
interdependence: security 7, 13, 19–23, 32, 35, 38
interface 5–6, 8, 13, 17–18, 23, 27, 28, 34–5, 38
Iran 60, 91, 135
Iraq 37, 96, 132–4, 137, 141–2

Kaliningrad 14, 112, 122, 125, 127–8
Khadafi, Muammar 84–5
Kosovo 28, 115, 127, 129, 135
Kozulin, Alexandr 58, 60

Landaburu, Eneko 45, 49, 51
Lukashenko, Alexander 57–61

Macedonia 67, 135, 140
Medvedev, Dmitry 109, 113, 118, 120, 122, 124–5, 130
Merkel, Angela 82, 123
Mohamed VI, King 86
Mohammed, the Prophet 45
Montenegro 68
Mubarak, Hosni 89–91

Nagorno-Karabakh 68, 70–2
New Transatlantic Agenda 16, 132
North Atlantic Treaty Organization (NATO) 3, 11, 15–16, 66, 69, 72, 74, 77, 112–13, 117, 119, 131, 134–5, 137, 140–2
Northern Dimension 15, 56, 108, 111, 129

Orange Revolution 69

Organization for Democracy and Economic Development *see* GUAM
Organization for Security and Cooperation in Europe (OSCE) 3, 15, 55, 57, 63–4, 71, 81, 120–1, 141

Patten, Christopher 42, 48, 53
peace (conceptualization of) 25–6, 30, 45–7, 81; *see also* stable peace
power 6–8, 10–12, 18–22, 32–6, 50–2
Prodi, Romano 45–6, 49
Putin, Vladimir 109, 111–16, 123, 130

Quartet 89, 93–4, 96, 99–100, 103, 108, 110, 121, 126, 134; *see also* United Nations

Rafah 94
recognition: logic 58, 12, 18, 27–31, 34
Reform Treaty 4, 149
region: conceptualization 8, 19–23, 25
regional security complex: European 10, 13, 37–8, 41; theory 7, 18, 20–2, 34, 37
Rehn, Olli 45
Rose Revolution 74
rule of law 43, 45, 48–9, 51, 58–9, 62, 64, 69, 72–4, 76–7, 81, 95, 97, 109, 121, 135–7, 139, 148

Saakashvili, Mikheil 65, 76–7
sanctions 50, 58, 60, 66, 79, 84–5, 131, 136
Sarkozy, Nicolas 118
Schengen 13, 14, 24, 82, 111–12
securitization 7, 8, 13, 20
security 3, 20; *see also* regional security complex; security community
security community 7–8, 13–14, 21, 23–6, 37–8, 81, 147, 149–50
Siniora, Fuad 97
Solana, Javier 42, 48, 53
South Ossetia 74–6, 116–20, 127, 136
stable peace 7, 13, 24–6; *see also* peace
strategic partnership 14, 43, 56, 60, 107, 109–10, 112, 121, 126, 130, 141

Tblisi Declaration 78
terrorism 8, 37, 41, 46–7, 72, 82–3, 86, 88, 90, 92–3, 96, 102, 108, 126, 134, 137
Transnistria 57, 61–3, 67–8, 79
trust 21–2, 25–6, 37, 71, 84–5, 100, 121–3, 130

Turkey 10, 11, 13, 23, 41–2, 56, 70, 72, 78, 81, 115

Union of the Mediterranean 56, 82
United Nations 80, 97, 100, 121, 131, 136, 139; *see also* Quartet

Verheugen, Günther 45–7, 49–51

World Bank 120, 138
World Trade Organization (WTO) 63–4, 83, 138, 142

Yanukovych, Viktor 65–6
Yushchenko, Viktor 65–6, 70

eBooks – at www.eBookstore.tandf.co.uk

A library at your fingertips!

eBooks are electronic versions of printed books. You can store them on your PC/laptop or browse them online.

They have advantages for anyone needing rapid access to a wide variety of published, copyright information.

eBooks can help your research by enabling you to bookmark chapters, annotate text and use instant searches to find specific words or phrases. Several eBook files would fit on even a small laptop or PDA.

NEW: Save money by eSubscribing: cheap, online access to any eBook for as long as you need it.

Annual subscription packages

We now offer special low-cost bulk subscriptions to packages of eBooks in certain subject areas. These are available to libraries or to individuals.

For more information please contact webmaster.ebooks@tandf.co.uk

We're continually developing the eBook concept, so keep up to date by visiting the website.

www.eBookstore.tandf.co.uk